Post-Traditional Societies

Essays by

S. N. Eisenstadt
Edmund Leach
S. J. Tambiah
Heinz Bechert
J. C. Heesterman
Ashis Nandy
Nur Yalman
Şerif Mardin
Ernest Gellner
Elbaki Hermassi
Abdelkader Zghal
Jacques Berque

Post-Traditional Societies

Edited by S. N. EISENSTADT

 W · W · NORTON & COMPANY · INC · *New York*

Copyright © 1972 by the American Academy of Arts
and Sciences

Library of Congress Cataloging in Publication Data
Main entry under title:

Post-traditional societies.

   Originally published as winter 1973 issue of Daedalus.
   1. Social history—20th century—Addresses, essays,
lectures. 2. Tradition (Philosophy)—Addresses, essays,
lectures. I. Eisenstadt, Shmuel Noel, 1923–   ed.
II. Daedalus.
HN16.P6   1974   300'.8   74–4323
ISBN 0–393–01108–9
ISBN 0–393–09303–4 (pbk.)

Published simultaneously in Canada
by George J. McLeod Limited, Toronto

Printed in the United States of America
1 2 3 4 5 6 7 8 9 0

To the memory of Harry Benda,
who should have been here

CONTENTS

THE TITLE of this volume is not intentionally ambiguous. It is a fact, however, that the term "post-traditional" is novel, and therefore requires some additional explanation. If the volume had carried the title of S. N. Eisenstadt's introductory essay, "Post-Traditional Societies and the Continuity and Reconstruction of Tradition," it would probably have been thought unwieldy, but it would have served to communicate a good deal more about what is implied by the term "post-traditional." As S. N. Eisenstadt explains: "The term 'post-traditional' has been coined to facilitate new ways of looking at certain central problems of modernization and development. Its appearance responds to a widespread dissatisfaction with many of the assumptions of the initial studies of modernization—especially with the dichotomy between 'traditional' and modern societies that emerged during the classical period of modern sociology and dominated the many studies of development and modernization made in the 1950's and 1960's."

The term "post-traditional" is not very felicitous. There is no reason to expect that it will come to enjoy common usage—it lacks precisely those rhetorical qualities that make certain other terms so beguiling—but it may serve to provide an additional incentive for looking at developing, modernizing (and even modern) societies with some concern other than that of finding those elements of congruence and uniformity that have already been achieved, or are about to be achieved. This volume, in short, casts doubt on those who imagine that all modern societies will in the foreseeable future sufficiently resemble each other so that earlier identities, expressed in differing traditions, will be virtually lost.

While it would be a mistake to speak of any single theme informing all the essays in this volume—the issue is perhaps most remarkable for the diversity of views represented—the greatest number do accept the idea that the contemporary world, including the so-called new nations, is not susceptible to meaningful social or political interpretation by analytical schemes that dwell principally on twentieth-century economic phenomena. Nor is it enough to make a modest bow to history, to include some consideration of the colonial and imperial economic experiences of the eighteenth and nineteenth centuries. A quite different kind of perspective is called for, and with it must come a more subtle analysis of the complex traditions—the "codes"—that have been transmitted, altered, or obliterated over time, and that provide a partial explanation of why specific societies have developed as they have, and how they have come to exhibit the social and political forms that they show today.

To many who have written for this volume, "tradition" is not a "passing" phenomenon, which can be represented as something that existed until very recently, and that will soon be recognized as belonging to the past. Implicitly or explicitly, many accept the view of J. C. Heesterman that "there hardly seems to be room for a conflict between tradition and modernity." As Heesterman explains: ". . . successful modernity does not mean the supersession of tradition or the superimposition on it of a different order." Tradition itself, he explains, is full of paradox; since it has to do with the way in which a society deals with the most fundamental questions, including those that touch the meaning of life and death, there can be no final formulations that are totally inflexible.

There is a constant effort made in this volume to reveal the complexity of tradition, to dwell on the continuities between the past and the present, and to recognize how these are often expressed in deep relations between politics and religion. S. J. Tambiah suggests that these relations ought to be seen "as constituting dialectical tensions or parameters rather than age-sanctified, unambiguous rules." Were there a slavish conformity to an earlier religious tradition, the possibilities of widely divergent political practices in societies of similar religious origins would be substantially reduced.

Whether the subject is a Buddhist society or one that is formally Islamic, the object is to study a wide variety of political and social systems and a great number of different uses that tradition has served. Nur Yalman, for example, is interested principally in those societies "which have cut their moorings with their traditional pasts and yet have been unable to start their economic engines." He believes that the concept of the "post-traditional" can be used also to "draw attention to these drifting vessels."

The term "post-traditional" clearly refers less to a characteristic common to specific contemporary societies than to a method that requires a kind of analysis that has not to date been at all common. If one asks what are the "post-traditional societies" that have been treated in this volume, they include India and Pakistan; the Soviet Union, China, and Japan; Burma, Thailand, Ceylon, Cambodia, and Laos; Turkey, Tunisia, Algeria, Morocco, Senegal—and these are only the principal ones. In the conference that led to the development of this volume, Spain and the states of Latin America also figured. To imagine that all these can be subsumed under a single rubric is to realize that the object cannot be to demonstrate significant identities between them, but to try, insofar as it is possible, to consider what is referred to in this issue as the "gargantuan dimensions of the task of transforming 'traditional' societies." Such transformation, in the 1950's and 1960's, was thought to be a relatively easy matter. It was thought to be a problem principally for the new states, for those which had recently been liberated from colonial rule. Both these opinions are implicitly repudiated by many of the articles in this volume. Tradition is not so evanescent as it was once believed. It is a measure of the distance we have come since dropping the supposedly pejorative label "underdeveloped societies" in favor of the more neutral term "developing societies" that this volume brings into question the adequacy of either definition. So long as the whole of a scholar's attention is focused on a mythical future to which societies are tending, there can be no adequate appreciation of the different origins from which all societies depart. So long as there is no attention given to origins, there can be no understanding of tradition, and therefore, in the view of these authors, no understanding of the contemporary world.

A great debt is owed S. N. Eisenstadt for pressing a "post-traditional" agenda on a group that met in Rome in June 1972 to discuss early drafts of the papers that are published here. Thanks are due also to the Ford Foundation for generous support of a study which unites history, anthropology, sociology, and the history of religions.

STEPHEN R. GRAUBARD

Post-Traditional Societies

S. N. EISENSTADT

Post-Traditional Societies and the Continuity and Reconstruction of Tradition

I

THE TERM "post-traditional" has been coined to facilitate new ways of looking at certain central problems of modernization and development. Its appearance responds to a widespread dissatisfaction with many of the assumptions of the initial studies of modernization—especially with the dichotomy posited between "traditional" and modern societies that emerged during the classical period of modern sociology and dominated the many studies of development and modernization made in the 1950's and 1960's. The modern and traditional societies that confronted each other in these analyses were for the most part depicted as completely "closed" types, described in various ways. Among the most famous were Tonnies' differentiation between *Gemeinschaft uud Gesellschaft* and Redfield's more anthropologically oriented distinction between primitive, folk, and urban societies. Out of such systems emerged the picture of traditional and modern societies preeminent in sociological thought for many years.

Traditional society was viewed as a static one with little differentiation or specialization as well as low levels of urbanization and literacy. Modern society, in contrast, was characterized as having thorough differentiation, urbanization, literacy, and exposure to mass media. In the political realm, traditional society was thought to be based on a "traditional" elite ruling by virtue of some Mandate of Heaven, while modern society rested on the wide participation of its population, which refused to honor the traditional forms of political legitimation and held rulers accountable in terms of secular values and efficiency. Traditional society had been conceived, above all, as being bound by the cultural horizons set by its tradition, and modern society as being culturally dynamic, oriented to change and innovation.

Behind many of these researches was the assumption, usually implicit, that the conditions for sustained growth in different institutional fields depended on continuous extension of specific sociodemographic or structural

1

indices of modernization. According to such views, a society's modernity related directly to its characteristics of structural specialization and to the various indices of social mobilization. The greater the specialization, the less traditional it was, and, by implication, thereby the better able to develop continuously and to deal with new problems and social forces.

But the experiences of the late 1950's and early 1960's called into question many previously held opinions or hypotheses about the conditions of continuous modernization. The implicit assumption that the less traditional society is more capable of sustained growth has been proved incorrect. The various sociodemographic or structural indices of modernization are now seen to indicate only the extent to which traditional, self-contained societies or communities became weak or disintegrated—the extent to which, to paraphrase the title of Daniel Lerner's book, Traditional Society Is Passing. In themselves, such indices do not reveal whether a viable new modern society, capable of continuous growth, will develop. Nor do they predict the kind of society that will develop or its institutional contours. Moreover, the development of a new society and the disruption of traditional frameworks—be they family, community, or political mechanisms—leads more often to disorganization, delinquency, and chaos than to a new viable modern order.

And, paradoxically, in many countries modernization has been successfully undertaken under the aegis of traditional symbols and by traditional elites. In such countries as Japan or even England, many traditional symbols have been retained—be they the Emperor, the Japanese Crown, or the symbols of the realm in Britain. When anti-traditional elites provided the initial impetus to modernization, an attempt, even a halting one, to revive some of the traditional symbols has often followed.

From these emerged the recognition that even if traditional societies are typologically different from modern ones, they may vary greatly in the degree to which their traditions impede or facilitate the transition to modernity. It thus became apparent that greater analytical distinctions had to be drawn among different types or elements of "traditions." Perhaps the first to employ this new focus was Marion Levy in his research into the premodern social structures of China and Japan and their individual courses of modernization. Subsequently, David Apter, in comparing Ghana and Uganda, set out to investigate what aspects of a certain tradition impede or facilitate the process of modernization; and many of the works of the Committee on Comparative Politics of the SSRC have followed along these lines.

Emphasizing the distinction between tradition and traditionalism, Edward Shils, followed by Hoselitz and Spengler, has defined traditionalism as a more extremist negative reaction to the impingement of forces of modernity, and tradition as a society's reservoir of behavior and symbols. The perceived persistence of strong traditions in modern or modernizing societies has further undermined the earlier dichotomy established to differentiate "traditional" and "modern" societies. Binding ways of behavior rooted in the past and to some degree referring to the past have been recognized as characteristic of certain modern or modernizing societies. And, conversely, several scholars, Singer and Rudolph particularly, have demonstrated that traditional forces or groups—be they castes or tribal units—tend to reorganize themselves in new, modern settings in effective ways.

Moreover, within many of the New States, whose politics were greatly shaped by modern models of politics, older traditional models of politics have tended to reassert themselves after the initial phases of independence. Consequently, there has been growing recognition of what may be called the systemic viability of so-called "transitional" systems, those being neither modern nor traditional. Indeed, partial "modernization" or development—that is, development of some institutional or organizational frameworks sharing many characteristics of modern organizations—may take place in segregated parts of a still "traditional" social structure, and their infusion may even reinforce those traditional systems.

The initial assumptions made in the early studies of modernization failed to explain the great variability of contemporary societies in their attempts to modernize themselves. This range was subsequently attributed by certain scholars to the ability of the various modern or modernizing societies to move or to "develop" in directions that do not necessarily lead to any single "end-state" envisaged by the various "evolutionary" models of modernization. The prime causative agent behind the great diversity has been located by other scholars in the uniqueness of both the tradition of the society in its continuous unfolding as well as the specific historical international situation. The spread of capitalism and imperialism and the consequent dependence of underdeveloped societies on the hegemonic metropolitan centers have been singled out as major explanations of these dynamics.

But too often in these analyses tradition was seen or defined as some general reservoir of experience that, although it contained a great variety of components—such as patterns of habitual behavior, symbols of social and cultural identity, patterns of legitimation of the social order—constituted a rather general undifferentiated whole. The growing accumulation of research has indicated the inadequacy of these "historicist" emphases as well as of the rather general definition of tradition implied in some of them. The term "post-traditional" was coined—perhaps not very felicitously—in order to point out some new ways of looking at these problems. Modern and contemporary settings, it is assumed, have specific character-

istics and create specific problems that distinguish their patterns of development from the changes that had continuously taken place in these societies in their traditional, historical settings. At the same time, contemporary
responses to these problems may diverge greatly from the initial "Western"
model of modernization. And, in the shaping of these responses, many
forces that develop from within a society's traditions may indeed be of
crucial importance. The indiscriminate use of the term "tradition" to explain "everything" in the development of these societies may entirely
invalidate the usefulness of this concept, however, and only a more differentiated use of this concept may prove to be of value.

Thus, instead of talking in a general way about "tradition" and its
unfolding, one must attempt to distinguish systematically between different aspects of what has often been called "tradition" and to analyze their
relation to social structure and organization. Only insofar as one takes
into account the interaction between the various aspects of "tradition," as
they influence the activities of different groups and societies in the new
modern settings, can one analyze the dynamics of the construction of post-
traditional orders in their social, political, and cultural dimensions.

Modern societies, as contrasted with more traditional systems, continuously face the crucial problem of the ability of their central frameworks to "expand." The demand for or expectation of such "expansion"
can develop in several different, albeit closely connected and interrelated,
directions: aspirations for the creation or maintenance of new, wider, political frameworks; for economic or administrative development or "modernization"; for greater societal responsiveness, especially in the elaboration
of new principles of distribution; for redefinition of the boundaries and
symbols of the collectivity and for more direct access to the center. While
the concrete contents of such demands vary greatly according to the
society's structural conditions—such as urbanization, agrarian technology,
educational expansion, and the like—general patterns of demands have
tended to develop that are in a sense specific to modern situations. First
of all, the number of demands has simply increased almost geometrically
and is closely related to a broader access to resources and to a greater range
of politically articulate groups and strata.

Beyond these quantitative aspects, there appears a tendency among
broader groups to make demands not only for concrete benefits based on
differential membership in ascriptive, closed subcollectivities, but also for
access to the center by virtue of membership in that subcollectivity.

These demands on the center are not issued simply in terms of the
dynamics of the respective spheres for which they speak—be they agrarian problems, urban problems, or labor problems. However important the
direct impact of such problems on the various social groups or strata,
they tend in modern societies first to become connected with demands in

the symbolic sphere derived from the participatory and consensual orientations inherent in the premises of modernity. They may then be articulated into themes of protest and into the broader political processes, subsequently impinging on the very centers of the social and political order. Around such demands and the center's responses to them emerge some of the major possibilities of conflict, cleavage, and crisis, that can undermine the respective regimes in modern societies.

As has so often been shown in the literature, traditional settings are also characterized by relatively less differentiated and specialized organizational structures than modern ones with their bureaucracies, parties, or popular movements—all of which can be used by rulers and the broader strata of society alike to cope with problems. Above all, modern societies and polities usually exhibit a wider scope in their political community, which has usually been created by different enterprising political and cultural elites.

These various discrete differences between traditional and modern orders converge into broader categories. In the cultural sphere all "traditional" societies, however great the differences among them, tend to accept the givenness of some past event, order, or figure (whether real or symbolic) as the major focus of their collective identity. This given sets the scope and nature of their social and cultural order, becoming the ultimate legitimizer of change and the delineator of the limits of innovation. Thus, official, normative limitations are placed on change and innovation in terms of reference to this past given. Access to positions of power is restricted, incumbents being recognized as the legitimate interpreters of traditions as well as the forgers of the legitimate contents and symbols of the social and cultural orders.

In traditional regimes, legitimation of the rulers has been couched in basically traditional religious terms. Moreover, the subject's basic political role is little distinguished from his other societal roles—such as membership in local kinship or "status" communities. His political role has often been embedded in such groups, and the citizen or subject does not exercise any actual, direct, or symbolic political rights through a system of voting or franchise.

Within the sociopolitical sphere the distinction between a traditional and a modern political or cultural order lies in the extent to which certain basic symbolic and cultural premises, with their structural and cultural limitations, do or do not maintain their centrality. The most important among these premises are the continuing symbolic and cultural differentiation between the center and periphery as well as the concomitant limitation on the access of members of broader groups to the political center or centers.

"Traditional" societies have, of course, varied greatly in the extent to which legitimation becomes a correlation between "pastness" and sacred-

ness. That past, moreover, has been conceived of in mythological, historical, or revelational terms.

But whatever these differences among them, traditional societies tend to
share the symbolic and structural frameworks outlined above. Thus, insofar
as changes in the connotation of tradition on central levels have taken place,
we witness the breakthrough—gradual or abrupt—to some sort of modern
or, rather, post-traditional, sociopolitical or cultural order. The crux of such a
breakthrough lies in the weakening of normative limitations on the contents
of the symbols of the center, in their secularization, and in the growing emphasis on values of human dignity and social equality. Larger groups demand participation—even if intermittent or partial—in the formulations
of the society's central symbols and institutions.

The processes of modernization are, therefore, unique in comparison
with other historical movements of change, because they have been
grounded on the assumption that it is possible to create a new sociopolitical order, an order based on premises of universalism and equality. The
spread of these attitudes has led to far-reaching changes in societal structure and organization, especially in the economic and political spheres.
Modernization has taken place throughout the world through a series of
social, political, and cultural movements that, unlike movements of change
and rebellion in many other historical situations, have tended to combine
orientations of protest and those of center-formation and institution-build-
ing. It has fostered the establishment of a universal civilization in which
different societies have served one another as mutual reference points. A
society judges both itself and others in relation to these premises of universalism and equality.

The continuous spread of these assumptions throughout the world in
a variety of guises—liberal, national, or socialist movements and ideologies—has greatly undermined the bases of legitimation found in historical
or "traditional" civilizations. This does not mean, of course, that modern or
modernizing societies are traditionless—that within them there is no attachment to customs and ways of the past or to various symbols of collective
identity in which primordial elements combine with strong orientations
to the past. It means, rather, that modernization has greatly weakened
one specific aspect of traditionality—namely, the legitimation of social,
political, and cultural orders in terms of some combination of "pastness,"
"sacredness," and their symbolic and structural derivatives. At the same
time, however, modernization has given rise to the continuous reconstruction of other aspects of tradition, often as a response to problems created
by the breakdown of traditional legitimation of sociopolitical and cultural
orders.

Many of these differences between "traditional" and "modern" social and cultural orders were, of course, stressed in the first literature on modernization. Yet, unlike the "classical paradigms" of modernization, the approach proposed here does not assume that "development" or "modernization" constitutes a "unilinear" demographic, social, economic, or political process, extending, even if haltingly or intermittently, to some plateau whose basic contours will be everywhere the same, despite differences in detail. Rather, modernization must be seen as a process or a series of processes with a common core that generates common or similar problems.

The structural and cultural parameters of these processes—those of growing differentiation, social mobilization, and the breakdown or weakening of traditionality—are unparalleled in the history of human societies. They pose before these societies basic problems of regulating the continuously developing and newly emerging groups and of integrating them within some common institutional framework. New foci of collective national identity must be formulated in which tradition, modernity, and change are to some extent combined. But the most general and common problem attendant on modernization is the development of a capacity to maintain an institutional structure that is capable of absorbing changes beyond its own initial premises and of dealing with continuously new and changing problems. This structure must also be able to foster participation, liberty, and some degree or type of rationality.

Although these processes of change and the problems they tend to create have certain common cores, the responses they evoke and the consequent types of social, political, and cultural "post-traditional" orders that develop vary greatly.

The range in response is evident not only in the degree of social mobilization and structural differentiation, but also in the symbolic and institutional reaction to the impact of modernity. Differences appear in the basic conceptions of the cultural and social order: the degree of commitment to participate in its formation; the relative autonomy of the individual vis-à-vis that order; and the relative autonomy of the social, cultural, and political order itself. Systems of stratification vary, both in the degree of class cleavage and conflict and in the conception of social hierarchy.

These differences have tended to become new "modern" traditions, particularly in the ways in which the parameters of these traditions are related to the extension of participation, liberty, or justice. In the formulation of responses to the challenges of modernization, the "traditions" of a society or a civilization have central importance.

II

The influence exerted by tradition is, however, neither unified nor homogeneous. The simplest example of the impact of traditional forces on the process of modernization is the resurgence of traditional groups—be they the *Ulema* in Islamic countries, the Buddhist *Sangha* in Southeast Asia, or the peasantry and aristocracy in many European and Asian countries alike. Such resurgence of "traditional," "conservative" groups may seem to go against the internal logic of the dynamics of modernization, since modernization, indeed every process of historical change, threatens many existing, entrenched groups and is seemingly oriented to their "liquidation." In some rather rare instances such groups may indeed disappear, at least from the center of the social and historical scene, as did the peasantry or urban artisanat in Europe as a result of the gradual development of new forces of economic organization. In more revolutionary situations, they can be obliterated or tolerated at the margin of society by a combination of legislation and coercion—as was the case to some degree for the aristocracy of Western Europe after the French Revolution and more prominently for the bourgeoisie in Russia or China.

Such groups may, however, also transform themselves, adapting to the new setting by adopting new tasks and organizational patterns and forming coalitions with the new emerging groups and centers of power—be they absolutist kings, a centralizing bureaucracy, the bourgeoisie, or a revolutionary elite and party.

The resurgence of traditional groups in situations of modernization does not merely testify to their capacity to survive in a new setting; it more basically connotes the fundamental transformation of the groups themselves as well as of their relations to other groups and centers of power.

But even in revolutionary situations, where old groups, classes, or status categories are obliterated, the new groups often exhibit a similar pattern of social behavior and cultural orientation. After the first upsurge of nationalist movements, the new elites of Burma or Ceylon, for example, tended to develop patterns of behavior very similar to those of the displaced traditional elites. Tocqueville long ago pointed to the persistence of bureaucracy in pre- and post-revolutionary France, and in the more recent revolutionary situation in Russia or China such continuity can be seen in the domination of State over Society and in certain of the modes of such domination.

Such continuity between the traditional and modern settings of a particular society has often been perceived in terms of the persistence of some broad cultural orientations, with little attention being paid to the more structural aspects of these societies. Recently, there have been more systematic attempts to link psychological variables to patterns of institutional behavior—an effort perhaps best illustrated in the concept of "political culture" developed by Almond and Verba, and subsequently employed in various studies by members of the Committee on Comparative Politics of the Social Science Research Council. It has now been recognized that tradition may persist through many historical changes not only in daily customs, folklore, or general societal symbols, but also in the more central structural and institutional aspects of a society. Such continuity finds its simplest expression in various discrete organizational patterns—as, for example, the "building" activities of the Ceylonese Kings of old that Leach compared to those of Mr. Bandernayke in the modern period of Ceylonese history.

Within the political sphere, important aspects of continuity can be found in the loci of centers of political decision and innovation as well as in the types of center-periphery relations prevalent within a society. Rulers or elites can demonstrate such continuity in the relative emphasis they place on the activities of centers and their components. Not only in its policies, but also in its political struggles and organization can a regime reveal persistent patterns.

In terms of stratification, continuity can be found in the attributes that constitute the bases of societal evaluation and hierarchy, in the access of various groups to such attributes irrespective of centers of the society, and in the degree of broader status association as opposed to status segregation of relatively closed occupational and professional groups. We shall attempt to trace such continuities in three types of society: the Western European, the Russian, and the "patrimonial."

Even with the constantly increasing importance both of mass parties and bureaucracies as arenas of decision-making in the pluralistic regimes of Western Europe, neither the parties nor the bureaucracies have become the only areas of political discussion, innovation, and decision-making. Executive and legislative organs have continued to maintain some of their positions of control—at least symbolically—as the main frameworks of independent public opinion and leadership and as the main areas in which political innovation become institutionalized.

The societies of Western Europe have also continuously been characterized by a high degree of commitment by centers and periphery alike to common "ideals" or goals, the center permeating the periphery in attempts to mobilize support for its policies and the periphery impinging on the center. Accordingly, both the traditional—the absolutist and "estate"—rulers of Western Europe and the leaders of modern "nation-states" have laid special emphasis on the development of common symbols of cultural and political identity, on collective political goals, as well as on a high degree of regulation in the relations among different, relatively independent, groups. Continuity has also appeared in the pattern of policies oriented to the creation or promotion of new types of activities and structures.

All these aspects of political systems are closely connected to patterns of political organization and struggle characterized in Western Europe by the development of relatively autonomous political groups—such as parties and organs of public opinion. They relate, as well, to highly autonomous political goals that have not been limited to struggles for access to goods and the resources of the center, but extend to attempts to influence, in an independent way, the very values and structure of the centers—thus proclaiming the autonomy of broader groups as the bearers of those values and attributes that the center claims to represent.

The "traditional" feudal or absolutist system of stratification in Western Europe was characterized by multiplicity in its hierarchies of status and patterns of status incongruity, as well as by strong tendencies to obliterate the legal distinction between free and servile groups. Most groups could participate in the center by virtue of their collective identities, as corporate or semicorporate bodies. Hence a countrywide "consciousness" or organization developed that was not confined to the higher groups, but could also be found among the "middle" or lowest free groups and strata.

Family and kinship identity tended to be closely related to collective-strata identity, with family and kinship groups representing important channels not only of orientation to high positions, but also of ascriptive transmission of such positions. The degree of access of different groups or strata to the center was not ascriptively fixed, but constituted a continuous "strata-conflict"—that is, conflict among different strata, as *strata* in classes, about their relative prestige and the scope of their participation in the center.

Each stratum, but especially the "middle" ones (and sometimes also the aristocracy), tended to encompass a great variety of occupational positions and organizations and to link them in some common way of life, resulting in a high degree of broad status association as against relatively narrow status segregation.

Political organization and social stratification in traditional (autocratic) and modern (communist, revolutionary) Russia show a pattern of organization in the political sphere that evinces crucial continuities across time, but differs markedly from the Western European. In the traditional Tsarist setting and in Soviet Russia alike, the executive predominates over the other organs of political organization, and the political elite monopolizes political innovation. In the traditional setting, political innovation and decision-making rest with the monarchy and, to some degree, the upper bureaucracy; in the modern one, they reside with the party and its leadership, and to a certain extent the bureaucracy. The legislature performs mainly ritual functions, while the executive (as distinct from the monarchy or party leadership), although important in several aspects, plays mainly only a secondary, routine role.

In both systems, the center permeates the periphery to a relatively high degree in order to mobilize resources and to control broader society-wide activities. The modern revolutionary center tries to stimulate commitment to its goals, but at the same time controls with strict coercion efforts of the periphery to impinge on it. Both systems strongly emphasize the formation of political and cultural identity as well as collective goals, but with greater monopolization of force by the center and less stress on the upholding of the internal-regulative activities of various groups than are found in Western Europe. Consequently, the policies developed by both the traditional and modern Russian centers have been mainly regulative and coercively promotive ones sponsored by the center with little autonomous expression of the goals of broader groups.

The patterns of political struggle and organization in different epochs of Russian history have been characterized by periods of a relatively high degree of organized political activity directed by the center with little possibility for the autonomous expression of such demands or activities that alternate with times of extremist political, ideological, and religious rebellious movements.

The elites of both Tsarist and modern Soviet Russia have tended to encourage among different local, occupational, territorial kinship groups the segregation of life styles and patterns of participation. These elites have attempted to minimize the "status" or "class" components of family or kinship group identity as well as the autonomous standing of the family in the status system. Especially with regard to the access to the center, they have tried to establish a uniform hierarchy of evaluation of major positions. They have aimed also at making this hierarchy a relatively steep one—within the center, between it and the periphery, and to some degree also among the peripheral groups—discouraging the development of any countrywide class-consciousness among most groups and strata.

Because semi-normative styles of life have been deliberately inhibited among the different strata, they tend (in Soviet Russia) to exhibit less emphasis on styles of life and family continuity, greater openness toward different new occupational or economic and educational activities, and greater readiness to approach the modern center.

Different occupational groups in Tsarist and Soviet Russia alike have also been inclined to social segregation and an emphasis on their own distinct occupational or professional goals. Such groups often tend to coalesce into relatively closed semistrata, each stressing its separateness from other groups, but at the same time espousing similar desiderata as well as using the same basic types of institutional commodities and means of exchange.

The monopolistic bias of the central elite tends to control severely the legitimation of the styles of life of each subgroup. The center continuously attempts to limit and to break up efforts of any stratum to transcend its own style of life beyond restricted parochial scopes or to claim legitimation for its style of life in terms of wider central values independent of the elite.

Accordingly, the central elite in these societies tries to minimize any tendencies to base such styles of life and differential access to positions on family transmission.

These tendencies necessarily affect the ways in which the different status groups participate in various spheres of social life. In principle most groups in Soviet Russia are allowed to participate in different spheres of life, but their success depends greatly on their relative standing with regard to the central elite. Common participation is possible in ritual-political or communal-sporting activities, which are controlled by the central elite, but impossible in the more private spheres of each stratum or in the more central spheres of the elite itself.

These general aspects of the system of stratification are paralleled by or manifest in crucial characteristics of the structure of the elites and the professionals alike. A high degree of dissociation appears both between the elite groups themselves and (in most respects) between them and the rest of society, with one elite group always trying to dominate the others. Similarly, the professional groups—not unlike the urban guilds of Tsarist times—evince little autonomy or autonomous commitment to a broader social order. They are characterized by a narrow conception of their technical function and a high subservience to the State, which supervises them closely.

Many of the "patrimonial societies," such as the Southeast Asian or Latin American ones, exhibit a similar continuity in the basic aspects of the systems of political and social-hierarchical regulation. The foci of political decision and innovation in the traditional regimes remain mostly in the hands of the rulers' household cliques, while in the modern ones usually in the executive branch of the government as composed of bureaucratic, army, or political cliques, and pressure groups. These central elites tend to monopolize central political activities and resources, attempting to limit any independent access of the periphery to such resources and activities as well as minimizing the direct independent political contact and participation of the periphery in the center. At the same time, however, they try to maintain minimal structural interpretation of the periphery.

The development of collective goals or the active formation of new symbols of collective identity, as well as the regulation of autonomous intergroup relations, tend to be much weaker than in Western Europe and Russia. Accordingly, the policies of the central elites are mostly prescriptive and distributive, especially those which aim at the accumulation of resources in the hands of the centers and on their possible distribution among the various groups of the society. Insofar as the rulers of these regimes engage in economic policies, they tend to aim at expanding control of large territories and not to be characterized by intensive exploitation within a fixed resource basis. Such distributive and extractive policies—

often coupled with ritual—aim to maintain the harmony between the cosmic and the social orders implicit in the ideal "image" of the King as the "keeper" of the welfare of the people. They also provide important resources for the maintenance of the ruler's power in the internal political game.

Structural and symbolic differences are relatively limited between the center and the broader peripheral groups or regions of society, connected as they are by the great ecological and symbolic magnet of the center. The links between the center and the periphery that have tended to develop in these regimes create little basic structural change either within the sectors or the strata of the periphery, or within the center itself.

The center impinges on the local (rural, urban, or tribal) communities mainly in the form of administration of law, attempts to maintain peace, exaction of taxation, and the maintenance of some cultural or religious links to the center. But most of these links and the attachment to the center are, with few exceptions, effected through the existing local kinship units, territorial and ritual. New types of mechanisms linking the center and the periphery seldom develop. Only a few new structural channels have appeared that undermine or attempt to change the existing social and cultural patterns of either the center or the periphery or to inject into them new common orientations, as is the case in Imperial systems or in the modern nation-states and revolutionary societies.

Political struggle within the center tends to take the form of direct bargaining as well as regulation of the access to channels of distribution and of mediation among various groups. It seldom takes place through more representative activities or the promotion of continuous uniform activities according to certain general principles or articulated goals and criteria. By the rules of the political game, coalitions tend to be mostly those of mediation and cooptation to, or exclusion from access to the center. There is little leeway for the development of autonomous access by these or other broad groups to the resources and positions controlled by the center.

Within these frameworks and patterns of coalition, the major means of political struggle tend to become more and more those of change or extension of the clientele networks. General popularistic appeals often accompany such struggle and are mostly made in terms of ascriptive symbols or values representing different ethnic, religious, or national communities. Such appeals can, however, easily precipitate outbreaks that serve as important signals for the inadequacy of the existing pattern of cooptation.

In the systems of stratification of traditional as well as modern patrimonial societies, the bases of evaluation are attributes of relatively closed groups, with the difference between "modern" and "traditional" being increasingly important distinctions of such attributes. Evaluation has also tended to be measured in terms of the control over resources, with functional "performance" or "service" as designated by the center playing a relatively smaller role.

Given the strong emphasis on such attributes as well as the center's predilection for strict control over the access to them, country-wide strata or class consciousness has tended to be weak. Instead, smaller groups—territorial, semi-occupational, or local—become major status units, all of them developing rather strong tendencies to status-segregation with little autonomous political orientation.

These societies also plan strong emphasis on the combination of "closed" restricted prestige and "power" as the major social orientations of the elites and the groups alike. In modern patrimonial societies, unlike the traditional, strong and usually ascriptive orientations and references to the center have tended to develop, however "segregated" various units may be. These groups attempt to convert their resources into media that might enable them to participate in the broader frameworks, but mostly in the ascriptive ones of the new center—tendencies that have many repercussions in the political field.

III

Significant continuities in the modes of political organization and social stratification are not limited to the "mere" persistence of random, discrete institutional features. These various characteristics are closely related to some crucial differences in the broader cultural orientations of these societies and may also persist through different periods in the history of the same societies or civilizations. Insofar as these societal thrusts have institutional impact, they are not broad cultural or value orientations, but seem to be much closer to what Weber has called *Wirtschaftsethik*—that is, general modes of religious, "ethical" (or rather general symbolic) orientation employed in a specific institutional sphere. These codes or orientations provide directives or choices with respect to some of the perennial problems immanent in the nature of human life considered in its social and cultural contexts. They offer the major ways of looking at the basic problems of human existence as well as at the social and cultural order itself.

It can, perhaps, be conjectured that the constellation of such codes operative in any group or society constitutes a crucial aspect of its "hidden" structure. In support of such a claim, one can point to the regularity evidenced in the ways these orientations relate to the more organizational aspects of social life. For example, the greater the tendency to perceive the social and cultural orders as being relevant to one another and mutually autonomous, the greater is the degree of political autonomy among different groups and the development of independent foci of political struggle, as is true in Western Europe. Conversely, when these orders are subservient to one of them, as in Russia, or dissociated from one another, as in many patrimonial societies, the degree of autonomy is restricted.

Similarly, when the center is conceived of as the single focus of broader cultural order, emphasis tends to be placed on functional attributes of status and closed segregated status groups. As the "adaptive" attitude to the center becomes more pronounced, so also do the degree of status segregation and the emphasis on the restricted prestige of closed communities. The commitment of broader groups to the social order necessitates greater permeation of the center into the periphery and focus on attributes of power in the system of stratification. Similarly, when autonomous access to the center and common commitment to a broader social order are stressed, the degree of status association and autonomy tends to be great.

Such sets of codes are highly correlated not only to discrete patterns within these societies, such as the structure of the political process or hierarchical organization, but also to the more "basic" aspects of the working of social systems. Moreover, they tend to influence the working of social and political systems in similar ways in "traditional" and "modern" societies alike.

Thus, for example, the modern socio-political order of Western Europe has been characterized by a high degree of congruence between the cultural and political identities of the territorial population as well as a high level of symbolic and affective commitments to the political and cultural centers. There has been a marked emphasis on politically defined collective goals for all members of the national community, while access of broad strata to symbols and centers has been relatively autonomous.

Certain patterns of participation and protest specific to the European scene have developed in close relation to these features. Both the political groups and the more autonomous social forces and elites have tended to crystallize in the complementary "units" or "forces" of "State" and "Society," continuously contesting their relative importance in the formation of the cultural and political centers of the nation-state and in the regulation of access to them. The processes of structural change and dislocation concomitant with the development of modernization in the periphery have given rise not only to concrete problems and demands, but also to a growing quest for participation in the broader social and political order.

Indeed, many concrete social, economic, and political demands have originated as part of this broader quest for participation in the formation of the social and political orders and their centers. One response to the convergence between concrete socio-economic problems and the demand for participation has been the development of the conception of "class society" and "class struggle."

Many of these characteristics of the European nation-states are similar to those that existed in their premodern sociopolitical traditions—those of the Imperial, city-state, and feudal systems. Strong activism derives to a large extent from the traditions of city-states, while the conception of the political order as being actively related to the cosmic or cultural order has its origin in many Imperial traditions or in the traditions of Great Religions. Ideas about the autonomous access of different groups to the major attributes of social and cultural orders find their sources, at least in part, in the pluralist-feudal structure. Continuation and expansion of these premodern structures and orientations have been greatly facilitated by the commerical and industrial revolutions as well as by the development of absolutism, on the one hand, and of Protestantism, on the other.

In the Imperial East European or Asian societies—such as Russia, Japan, or China—the pluralistic elements have been much weaker than those found in the feudal or city-states of the traditional Western European order. Their political traditions have rarely entailed a dichotomy between State and Society. Rather, they have tended to stress the congruent but often passive relations between the cosmic order, on the one hand, and the socio-political order, on the other. The interrelation between the political and the social orders is not stated in terms of an antithesis between these entities, but envisaged as the coalescence of these different functions within the same group or organization and with a common focus in the cosmic order.

In Russia, for example, the constellation of attitudes has encouraged neither the conception of relatively autonomous access for the major strata to the political and cultural centers nor the autonomy of the social and cultural orders in relation to the political one. Accordingly, demands of the broader groups for access to the center are, on the whole, either couched in terms of possible participation in a social and cultural order as defined by the center or expressed in attempts to overthrow the existing center and establish a new one similar in its basic characteristics. Autonomous access to the center is seldom sought, nor must the center face continuous struggle about the relative influence in the formation of such order. As a result, the situation in Russia and similar societies has not fostered the development of the autonomous class-society, "class-consciousness," and class struggle characteristic of Western Europe. Demands are made on the center by major groups in these societies, especially for greater distribution of resources by the center. But such demands do not necessarily advocate actual participation in the political-cultural order or discuss the possibility of such participation.

In traditional as well as modern patrimonial regimes, the broader social or cultural order is perceived mostly as something to be mastered or accommodated, not as something commanding a high level of commitment. Within these societies, acceptance of the givenness of the cultural and social order tends to be strong, while the possibility of active autonomous participation is barely perceived by any social groups that could shape the contours of that order, even to the extent that such shaping is possible in traditional systems. Tension between a "higher" transcendental order and the social order seldom appears; and when it does, it constitutes an important element in the "religious" sphere proper but not in the political or social ones.

Such societies place little emphasis on the autonomous access of the major groups or strata to the major attributes of these orders, access usually being seen as mediated by ascriptive individual groups or ritual experts who represent the "given" order and are mostly appointed by the center or sub-centers. The connection between broader universalistic percepts—be they religious or ideological—and the actual social order tends to be weak. Ritualistic participation in the society's broad orientations plays a more prominent role than deep commitment to such concepts. The basic premises of the cultural order are accepted with relative passivity, while the givenness of that order often goes unquestioned.

As a result of these perceptions of the social-political order, the inclination to active participation in the centers of these societies is weak, while the center is depended upon to provide resources and to regulate internal affairs insofar as these are related to the broader society. The development of autonomous mechanisms of self-regulation is inhibited in such situations.

Demands on the center have not abated at all in these societies with the spread of the basic assumptions of modernity. But such demands have usually focused not on control of the center, but on change in its contents and symbols or on the possible creation of new types of social and cultural orders by the center.

The characteristics of the various social orders coalesce—in the traditional and modern setting alike—into broader models of socio-political orders, producing patterns that have been designated as the "absolutist" and "estate" and "nation-state" models of Western Europe, the autocratic-Imperial and revolutionary-class models of Russia (or China), and the patrimonial and neo-patrimonial models. Each model or system of codes contains within it several inherent foci of tension. Such tensions are inherent in the contradictions that develop within any system itself, in its application to broad institutional complexes, and in the differences between it and other types of cultural constructions. Indeed, any construction of cultural reality implies posing certain kinds of questions about the basic problems of human existence. The range of acceptable questions as well as permissible answers is thereby defined. Thus, for example, any cultural model usually emphasizes certain dimensions of human existence—be they the aesthetic, the political, or the ritual experiences. In this process it may suppress other dimensions or relegate them to secondary or "subterranean" levels.

Moreover, within any tradition or social order, the possible relations among its different components are not exhausted by their actual coalescence in the given institutionalized system. The very specification of the basic parameters of a cultural tradition in its relations to various collectivities is open, therefore, to redefinition and recrystallization in terms of any of these parameters or of new orientations that may develop from them. Similarly, attempts at such redefinition may focus not only on the degree to which any given collectivity becomes the embodiment of the major orientations, but on the relative evaluation of the different dimensions of human existence as well. The processes whereby the various dimensions of tradition become institutionalized are in continuously close relation to the organizational aspects of social division of labor in general, thereby sharpening the tensions implicit in any social order.

The contradictions inherent in the complex of codes operative in any society and in their applicability to broader institutional patterns tend to cluster around certain poles involving their perception and formulation on the symbolic level. Among such themes or poles the most important are the varying ways of structuring the differences in human life between nature and culture; the perennial encounter between the quest for solidarity and the exigencies of division of labor and of political struggle; the tension between the givens of power and its exercise and the search for more transcendental types of legitimation of the social order; and the degrees to which various models of cosmic, human and social order can provide foci for meaningful human endeavor. Such themes influence concrete institutional and behavioral patterns mainly through the provision of guidelines for the choice of goals and the means for their attainment by individuals. They determine, for the most part, the normative specifications of the limitation on the goals available or permitted to the members of a certain group. Controlling the organization of directives and mechanisms that regulate the flow of resources, they set the pattern of exchange and interaction that takes place within the major institutional spheres of a society.

The concrete specifications of such guidelines are effected through sets of rules of transformation that indicate or specify the ways members of different groups in a society are expected to pursue such goals in the course of their lifetime. They also concretize how different rewards and sanctions, especially of various combinations of solidary instrumental rewards and power, are distributed among the different sectors of any group and how such distribution is legitimated. On the macro-societal level, of special importance here is the specification not only of goals, but also of the centers and collectivities as against the secondary, "sub-cultural," and "counter-cultural" groups that may be caused by movements of heterodoxy and rebellion.

Insofar as such a constellation of codes exists or persists in the "same" society in different periods of its development, cutting across levels of social differentiation and changes of regimes, it may be seen as one crucial aspect of "tradition" and continuity. But such continuity or similarity differs fundamentally from that which characterizes boundary-maintaining systems, such as political systems and regimes or cultural and ethnic communities bound together by common symbols of collective identity. Truly enough, such different aspects of "tradition" tend in a given historical situation to coalesce, but they need not vary always to the same degree. Moreover, each may have distinct structural bases and carriers as well as different modes of operation.

Different structures of codes may be institutionalized in a great variety of concrete ways and may persist beyond changes in the political system or the boundaries of collectivities. Thus, the ways in which basic problems and dilemmas are defined and resolved in articulated cultural models do not necessarily correspond to the specific methods of institutionalization. Codes that usually tend to specify the general type of relations between, let us say, the political and social or cultural order can leave undefined the concrete settings or boundaries of such organizations and units.

For example, while the general idea of the importance of the fusion of the political and cultural communities is basic to all of Islam, the way in which it can be institutionalized has varied greatly from one situation to another—from the tribal setting of Arabia, to the centralized Empires of the Middle East, to the more shifting centers of North Africa. Within each such situation, rather different rules of transformation can operate, and in each situation different cultural themes can be emphasized.

Even in more "compact" traditional societies, like China, Japan, and Burma, where there is greater coalescence between the cultural and the political orders, these codes have been institutionalized in various ways. Thus, in China, the tension between the ideals of sociopolitical and of inner harmony can be played out in the distinction between the lonely scholar and the bureaucrat, on the one hand, or between the legalistic-official and the Taoist-Buddhist, on the other.

But the diversity in the ways in which these codes can be institutionalized, however great, is not endless. It is bound by some internal structure which provides coherence to such codes and makes it possible to talk about their continuity in different situations and across various levels of structural differentiation. Such continuity depends largely on certain structural conditions. The differences in this respect stand out between traditional and modern settings of the "same" societies or civilizations as well as within different traditional settings.

In most of the traditional civilizations discussed earlier, there has been relatively great continuity in cultural models and especially in the systems of codes. Although the concrete setting fostered by any given political community or by a certain level of economic resource does constitute an important "selector" of codes, it does not, on the whole, tend to change the major contents of these codes or their rules of transformation.

This characteristic seems to have been due, in part, to the relatively limited level of resources available for the building and construction of new institutional complexes. It has also been supported by the prevalence within these societies of traditional legitimation. Some combination of "origin," pastness, and sacredness, usually represented by some great figure or historical event, tends to be accepted as the major source of the legitimation of an immutable cultural model and social order.

Thus, however varied the symbols of collective identity within these civilizations, they all contain some references to these common symbols of tradition—thereby limiting their possible variability. Similarly, such legitimation restricts the level of demands, especially for participation in the cultural and political centers and for possible far-reaching changes in their contents.

Such limitations—the structural and the symbolic—on levels of resources and demands reduce the range of variability in the selection of codes. Limits are manifest in and reinforced by the structural and the ideological orientations of movements of heterodoxy, on the one hand, and of rebellion, on the other and especially by their tendency to be separated from one another.

IV

The development of a post-traditional modern order creates a setting in which the interrelations among specific aspects of tradition become not only more complex, but also more sharply articulated. Moreover, within many societies and cultures new codes and cultural models can emerge in such situations through a variety of mechanisms of cultural diffusion. Modernization is viewed not simply as a given process, but also as a goal—in the transitive sense.

Concomitant with modernization, for example, has been the reevaluation of the political dimension of human life and, as a result, increasing politicization and greater sensitivity to political demands. For the relative late-comers, as opposed to European societies, the break with the traditional bases of legitimation may also imply a possible rejection of their own heritage.

Any attempt to establish and maintain a new post-traditional order creates problems, conflicts, and tensions unparalleled in other situations of change. The transition to a modern, post-traditional order constitutes a focus around which severe conflicts and struggles tend to develop—borne most visibly by social movements, political elites and groups, and different social and political coalitions. Through such processes of struggle crystallize most of the contours of post-traditional orders—such as the ability of the post-traditional order and political regime to institutionalize new types of center-periphery relations as well as new patterns of institutionalization.

Obviously, the establishment of such an order does not necessarily obliterate traditional forces in general or arrest the continuity of traditional cultural models in particular. Nevertheless, the problems attendant on the institutionalization of new cultural models and their impact on the working of their respective societies are much more complex in modern settings. They become closely interrelated with the construction of symbols of tradition in general and those of collective political and cultural orders in particular. Such construction does not take place through a "natural" unfolding of the traditions of these societies; these processes contain strong elements of choice. Whereas the range of choices is not unlimited, their concrete crystallization in any specific situation is not entirely predetermined either by structural developments or by the "tradition" of a society. Even in structurally similar situations, there is always some range in the alternatives available.

Choices are manifest on different levels, being perhaps most visible with respect to the types of political regimes that may develop within the framework of the broader models of socio-political order. On a level somewhat less fully institutionalized and formalized, but not necessarily less pervasive, such choices emerge in the patterns available for reconstructing the traditions of such post-traditional societies, especially the ways in which various symbols of collective identity are to be shaped. The situation can be perceived in terms of cultural continuity or discontinuity, and various "existing" traditions and symbols of collective identity can be discarded or incorporated into the new symbolic frameworks. Such elements of choice are especially prominent in the reconstruction of the symbolic frameworks that designate a society's self-conception.

Rarely are such symbols taken as given from the existing tradition; rather, a process of re-constitution or re-construction of such symbols tends to take place. In all situations of far-reaching change, cultural traditions, symbols, artifacts, and organizations become more elaborate and articulated, more rationally organized or, at least, more formalized. As different groups and individuals in the society become increasingly aware of these traditions and symbols, "tradition" becomes differentiated in layers. Simple "given" usages or patterns of behavior may become quite distinct from the more articulated and formalized symbols of the cultural order—such as the great ritual centers and offices, theological codices, or special buildings. The layers of tradition tend to vary also in the degree and nature of their prescriptive validity and in their relevance to different spheres of life.

These processes are often related to a growing "partialization" and privatization of various older existing traditions or customs. Even if the "old" customs and symbols are not negated or "thrown out," they undergo far-reaching changes. What had been the totality of sanctioned patterns in any given community or society tends to become only partial in several respects. It may persist as binding only for certain members or for certain spheres. Even the validity of its prescriptive power or its use as the guiding symbolic templates in these spheres of life change greatly and become differentiated.

The transition to modernity poses, even more than in other situations of change, the question of whether the old or the new traditions represent the true tradition of the new social political or religious community. It must be determined how far any of the given existing traditions can become incorporated into the new central patterns of culture and "tradition" and the extent to which it is possible to legitimate this order in terms of those existing traditions.

As a reaction to the possibilities of erosion, the tendency known as "traditionalism" can develop, preparing the soil for potential dichotomy between "tradition" and "traditionalism." Traditionalism is not to be confused with a "simple" or "natural" upkeep of a given tradition. Rather, it denotes an ideological mode and stance oriented against the new symbols; it espouses certain parts of the older tradition as the only legitimate symbols of the traditional order and upholds them against "new" trends. Through opposing these trends, the "traditionalist" attitudes tend toward formalization on both the symbolic and organizational levels.

It is possible to distinguish, even if in a preliminary way, several major patterns of reconstruction of tradition in situations of social change in general and of modernization in particular. One such pattern segregates "traditional" (ritual, religious) and non-traditional spheres of life without, however, developing any appropriate connective symbolic and organizational bonds between the two. In other words, new percepts or symbolic orientations do not develop that might serve as guides to the ways in which the various layers of tradition could become connected in meaningful patterns. At the same time, a strong predisposition or demand for some clear unifying principle tends to persist, with uneasiness and insecurity becoming pronounced when it is lacking. As a result, a tendency can develop toward "ritualization" of the symbols of traditional life, on the personal and collective levels alike. Increasing attempts to impose traditional symbols on the new secular world in a relatively rigid, militant way may then alternate with the total isolation of these traditional symbols from the impurities of that world. This mode of persistence of traditional patterns is usually connected with the strengthening of ritual status images. It is often accompanied by an intolerance of ambiguity on both personal and collective levels as well as by apathy and the erosion of any normative commitments because of such apathy.

Groups exhibiting these tendencies do not normally incorporate their various "primordial" symbols of local, ethnic caste or class groups into the new center of the society, and the reformulation of these symbols on a new level of common identification is difficult and problematic. Rather, they tend to become foci of separateness, of ritual traditionalism. On a macro-societal level the responses of this pattern are usually characterized mainly by conservative ideologies, coercive orientations and policies, and an active ideological or symbolic closure of the new centers, with a strong traditionalistic emphasis on older symbols.

A second major pattern yields a continuous distinction and differentiation among the various layers of tradition and between the traditional and non-traditional ("religious" and "non-religious") spheres of life. This segregation, however, is less total and rigid than that characterizing the first pattern; there tends to be more continuity between the different spheres, with greater overflow and overlapping, although this continuity does not ordinarily become fully formalized or ritualized. There is not usually any strong predisposition toward rigid unifying principles, and in this way greater tolerance of ambiguity and of cognitive dissonance is built up.

The members of the group or society tend to be predisposed to making a positive connection between their personal identity and the symbols of the new political, social, and cultural order. The members thus accept the new symbols as the major collective referents of their personal identity. These symbols provide guiding templates for participation in the social and cultural order and lend meaning to many of the new institutional activities.

The groups or elites exhibiting this pattern tend to distinguish between different layers of traditional commitments and motivations and to draw on them all, insofar as possible, in the development of new tasks and activities. The first of these layers is the persistence, however flexible, of certain poles or basic modes of perception of the cosmic, cultural and social orders. The second is the persistence of autonomous symbols of the collective identities of major subgroups and collectivities, however great may be the concrete changes in their content. Traditional symbols may be transposed into new broader frameworks by groups or elites with tendencies to innovate new central symbols of personal or collective identity. Major differences develop, however, between non-coercive and coercive elites of this kind. The first tend to facilitate or encourage the rise of new groups or collectivities, especially the more differentiated, specialized ones committed to new institutional goals. As a result, continuity of tradition may be maintained mostly in terms of general orientations, but not of full commitment to their content, which may continuously change.

With a coercive elite, the situation is more complex. Once in power, it is in a position to destroy most of the concrete symbols and structures of existing traditions, strata, and organizations and to emphasize a new content and new types of social organization. At the same time, however, it may preserve considerable continuity with regard to certain basic modes of symbolic and institutional orientations. Coercive elites attempt to unleash and to control, in a new way, the primary motivational orientations inherent in the older systems, while changing their content and basic identity.

The processes through which any of these patterns of reconstruction of tradition become predominant comprise elements of struggle and resolution of conflicts as well as a certain element of choice. Patterns and types of political regimes demonstrate affinity with these patterns of reconstruction in their shared attitudes about the processes of change. Thus, groups or elites that are totally passive, negative, or actively resistant to change through an organized "traditionalistic" response tend to adopt a pattern of reconstruction characterized by ritualistic segregation between different layers of tradition. On the whole, they are most able to develop with authoritarian regimes. Groups or elites that evince more positive orientations incline to open segregative patterns of reconstruction. Such groups tend, in their turn, to be most closely attuned either to a variety of pluralistic regimes or, in the case of the coercive orientation, to totalitarian or semi-totalitarian regimes.

But although there is noticeable affinity between types of regimes and patterns of reconstruction of tradition, the latter seem to be more variegated than the former. Thus, any given type of political regime tends to develop a certain heterogeneity in its patterns of reconstruction of tradition. Such heterogeneity, while constrained by the type of regime, is not entirely bound by it and may even prove to be an important focus of political change.

The various "choices" of political regimes have even less of a direct correlation with the alternative patterns of reconstruction of tradition and especially of continuity and discontinuity of various codes. Constellations of codes may persist in a given society, whatever the regime or the pattern of reconstruction that becomes most prevalent within it. Thus, for example, it may be claimed that similar constellations of codes characterized both the "nationalistic" and "revolutionary" regimes in China, the modernizing, autocratic, and revolutionary regimes in Russia, or the constitutional and caudillo regimes of countries like Venezuela. The concrete problems with which the structural derivatives of these codes coped as well as the concrete contours of these derivatives differed greatly between such regimes, yet these concrete problems were indeed shaped by the types of regimes and patterns of reconstruction of tradition that became prevalent in the society.

Whatever the exact relations among the different "choices" as they develop in post-traditional orders, their direction is greatly influenced by the predominance of coalitions between the various elites and major social and economic groups. But these patterns of coalition may, in their turn, be influenced to some degree by the different codes that have been predominant in the traditional settings. It is this combination of various aspects of tradition at work, of selection of patterns for reconstruction of tradition, and of struggle leading to the establishment of political regimes that explains at least some of the dynamics of different socio-political orders. At this stage it is not possible to present more than a distant preliminary hypothesis with regard to the ways in which such combinations operate. It may, perhaps, be postulated that the ability to institutionalize any post-traditional order and political regime is influenced mainly by the respective power-relations among the groups participating in this struggle, by the internal cohesion of the major elites that become predominant in the situation of change, and by the severity of the solidary relations between the predominant elites and the broader strata.

One can also assume that the concrete political regimes as well as the patterns of reconstruction of tradition that become institutionalized in a post-traditional society are determined mostly by the composition and orientation of the elites or strata that become predominant in that post-traditional order. Concomitantly, the constellation of codes operative within the society shapes the development of different broader models of post-traditional societies—be they "nation-state," patrimonial, or whatever. These constellations determine not only the specific types of conflicts to which the societies are especially sensitive, but also the conditions under which such conflicts become articulated into more specific boiling points, threatening the stability of the regimes. Such codes define the means available to the regimes when coping with these conflicts, especially the ways of incorporating various types of political demands, those for growing participation in the political order in particular. Not only the intensity of such conflicts and the perception of their acuteness, but also the range of "flexibility" or rigidity in response seem to be determined primarily by combinations between, on the one hand, the different patterns of construction of tradition and new symbols of collective identity and, on the other, the relative balance of forces among groups with different socio-political orientations.

These hypotheses all indicate that the social and cultural forces of what has often indiscriminately been called tradition, as well as other more "structural" processes, need not always vary in a direct relation or unfold in a preordained direction. It has frequently been assumed, even if only implicitly, that changes in codes, regimes, and levels of social power and differentiation are always directly correlated. The dichotomy posited by earlier researchers between modern and traditional societies was, to a very large extent, based on this assumption.

The analysis presented here, however, indicates that the populations that live within the confines of what has customarily been designated as a "society," a macro-societal order, are not usually organized in one "system," but rather in several different ways and on several levels. These various levels may be carried by different parts of the populations as well as through different mechanisms and structures. The movements of the "same" or of closely related populations through such systems may also vary to some degree independently of one another. Finally, these aspects of the social order differ greatly and evince different patterns of organization, continuity, and change; they may change within the "same" society to different degrees or in different ways in various areas of social life.

Of special importance, from the point of view of comparative macro-sociological analysis and the analysis of social change, are, first, different collectivities and organizations, organized as "systems" or congeries of "systems" with their respective boundary-maintaining mechanisms; second, various socio-ecological systems; third, broader collectivities, communities, or socio-cultural orders that are not necessarily structured as organizations, but are focused on various symbols of collective identity; fourth, different levels of structural differentiation of social activities; and, last, cultural orientations and "codes." Each of these aspects of the social order "organizes" the social activities of the respective population from a distinct point of view and in a distinct pattern, also evincing different patterns of continuity or change.

Such observations have certain far-reaching implications for comparative macro-sociological analysis in general and for the analysis of change in particular. The major differences not only between the various types of "traditional" societies (such as "archaic" or "historical"), but also between traditional and modern societies have usually been constructed in sociological literature according to criteria of structural differentiation or the contents of different cultural symbols of spheres. Such aspects are obviously of great interest for macro-sociological comparisons, but more importantly, perhaps these different levels of differentiation can serve to point out the nature of the constellations of forces generated in any society that impinge on its collectivities or systems, creating concrete problems but also providing resources through which such problems can be resolved.

In situations of change there develops not just one possibility for restructuring resources and activities, but rather a great variety of possibilities. Within each "type" of traditional or modern society, different models of social and political order emerge which define the parameters of traditionality and modernity. The variability of these aspects of social order is not, however, entirely random. Indeed, these considerations call forth a series of new questions: Who are the carriers and what are the mechanisms of the different aspects of social order? What are the relations among them? What are the structural conditions that facilitate the development of different types of codes and the continuous maintenance of their major structural derivatives? What are the conditions under which the relative importance of different codes within a society change? Is the "transition" from one type of society to another—from a "traditional" to a modern one—dependent on change in the existing constellation of codes or is it possible to envisage such transitions simply through changes in cultural contents or through structural differentiation?

Some of the initial theoretical considerations on the dynamics of traditions exposed here can be found in greater detail in the author's "Intellectuals and Traditions," *Daedalus* (Spring 1972), pp. 1-19; and "Some Observations on the Dynamics of Traditions," *Comparative Studies in Society and History*, Vol. 11, No. 4 (October 1969), pp. 451-475.

EDMUND LEACH

Buddhism in the Post-Colonial Political Order in Burma and Ceylon

I WAS asked to write about the influence of traditional (especially Buddhist) conceptions of the political order on the political orientations of the national movements and especially on the formation of post-colonial political orders in Burma and Ceylon. In fulfillment of this task, I shall switch the reader's attention back and forth between the two countries rather rapidly; to lessen confusion let me start with a list of names. Since the end of World War II the most significant political leaders in Burma have been Aung San, U Nu, and Ne Win. In Ceylon leadership has been more confused, but we may note in particular: D. S. Senanayake; his nephew, Sir John Kotelawala; his son, Dudley Senanayake; S. W. R. D. Bandaranaike; and the latter's widow, Mrs. Bandaranaike. At the present time (Autumn 1972) Burma is ruled by a military dictatorship headed by Ne Win; Ceylon is ruled by a nominally democratic government headed by Mrs. Bandaranaike, which exercises dictatorial jurisdiction under a special powers act. Of the persons named, Aung San and S. W. R. D. Bandaranaike both died by assassination.

Before I examine the evidence which the careers of these people provide, let me make some brief definitional comments on the words "political" and "national." A man is engaged in *political* action whenever he behaves in such a way as to rally others to support a cause in which he is interested. This is a very wide definition; for my present purposes, I shall assume that we are talking about politics at a relatively "high" level and that what is at issue is the control and orientation of the policies of state governments.

The term *national* is more complicated. Politicians may engage in one or other of two major types of enterprise; either they seek to lead or participate in a *rebellion,* hoping to seize power in the existing system and then to run the whole organization much as before, or they promote a *revolution,* which entails (or at least is expected to entail) a radical change in the existing order. Since the advocates of revolution wish to destroy what exists, they must be prepared to suggest alternatives. These alternatives again fall into two types: the millenarian dream which looks forward to the creation

29

of a New Heaven and a New Earth, and the mythical restoration which seeks to recreate the Golden Age of peace and plenty and brotherly love. The difference between those who harness their ambitions to an imaginary future and those who seek to recover an imaginary past is not, in practice, very great, but certain kinds of symbolism are more readily adapted to the one frame of reference than to the other. Political movements which come to be labeled *nationalistic* are always revolutionary in their grand objectives, but they are fairly consistently backward-looking rather than forward-looking. The nationalist credo is: "We are one nation because we share a common origin." That origin may be either physical or cultural or territorial.

Let me cite some examples. Hitler's National Socialists saw their identity as that of a mythical Aryan race, the *Deutsche Volk*. It was this imaginary racialist self-identity which served to justify their very unimaginary racialist persecution of the Jews and the Gypsies. Similarly, in present-day Great Britain Enoch Powell's nationalism takes the form of the wholly imaginary thesis that true Englishmen are all of common genetic stock. This has the logical consequence that he does his best to encourage rabid hostility against all those whose visible appearance seems to contradict his thesis.

The myth of common breed can quickly switch to a myth of common culture. In recent times the French, the Irish, the Welsh, the Sinhalese, and the Indian National Congress have all, at different levels and in different ways, tried to use "the cultural tradition of a common national language" as a symbol of political solidarity. Likewise, the practical, as distinct from the theoretical, limits of Hitler's *Deutsche Volk* were largely *linguistic*; hence the thesis that the Austrians, the inhabitants of Bohemia (Sudetenland), and even the German speaking Swiss "ought" to be incorporated into a Greater Germany, despite the fact that many of the greatly varied dialects of the German language are mutually incomprehensible.

This, of course, is an oversimplification. The growth of a sense of national German identity during the nineteenth century was the product of a complex of historical forces. My point is simply that in all countries demagogic politicians who wish to exploit nationalist feelings repeatedly revert to the same key symbols, and common language is one of these.

The emotional value of this "language = common culture" thesis is very great, but as a political instrument it is double-edged. The sovereign states of the late twentieth century are invariably defined as units of territory with precisely defined boundaries, and these boundaries are complex products of history and geography; it is unusual to find that all the citizens of such a state speak the same language or that the speakers of a particular language are all citizens of one state.

The same is true of another major cultural parameter, religion. Sectarian solidarity is so emotive that the nationalist politician is at all times greatly tempted to disguise his gospel of revolution as a summons to a Holy War, but the practical boundaries of natural geography, speech community, and sectarian affiliation very seldom fit together. Political propaganda commonly seeks to mask this discrepancy, but it is an important fact which should not be overlooked. At no time in past history have Burmese Buddhists or Ceylonese Buddhists ever occupied more than a fraction of the geographical areas which are labeled on contemporary maps as Burma and Ceylon.

All that I have said so far expresses a personal, prejudiced point of view. There would be no general consensus among social scientists that "political movements which come to be labeled as nationalistic are always revolutionary." Quite to the contrary, many scholars write as if a nationalist credo might characterize a thoroughly conservative, functionally cohesive social system. Others would repudiate my thesis that nationalist movements are consistently backward-looking. But such disagreements stem from issues of definition. For example, I agree that the arrogant contempt for foreigners which was frequently exhibited by Oriental despots even in quite recent history, as well as the bellicose patriotism referred to as "chauvinism" or "jingoism," have their roots in a sense of national self-consciousness and pride. I agree, too, that such attitudes are often adopted by persons who appear to be in secure positions of power. But these are styles of behavior rather than political doctrines. I claim that when a whole political movement prides itself in its "nationalism" it is always seeing itself as being on the defensive or in opposition, and even the most aggressive actions against neighbors are justified by the plea of self-preservation. As to the question of whether such nationalism is necessarily backward-looking, I may cite the views of an authority who takes a different view.

D. E. Smith[1] claims that "independent Burma inherited not one but two nationalist traditions." The first, which he calls "traditional Burmese nationalism" was "based among other things on a common race, language and religion." This kind of nationalism, represented in the person of Prime Minister U Nu, was a continuation of the nationalism of Saya San, the ex-monk who led an unsuccessful rebellion against the British in 1930-1931, and was even proclaimed King. It was also in line with the explicitly Buddhist militarism of the agitator monk U Ottama (1921) and with King Thibaw's proclamation, at the beginning of the Anglo-Burmese war of 1885, to the effect that the invading British were "heretic barbarians" who threatened Burmese religion, national customs, and race. Smith's second kind of Burmese nationalism is that of General Ne Win, which he claims is a continuation of the nationalism of Aung San (assassinated in July 1947) and of the Thakin movement formed in 1935. Smith describes it as "militant in its opposition to foreign rule but with a considerable regard for western political institutions, secular and Marxist-inclined in its ideological orientation."

Smith's view, then, is that the nationalism of Aung San and of Ne Win is forward-looking rather than backward-looking. Now it is quite true that Aung San proclaimed "progressive" objectives, but he was not particularly successful at grafting these objectives onto the nationalist cause. "A nation," he once declared, "is a collective term applied to a people, irrespective of their ethnic origin, living in close contact with one another and having common interests and sharing joys and sorrows together for such historic periods as to have acquired a sense of oneness. Though race, religion, and language are important factors, it is only their traditional desire and will to live in unity through weal and woe that binds the people together and makes them a people."[2]

But this is just wishful thinking. History offers a variety of instances, Athens and Venice are examples, in which a closely packed, polyglot, ethnically diverse population has developed a sense of national identity by loyalty to a well-defined locality, a named City State, and it might perhaps be claimed that in such cases it is "a traditional desire and will to live in unity" which generates a sense of nationalism. But, where sovereignty is on a larger scale and the limits of national territory more vague, the forces of social cohesion operate the other way around; a sense of nationalism, which draws its strength from a belief in common origins, as symbolized by race, religion, and language, generates the will to live in unity.

In any event, Smith's view is a drastic oversimplification. The political ideologies of U Nu on the one hand, and of Aung San and Ne Win on the other cannot be polarized in the way he suggests. All three men had been close friends in their student days and they were all colleagues in the original Thakin movement. In their private capacity Aung San and Ne Win were both of secular disposition, but such political success as their movement achieved prior to 1940 was entirely due to the support of politically active Buddhist monks. It is quite possible that, right from the start, Aung San sincerely believed in the possibility of a National secular State in which Burmese, Shans, Karens, Kachins, and Chins could all participate on a basis of equality, but, if so, very few of his associates can have thought along these lines. The original emphasis of the Thakins was on their status as an intellectual elite and on their indignation at being treated by the British as socially and culturally inferior. In the days when the movement was called the Do Bama Asiayone (The We Burmans Association), it was basically a clique of Rangoon University-educated intellectuals. During the 1941-1945 war it turned into a military organization, the Burma Independence Army, which at first supported the Japanese but remained almost exclusively Burmese Buddhist, with the Shans, Karens, Kachins, and Chins holding aloof.

After the war, perhaps with the hope of lessening the suspicions of the cultural minorities, reference to Burma was dropped from the title and the political party to which the British finally handed over power was called the Anti-Fascist People's Freedom League (A.F.P.F.L.). It was probably

Aung San's hope that, under this label, the appeal of his program would override cultural, linguistic, and religious frontiers, but he was assasinated before he was able to put this thesis to the test. After Aung San's death, U Nu turned the A.F.P.F.L. into a passionately sectarian, backward-looking party devoted to the advancement of Buddhism as the state religion of Burma. In this form it completely alienated the leadership of all the non-Buddhist, non-Burmese speaking minorities. Under Ne Win the regime has again adopted secular forms, but it remains highly intolerant of cultural diversity. Several of the ethnic-religious minorities appear to be in a state of more or less continuous revolt.

The historical facts surrounding Aung San's rise to power are complex, but it can hardly be denied that the dead Aung San is now remembered as a nationalist hero of the backward-looking kind. Even while he was alive the forward-looking, universalist, non-sectarian speeches which appealed so strongly to his Western admirers had little relevance for his Burmese followers. The Nationalist-patriotic and the modern-international-statesman components of Aung San's post-1945 public image were not compatible.

The political appeal of nationalism is precisely that it binds its adherents together in tight and passionately aggressive solidarity rather than in universal amity. The intolerance for opponents which nationalists consistently exhibit is their greatest strength, but this intolerance springs from a sense of inferiority and impotence. Once the revolutionary victory has been achieved, the practical problems of administration call for compromise. This difficulty is very apparent in both the countries with which this essay is mainly concerned. Nationalism in Burma and Ceylon originally developed as a reaction to colonial domination. With independence achieved, the nationalist credo of the politicians who had inherited the reins of government ceased to be appropriate. The populations they were required to govern are diverse in speech, general culture, and religion. In practical terms, the slogans of unity on which the nationalist political parties had come to rely no longer made sense, but they could not be abandoned overnight; they have not been abandoned even now.

Let us start with the thesis advanced in Clifford Geertz's *Islam Observed*.[3] A religious system is not a thing in itself, but a facet of the total culture in which it occurs; it permeates other institutions and is in turn permeated by them. The doctrinal orthodoxy of Islam can be determined by reference to the scriptures, but the significance of Islam for Moroccans is quite different from the significance of Islam for Indonesians. And the same is true of Christianity; Mexican and Belgian farmers may recite the same prayers but they do not mean the same thing. But Geertz's argument goes much further than this. It is not simply that the Moroccans and the Indonesians have adapted "the same" religious tradition to fit the circumstances of their respective traditional cultures in quite different ways, but that each has acquired, over the centuries, a separate traditional mode of adapting its traditional religion to changing circumstances. Muhammed V and Sukarno were, respectively, the "makers" of modern Morocco and modern Indonesia, and, in achieving that status, each achieved success through the exercise of personal charisma.

But the charismatic leadership was successful because Muhammed V managed to exercise his leadership in a traditional Moroccan way, while Sukarno exercised his leadership in a traditional Indonesian way. Both leadership styles are Islamic, both are traditional, but neither can be inferred from a study of Islamic scripture. The same applies to the countries in which Theravada Buddhism has traditionally flourished. In each of them there is a long tradition about how religious argument and religious institutions may be manipulated to serve political ends, or to meet changing political and economic circumstances.

In Burma and even more in Ceylon, prior to the Colonialist phase, the secular head of the state was always treated as an absolute despot. In most cases supreme power was achieved by usurpation rather than by natural succession so that "it was the monarch's unique role as defender and promoter of the Buddhist religion which in the final analysis confirmed his legitimacy."[4] Present-day Sinhalese often talk as if "the Tamil problem" was something that was maliciously invented by the European colonial powers on the principle of "divide and rule," but in fact the Holy War which defends the Buddhist Sangha against Hindu-Tamil encroachment is the most basic of all Sinhalese nationalist traditions. The supreme hero in Sinhalese saga is the usurper, King Duttha-Gamani (second century B.C.), whose role was to expel the Tamils and restore the true faith. His battle cry was "Not for the Kingdom, but for Buddhism."[5] Down the centuries all of the legendary hero Sinhalese Kings are constructed to the same model. Dhatusena (436 A.D.) usurps the throne, drives out the Tamils, restores the faith, and republishes the gospels. The record provides an enormous list of Dhatusena's meritorious works, all of which are concerned with the construction and repair of Buddhist temples, the distribution of Buddhist texts, the provision of revenues for the monks, and the construction and repair of irrigation works.[6] The Burmese pattern is strictly comparable. The Kings exhibit their secular power by arbitrary tyrannies of the most ruthless kind, but they also squander enormous sums of money on the construction of Buddhist shrines, the acquisition of relics, and the publication of Buddhist texts.

These traditional modes of using religious values for political ends are still at work. In Ceylon, expenditure on irrigation works is still the most popular form of public investment. In Burma, the Sixth Great Buddhist Council of 1954-1956, sponsored by Premier U Nu, involved among other things the construction of a cave temple costing over two million dollars and the publication of vast amounts of Buddhist literature (printed on presses provided by the Ford Foundation). It was a close copy of the Fifth Great Buddhist Council of 1871 held under the patronage of the tyrant, King Mindon, which was no doubt in turn a copy of earlier Burmese Buddhist Councils, and so on. Politico-religious activities such as these constitute an important factor among the many forces which determine how these countries will adapt (or fail to adapt) to the pressures of "modernization," yet, on the face of it, they seem to be quite at variance with Buddhist precept.

The metaphysics of strictly orthodox, canonical Buddhism are very complicated, but, taken at its face value, the Buddhism of ordinary Burmese and Sinhalese laymen is a creed of *personal* salvation. It is not concerned with the future welfare of any collectivity such as the State or Human Society. Formal doctrine, as popularly interpreted, implies that all secular human activities are a source of cumulative corruption. Personal salvation can only be attained through the slow dissolution of the load of sin that has been piled up through past and present existences. This end may be served by the performance of works of merit—a closely defined range of activities of a ritualistic kind most of which would have been classed by Veblen as non-productive "conspicuous consumption." Otherwise the best hope for the potential saint is to be found in persistent non-involvement in the secular affairs of the world. Logically, this would imply that everyone who aspires to be a good Buddhist, but more particularly anyone who becomes a monk, should be totally disinterested in politics. Formal doctrine, as enunciated by present-day Buddhist monks, makes this quite explicit. Yet both the historical and contemporary facts are quite otherwise.

The varieties of Buddhism are as complex as those of Christianity, but the Theravada Buddhism which is today the dominant religion in Ceylon, Burma, and Thailand (Siam) is at least as unified as European Calvinism. There are sectarian differences but they are minor. All three countries have had a similar history in that, in an epoch around the eleventh century, they were all centers of affluent Buddhist Kingdoms, the architectural ruins of which survive to the present day as reminders of past splendors. It is relevant that most of what is commonly asserted about the "history" of these Kingdoms is derived from temple inscriptions and from "epics," such as the Sinhalese Mahavamsa, which were more concerned with the glorification of religion than with the accurate recording of events. Furthermore, the archaeological service is, in each case, a Department of Government which lacks scientific objectivity. The stupendous ruins have nearly always been interpreted in such a way that they appear to demonstrate the historical truth of the Buddhist sagas. In all three countries, any young, educated, potentially nationalistic man or woman is bound to feel that the evidence of past glory lies all around; and this past glory was Buddhist.

The degree of self-deception that is necessary to bring this mythological past into relation with the facts of the present day varies as between the three cases. In Ceylon more than a third of the population are either Tamil speaking Hindus or Tamil-cum-Sinhalese speaking Christians. It follows that a genuine Buddhist state could, at the present time, only be erected on a base of ruthless religious persecution. In Burma large parts of the geographical state are inhabited by non-Buddhist hill tribes, but their total numbers are not very great. The Thailand situation is similar, but with the added complication that the population includes a large and economically powerful faction of Chinese immigrants. The Buddhism of the latter is distinctly off-beat in terms of "normal" Theravada Buddhism.

In any case, the "great" period of the legendary Buddhist Kingdoms is remote. The more recent phases of pre-colonial history are shadowy; the colonial phase itself is humiliating. Hard evidence suggests that in the phase of "traditional independence" immediately prior to the nineteenth century era of European colonial expansion, all three countries had a similar and rather distinctive model of the ideal form of political organization, namely a weakly centralized Kingship balanced by a weakly centralized Buddhist "papacy."[7] The following quotation from M. E. Spiro, though intended to refer only to Burma, might be treated as an ideal type pattern for all three countries; I do not believe that it relates at all closely to the historical facts of any of them:

The relationship between state and Sangha during the monarchy was a reciprocal one. By supporting the monks, on the one hand, while on the other purifying the Order of dissident elements, the government minimized the potentiality of the Sangha for becoming an independent nucleus of political power. On the monastic side, by upholding the legitimacy of the government, while at the same time protecting the people from tyranny, the Sangha exercised a restraining influence . . . on excessive abuse of power by the government.

It should be emphasized, however, that both Church and State were loosely structured and that the kind of mutual interdependence which Spiro postulated depended on this fact. If the Church had been more closely organized it would have been brought more readily under political control. This point has been perceptively argued by E. M. Mendelson[9] who suggests that the enthusiasm shown by both the Burmese and the Ceylonese governments for sponsoring a Buddhist revival movement in connection with the supposed 2500th anniversary of the Buddha's death (1956) might be interpreted as a political attempt to impose on the Church a more formal bureaucratic structure than it normally possesses so as to bring it more fully under the control of the secular power. If this is a fair analysis, then one can only comment that, as in the past, the authority of the secular power has proved too evanescent to bring its plans to fruition.

This overall uniformity of political pattern was hardly "caused" by the presence of Theravada Buddhism, but the conjunction of political style and religious ideology was not accidental. The Political and Religious Orders were suited. During the colonial era the pattern was more diverse.

Ceylon was first partly colonized by Europeans towards the end of the sixteenth century; the process was completed in 1818. Burma lost its independence by stages during the nineteenth century. Because of the rivalry of the European great powers, Siam-Thailand maintained its nominal independence. The recent nineteenth and twentieth century experience of the three countries has varied accordingly.

Until 1940, the overall progress of Siam-Thailand might have been described by a Western observer as "slow but steady." The country was not a European colony but it lay within a European sphere of influence. New bureaucratic institutions of an administrative kind in such fields as law, communications, health, and education were consciously copied from European models. The economy developed along colonialist lines with rice exports, mining, and timber extraction forming the mainstay. Local industrial development was negligible. Even so, the absence of any alien paramount power had crucial significance. Although the autocratic despotism of the reigning monarch gradually eroded in the face of Western expectation concerning "civilized" political behavior, major decisions about the pace and overall direction of politics continued to be made by indigenous Thai leaders whose assessment of the relative merits and relative strengths of the rival great powers was often remarkably shrewd.

Latterly, Thai politics have become much more difficult. The chaos of 1942-1945 has been followed by the long drawn-out horror of Vietnam. From some points of view the latter might be considered a "benefit" to Thailand, since American military involvement has led to vast capital expenditure. But the resulting industrial development has been erratic and quite unbalanced; the long term viability of most of it is highly questionable. It is obvious that the consequential inflationary pressures have imposed great strains on all aspects of the Thai social system. Yet, so far, there has been no major disintegration, and indeed the relative political stability of Thailand since 1945, as compared with Burma and Ceylon, is very striking. It cannot be demonstrated that Thai Buddhist institutions have played any particular role in this adaptive adjustment to what is clearly a most uncomfortable form of modernization, but it is a fact that, in Thailand, the traditional ideal type relationship between Church and State has continued to have at least formal existence, whereas in modern Burma and Ceylon it does not.

The pattern in Ceylon and Burma has been, in some ways, the converse to that of Thailand. During the Colonialist era, prior to 1940, local politicians had no practical influence upon the overall course of development. Government existed to serve the interests of European and Indian entrepreneurs. In Ceylon it was mainly a matter of developing plantation products—first cinnamon, then coffee, then tea, rubber, and copra—for export. The Government was quite uninterested in the possibility of local industry. Likewise in Burma, after the opening of the Suez canal, the

southern Irrawaddy Delta region was opened up for large scale rice production *for export*. This trade was mainly financed with Indian capital.[10]
In Burma the British concentrated on the direct exploitation of natural
resources—teak extraction, oil production, mining. These trades made
little use of local labor and did not result in the emergence of a technically-
qualified middle class.

Both countries, but especially Ceylon, have a long tradition of literacy
though the uses to which this literacy was put in the pre-colonial era was
very limited. However, under the influence of the Christian missions a
number of schools developed curricula of a Western type. These mission
schools had limited objectives. They sought to train clerical staff for the
Administration and for commercial agencies; they did not produce scientists or engineers. In Ceylon, two particular boys' schools—St. Thomas and
Royal College—aimed at a higher standard and were, in effect, the equivalent of English public schools, but even here the objectives were nontechnical. In any event, in both countries wealthier parents sent their children
to finish their education in England, preferably as lawyers and doctors.
Even in State enterprises such as the railways and the post office, technical
operations were somehow kept out of the hands of the ordinary local inhabitants. In both countries, as was the case in India, the small Eurasian
community had privileged access to all occupations of this kind. The circumstance that a large proportion of this low status but technically qualified community has, since independence, preferred to emigrate rather than
accept local nationality has had serious implications and bears on the
striking absence of industrial development in both countries.

Yet, despite the limitations on economic and educational opportunity,
the general public derived many indirect advantages from the presence
of the colonial regime. Both in Ceylon and Burma the roads and railways were extended further and faster than was the case in Thailand; the
notorious efficiency of the colonial British in fields such as ordnance survey,
police organization, tax administration, and the administration of justice
was a benefit to all. Health services were thin on the ground but at least they
did exist. Higher education in the Western sense was restricted in its
availability but the best was very good indeed. Rangoon University in
1940 and the University of Ceylon in 1952 were both excellent institutions
of considerable academic distinction. The medium of instruction in both
cases was English.

Paradoxically, the very effectiveness of the Western style education
of the elite was partly responsible for the chauvinist character of the
subsequent nationalist reaction among those lower down the social scale.
G. C. Mendis, a senior Ceylonese historian, has commented:

The Sinhalese educated Buddhist community realized that the grant of adult franchise had enabled them to capture the government just as the English educated
middle class had captured it from the British. . . . Buddhism was in a backward

state. . . . It had to reorganise itself, but the obstacles in the way were great. Above all it had to compete with Christian organisations which had . . . established themselves firmly under British rule. . . . The Sinhalese-educated Buddhists thought that the only way they could preserve Sinhalese was by making it the language of government and the medium of education up to university level.[11]

A point that deserves notice in this formulation is the ambiguity of the "tradition" that is being evoked. Buddhist nationalism is in its essence backward-looking and this has reactionary consequences. In Ceylon, respect for tradition has forced the state to support schools of Ayurvedic medicine in competition with schools of Western medicine; likewise, there are now at least two state-sponsored Buddhist universities awarding degrees which have national parity with those of the Western style University of Ceylon. But for the ordinary Sinhalese this is a kind of voluntary self-deception. When Sinhalese parents seek higher education for their children, they mean Western style higher education; but at the same time they want their children to grow up as Sinhalese and not as second class Europeans—and on this point there is ambiguity. For what does "growing up as a Sinhalese" really imply? It is an evocation of the past, but of what past?

Here it is important to remember that both Ceylon and Burma had over a century of colonial experience. The "good old days" which older people now remember had nothing to do with the past glories of Anuradhapura; they belonged to the era of colonial government. Today, twenty years after Independence, the colonial era has itself become a tradition, which is merged with other traditions. A nostalgia for law and order evokes images of a Governor General supported by troops in khaki uniform rather than the picturesque nonsense of a medieval kingship. It is surely understandable that nostalgia of this sort should be widespread. For both Ceylon and Burma, the colonial era ceased immediately after World War II. In both cases the subsequent period has been one of steady economic decline, and the most obvious cause of this decline is the continued lack of industrial development.

The background circumstances of this failure to industrialize in Burma are inadequately known, but in Ceylon's case, despite verbal declarations to the contrary, it has resulted from clear-cut political choice. Ever since Independence, Ceylon has been the beneficiary of very large amounts of international aid and the total public sector investment has been substantial, but the politicians have preferred to build grandiose irrigation works rather than factories. In following this course they were reverting to classical tradition. D. S. Senanayake, the nationalist leader and first Prime Minister of independent Ceylon and prime sponsor of the immense Gal Oya irrigation project, quite explicitly saw himself as following in the footsteps of the thirteenth century hero—King Prakrama Bahu II!

Fantasy apart, there is in fact very little in the present-day political

organization of either Burma or Ceylon which derives directly from the
traditional forms of pre-colonial centralized Kingship. In Ceylon most of
the country has been subject to Roman-Dutch law for over 350 years, and
even the former Kingdom of Kandy has been administered in a British
style for over a century. The descendants of Kandyan feudal aristocrats
sometimes held office in sinecure posts even under the British, but there
was no serious attempt at indirect rule. On the contrary, the Colebrook-
Cameron "reforms" of 1832, which abolished the feudal rights of secular
grantees, effectively sequestered all their lands to the Crown. These
Crown lands were subsequently sold to the (mainly British) plantation
developers. By 1935 all the residual political rights of the Kandyan chiefs
had been eliminated. However, in sharp contrast, the very similar feudal
rights which had adhered to the "chief priest" of endowed Buddhist temples were, from the start, left severely alone. In 1956 in the Kandyan
area alone, temple lands still covered 376,000 acres, a fact which gave immense political and financial power to the monks and to the lay temple
officials who controlled the revenues.

During the latter part of the colonial period, the social discrepancy
between those who could afford to give their children an English education and those who could not became very marked. By the second decade
of this century, the whole of the Ceylonese middle and upper social class
had been very thoroughly anglicized. Most of the children learned English
as their mother tongue, were educated in English language Christian
schools, and attended British Universities. It is members of this same English speaking elite who are now "at the top" both in politics and in the
Civil Service. It is an index of the ambiguity of values to which these individuals are subjected that until very recently, in nationalist independent
Ceylon, in imitation of Westminster, the daily reports of Colombo parliamentary proceedings were officially known as "Hansard"! Such details are
not just theater; they reflect the fact that up to now the whole structure of
"modern" Ceylonese politics has been thoroughly British. Dr. N. M. Perera,
the dominant personality in the present Government, sometimes described
by Western journalists as a "left wing Marxist," is an elderly and wealthy
plantation owner; he holds a London University D.Sc. and first learned his
politics from Prof. Harold Laski at the London School of Economics.

There are many similar instances. A good example is the case of Mr.
Philip Gunawardena whose obituary as printed in The Times (London)
on March 28, 1972 is given below. This brings out very well the point that
European categories such as "Trotskyist," "Socialist," and "Conservative"
have little relevance as descriptive labels for Ceylonese political allegiance:

Mr. Philip Gunawardena, a former Ceylon minister and for many years a col-
ourful figure in the political life of his country, has died at the age of 71.
He founded the Trotskyist Lanka Sama Samaja Party, which is now led by the
Finance Minister Mr. N. M. Perera.

Educated at Ananda College and the Ceylon University College, he later went to the Universities of Wisconsin and Illinois where he read economics and agricultural science. In 1936 he entered the second State Council as Member for Avissawella. During the war he, with several other Socialist politicians, was detained under the Emergency Regulations introduced by the British Government. Two years later, together with his comrades, he escaped from detention and fled to India.

In 1956, he formed the Mahajana Eksath Peramuna (People's United Front) and closely allied himself with S. W. R. D. Bandaranaike in the General Election Campaign of 1956. When the Coalition Government was formed in April 1956 he became Minister of Agriculture and Food. In 1959 he and his party left the Coalition owing to differences with the Sri Lanka Freedom Party, and he went over to the Opposition.

Retaining his seat in the General Elections of March and July 1960, he and his party opposed the S.L.F.P. government of Mrs. Sirimavo Bandaranaike. After the elections of March 1965 he joined the National Government of Dudley Senanayake and held the portfolio of Industries and Fisheries, until 1970.

Yet, behind the anglicized façade, things are not so simple. Some of Dr. Perera's present colleagues have quite different roots. The Prime Minister, Mrs. Bandaranaike, is, in her own right, an aristocrat of aristocrats. Indeed, it has been claimed that if someone were to decide that it would be appropriate to reestablish the Sinhalese Kingship and were to search for a legitimate hereditary heir to the throne, Mrs. Bandaranaike herself would have serious claims to office. In the more traditionally-oriented parts of the country many of her political supporters are well aware of this fact. But here I refer to the traditions of Ancient Ceylon rather than to the traditions of the British Empire or of the London School of Economics.

Apart from W. Dahanayake, who only held office for a few months as a stop-gap measure after the assassination of S. W. R. D. Bandaranaike, there have been five Prime Ministers of independent Ceylon: D. S. Senanayake; his son, Dudley Senanayake; his nephew, Sir John Kotelawa; S. W. R. D. Bandaranaike; and the latter's widow, Mrs. Bandaranaike. All five are related by blood, marriage, or both, and several commentators have remarked that changes of government seem to have more in common with the succession disputes of the Wars of the Roses than with ordinary, Western, party government.[12]

Since Burma's full incorporation in the British Empire was of relatively short duration, predictably, the echoes of the former Kingship are more obvious. U Nu's "royal" sponsorship of the Sixth Great Buddhist Council has already been noted. U Saw, Chief Minister under the British in 1940, Dr. Ba Maw, who held the puppet office of Head of State during the Japanese occupation, and U Nu, Prime Minister for most of the period 1951-1962, all made a point of engaging in rituals ("ceremonial first ploughing") which were traditionally supposed to be "religious duties" of the King as Head of State. It is relevant that this particular piece of play acting was "religious" in a very special sense. Many of these ceremonies are concerned with the worship of guardian spirits ("the 37 Nats") and are not, properly speaking, Buddhist at all.

This again illustrates the ambiguity which is present in all "nationalist" symbolism. Nationalism proclaims the values of the past, but of what past? Conflict of political opinion can very quickly get transformed into a heresy hunt centered on just this issue. The devoutly Buddhist U Nu, when Prime Minister, was wont to engage publicly in all kinds of "nat ceremonies." His evident concern was to emphasize that his government was a national government concerned with the affairs of ordinary country people. When the secular minded Ne Win assumed control of events, first as Prime Minister in 1958 and later as military dictator in 1962, he suppressed U Nu's state-sponsored nat ceremonials. But he proclaimed that he did so in the interests of religious purity! "True Buddhism," it was argued, "is rational and opposed to all superstition, supernaturalism and magic; what U Nu had been advocating and practising was bogus Buddhism."[13] In seventeenth-century England, Cromwell disposed of his more liberal minded, but certainly more devoutly Christian associates by very similar arguments!

In Burma, the East-West clash of cultures is much less pronounced than it is in Ceylon. Burma came under colonial rule only piecemeal and the central core of the country was genuinely independent until 1885. In consequence, the "anglicization" of the indigenous upper class did not proceed as far as it did in Ceylon. When Independence was regained in 1947, comparatively few of the leading politicians had received their education overseas and hardly any of them spoke English in their homes. Parliamentary democracy of the Western sort, which had already established extensive roots in Ceylon, was in Burma still an idea rather than a fact, and even the idea disintegrated rather rapidly.

Although the colonial British were only in Burma for a relatively short time, they did manage to make a very thorough job of the destruction of indigenous political institutions. Most of the potentially legitimate claimants to the throne had been systematically eliminated even before 1914, and by 1940 there was scarcely the semblance of a surviving traditional aristocracy. As in Ceylon, "native law and custom" was only allowed to apply to a very limited range of domestic disputes of a very non-political kind.

One consequence of this thorough eradication of the earlier political structure was that, in the immediate context of post-war independence, although Buddhism might serve as a symbol of Burmese national identity and ritual performances formerly exercised by the reigning monarch could be transferred to the ruling Prime Minister, Kingship as such did not present itself as a viable political possibility.[14] The only alternative to the new-fangled notions of British parliamentary democracy was some variant of the more familiar, paramount power bureaucracy with a local military General replacing the British Governor General.

Ne Win's military dictatorship needs to be viewed in this context. In his speeches Ne Win himself interpreted the familiar thesis "the Government must cleanse the Sangha" to mean "the Government must remove the Sangha from politics." But the more positive objective, at the outset of his regime, was to reject the ideologies of both Western democracy and Buddhist para-theocracy in favor of rational efficiency (bureaucratic government). The fulfillment of this program entailed nationalizing almost everything, but, apart from jargon, the details of the resulting structure do not seem to owe very much to either Russian or Chinese models. On the contrary, it could be argued that, whatever his intentions, Ne Win has been very traditional. Taking his cue from E. Sarkisyanz,[15] H. Bechert[16] observes that "under the regime of the Burmese kings most of the more important business activities were State monopolies. The export trade was severely restricted by decree. Land could not be sold and all belonged—theoretically—to the King, (i.e. the State). . . . Thus the nationalization of business and of the land is just as much 'traditional' as it is 'Marxist.'" As yet very little is known in the West about how this experiment in non-traditional traditional politics has really worked out, so further comment is difficult.

In any case, the fact that independent Ceylon and independent Burma have both retained a great deal of the bureaucratic apparatus of the British colonial administration has probably had negative consequences for the political influence of the Sangha. As I have already indicated, the traditional pre-British Buddhist church was in both countries very loosely organized. The secular structure of government was feudal in that the occupant of land owed dues and services to his immediate overlord rather than to the central exchequer, but autocratic in that comparatively few of the superior feudal offices were ever held for long in hereditary succession. The secular offices were in the personal gift of the King; the office holder was a tax collector serving his own interest—a *myosa*, "an eater of the town," as the Burmese title put it. Such personal office holding was precarious; in contrast, the feudal tendencies of the temples were permanent. In these circumstances the loosely knit hierarchy of the Sangha gained in significance. "[The Buddhist monk] who theoretically had nothing to do with politics, or things of this world was really a political power, the only permanent power in a system where office was . . . transient and evanescent."[17] Correspondingly, the influence of the Sangha tends to wane as the permanence of the bureaucracy becomes more secure.

I think that enough has now been said to indicate why Buddhism should, in both countries, serve as the "national" symbol *par excellence*. In Burma it is the religion of the oppressed majority who have struggled to be free, free of political domination by English Christians, free of economic exploitation by Hindu, Sikhs, and Muslims from India. It is also the religion of a literate people who can thereby feel superior to the backward tribesmen of the surrounding hill country. Here it deserves note that in 1945, because of the activities of Christian missionaries, individual "backward tribesmen" were more likely to have had a Western style education than were the Burmese themselves!

Comparably in Ceylon, Buddhism is the religion of people who feel themselves to be an oppressed majority. They feel oppressed not only by the colonial British but also by their own Christian-educated, English speaking upper class and by their economically more resourceful neighbors, the Hindu Tamils of the North and East coasts.

Buddhist nationalism in these contexts does not fit at all conveniently with geography; state boundaries and religious boundaries do not go together. But on the whole, provided the facts are not examined too closely, it fits quite well with language. Thus, in both countries national Buddhism is closely identified with a sense of linguistic community, Burmese in the one case, Sinhalese in the other. To claim to be a Burmese and yet deny that you are a Buddhist would be, for most native born Burmese, almost a contradiction in terms. In Ceylon the bitter factionalism between Sinhalese speakers and Tamil speakers, which in 1958 led to the declaration of a state of emergency, operates on similar principles. The slogans run: "Sinhala (Ceylon) for the Sinhalese." "All Sinhalese are Buddhist." And what is meant by "a Sinhalese" is someone who speaks the Sinhalese language as his mother tongue.

The fact that about a third of the Ceylonese population do not speak Sinhalese and that a substantial and influential minority of those who do speak Sinhalese profess to be Christian rather than Buddhist in no way lessens the emotional appeal of such battle cries. Buddhism is thought of as a way of life rather than as a religious society. The political implication is crucial; although the Christian-educated, English-speaking elite still hold the reins of power, they cannot at any point afford to ignore, or even to neglect, the "national consciousness" of Sinhalese-speaking Buddhists.

The complexities of the underlying contradictions of cultural identity, part "traditional," part "modern," are well illustrated by the record of the martyred Prime Minister of Ceylon, S. W. R. D. Bandaranaike (born S. W. R. Dias). The particular relevance of this example is that it shows that, in the context of Ceylon, which was first colonized by Europeans in the sixteenth century, the polarization of *traditional* versus *modern* does not fit at all tidily with either of the alternative polarizations, *old* versus *new*, or *Asian* versus *European*.

Bandaranaike's family had been Mudaliyars—Native Government Agents of the highest rank—from the earliest days of European colonization. Like the Vicar of Bray they had always loyally supported the paramount power —Portuguese, Dutch, or British. A portrait of Dom Solomon Dias, Bandaranaike, Gate Mudaliyar, (great grandfather of S. W. R. D. Bandaranaike) who died in 1859, appears in J. E. Tennent[18] where the reader's attention is drawn to the "gold chains and medals by which his services have been recognised by the British Government." S. W. R. D.'s father, Sir Solomon Dias Bandaranaike, Kt., C.M.G., Maha Mudaliyar, served as Native A.D.C. to the Governor of Ceylon and extra A.D.C. to King George V. The whole family had been staunchly Christian for over a century. Around 1920 all of them seem to have been known by the simple surname Dias; in 1950 about half had reverted to a hyphenated Dias-Bandaranaike; only S. W. R. D. seems to have suppressed the Dias to an initial. S. W. R. D. himself only learned to speak Sinhalese after taking his degree at Oxford and qualifying as a Barrister in London. And like other contemporaries he did this to further his political career.[19] Yet despite his apparently Anglophile Christian background, Bandaranaike managed in the early 1950's to present himself to the electorate as the devoutly chauvinistic leader of Sinhalese Buddhists under the slogan: "Sinhalese is the national language of Ceylon; Buddhism is our national religion."

Bandaranaike's success in the 1956 elections was, without any question, mainly due to the well-organized and well-financed campaign of the Eksath Bhikku Peramuna (E.B.P.), a specially recruited team of political monks which was active in every Sinhalese constituency throughout the country. The E.B.P. was the brain child of the Venerable Mapitigama Buddharakkhita, the presiding monk of the very wealthy Kelaniya Temple. Various aspects of Buddharakkhita's murky political background and financial dealings are given in considerable detail by Smith[20] and Bechert.[21] Here it will suffice that Buddharakkhita owed his position in the Kelaniya temple to close personal ties with a variety of wealthy politicians, some of whom were his relatives. The network of kinsfolk included Bandaranaike himself.

Once in power, Bandaranaike was greatly embarrassed by his personal debt to Buddharakkhita. Buddharakkhita's mistress was made Minister of Health and Buddharakkhita himself was given an appointment under the Ministry, but Bandaranaike was unable to fulfill his lavish pre-election promises to the Sangha as a whole. The Marxist M.E.P. members of his coalition government refused to accept the communal, anti-Tamil implications of a flat declaration that Sinhalese was the national language and Buddhism the national religion. Bandaranaike was also unable to give Buddharakkhita and his relatives the financial perquisites which they had apparently been led to expect.

As a consequence of this backstage quarrel, Bandaranaike found that the political support he had previously received from the Sangha was fading rapidly. However, the quarrel was not public. Although the relations between Buddharakkhita and the Minister of Health were a topic of gossip and scandal, the Prime Minister still treated Buddharakkhita with the greatest public deference. Under the circumstances, it seems altogether astonishing that in September 1959 Bandaranaike should have been assassinated by a relatively junior monk acting on orders from Buddharakkhita

and that the latter should subsequently have been condemned to death
for complicity in murder. (The sentence was later commuted to life imprisonment.) Bandaranaike's posthumous career has conformed to a well-
established tradition concerning the sanctity of murdered religious leaders;
he is now variously worshipped as a god (*deviyo*) and revered as a
Bodhisattva (future Buddha).

What is astonishing is not that there should have been an assassination
but that the shrewd Buddharakkhita should have so misjudged the consequences. Overnight, the unpopular Prime Minister became a martyred
hero. For the first time in living memory Buddhist monks were stoned in
the street. The Sangha had lost every advantage it had gained in the past
ten years. But, even in this crisis, public reaction took a predictable and
traditional form. The newspaper editorials carried the banner, "Let us
cleanse the Sangha!"

There are some striking parallels with the assassination in July 1947 of
Aung San, who was just about to become the first Prime Minister of independent Burma, by U Saw who had been the last Chief Minister of Diarchy
British Burma in 1940-1941. Though he was reviled in retrospect, U Saw's
record was that of a genuine nationalist. He called his personal political
following the Myochit, that is "the Patriots." He was one of the defense
attorneys at the trial of leaders of the Saya San rebellion in 1931 and in
1940 declared that his Government would give official support to the Sangha.
He had a considerable personal following among the Buddhist peasantry.
U Saw was arrested by the British authorities in January 1942 on suspicion
of treasonable contacts with the Japanese and spent the rest of the war in
an internment camp in Uganda. He was released in 1946 and immediately
resumed his role as a leading Burmese politician. At first he became a
member of the Interim Government which had the confidence of the
British civil administration, but soon afterwards he went into opposition.
He then teamed up with Dr. Ba Maw, who had been puppet Head
of State under the Japanese, and Sir Paw Tun, who had been a member of
the (British) Burma Government in exile, to form the "Nationalist Opposition Front" (in opposition to Aung San). Even before this, in October
1946, the Communist leaders were denouncing Aung San for being "a tool
of British imperialist duplicity,"[22] and there was plenty of evidence that
Aung San had influential "protectors" among the British military.[23] It was in
this context that U Saw reverted to a more traditional style of politics. Even
so, as with the case of Buddharakkhita, it seems extraordinary that U
Saw should not have appreciated that political assassination would be just
as disastrous for the assassin as for his victim. U Saw was hanged in May
1948.[24]

But if U Saw may be compared with Buddharakkhita, Aung San may
be compared with Bandaranaike. Aung San was a well-educated man, in
the Western sense of the term, whose best skills were exhibited in the
field of international diplomacy. But in the Burmese countryside he is now

remembered as a man of the people, a victorious military genius appearing from nowhere in the classic Burmese style of King Alaungpaya (1752-1760) who drove the hated Talaings from Central Burma and went on to create a Nation. A detailed, scrupulously documented account of Aung San's actual career is to be found in F. N. Trager,[25] but that author's self-righteously anti-British stance leads to some very strange interpretations. The reader gets the impression that all of Trager's Burmese informants moved in or near Government circles in Rangoon. In any case, I believe that Trager has been misled by post-assassination propaganda to exaggerate and misrepresent the influence which Aung San exercised during his lifetime.

Aung San was a leader of the Thakin movement and a colleague of U Nu from 1936 onwards, but he lacked the latter's Buddhist enthusiasms. The Thakins drew their main support from educated intellectuals; they aroused enthusiasm in the countryside only on those occasions when they received the collaboration of the Sangha. Trager's statement that "the Thakins succeeded in doing what the preceding generation of nationalist leaders had failed to do: they brought together, organised and led a mass base of workers and peasants"[26] is entirely mythological. Aung San was in touch with Japanese agents from around 1938 and, when threatened with arrest in 1940, he escaped to Tokyo. He returned to Burma with the invading Japanese army in 1941. Contrary to legend, the Burma Independence Army, which Aung San then organized, was originally an insignificant group to which the Japanese offered little support. It is extremely doubtful whether this "army" ever engaged in any form of combat. Its expansion in 1944-1945 was largely achieved by assistance from "Force 136," a British special operations unit. This "cloak and dagger" organization was controlled directly from Whitehall and not by the (British) Burma Government in exile, who viewed most of its activities with extreme disapproval. In the spring of 1945 Aung San, who had previously been denounced by the British authorities as a dangerous traitor, was suddenly recognized by Admiral Mountbatten (on advice from Force 136) as "the leader of anti-Japanese resistance in Burma." Without this recognition Aung San would very likely have disappeared without a trace. The subsequent build up of Aung San's reputation as "Burma's popular hero" was very elaborately engineered. It is arguable that he was assassinated because, in the eyes of his assassin, who knew all the background facts very well, he was a British stooge. "Truth" in such situations is very complex. Aung San was certainly a devoted patriot, but he was also an opportunist and a very practical politician. In this sense "Aung San the very undercover British agent" is possibly closer to the mark than "Aung San the heroic anti-imperialist" whom Trager and all official historians, whether British or Burmese, present for our admiration. In any event, both Bandaranaike and Aung San seem to have perished because, having ridden to power on the crest of a militant Buddhist nationalist wave, they would both have liked to reach some compromise agreement with the kind of Western "modern" society which, in their hearts, they both really admired.

The point that I want to emphasize in these summaries of the careers of Bandaranaike and Aung San and the still more summary references to the careers of their murderers is not the cynicism involved in rapid changes of faith and political allegiance, or the corrupt immorality of the outstanding Ceylonese Bhikkhu of his day, but rather the fact that the realities of Ceylonese and Burmese politics make behavior such as Bandaranaike's not merely appropriate but essential. In one way or another almost every successful operator in the field of politics in either Ceylon or Burma during recent decades has attempted (sometimes with considerable but short-lived success) to exploit Buddhist religious enthusiasm in the interest of party politics. This is not a new phenomenon. It is not the case that all good Buddhists are politicians, but it is nearly true that all effective politicians in Buddhist countries have, for centuries past, found it expedient to claim to be good Buddhists.

But the concept of "good Buddhist" is here ambiguous. Although canonical Buddhism is pacifist, the popular religion embodies in some of its manifestations the idea that the perfect secular ruler should be a world emperor, a *cakravartin,* who will become, in some future existence, a Buddha.[27] Thus, although canonical Buddhism formally recognizes no god, there is a sense in which the traditional Buddhist kingship was a theocracy. This traditional political involvement of "the living Buddha" accounts for the paradox whereby the expansion of pacifist Buddhism into Southeast Asia in the early centuries of the Christian era took place in a context of military conquest.

It also accounts for the strongly held tradition which prevails in all Theravada Buddhist countries that rebellions and revolutions are led by puritanical religious reformers. They represent themselves as adherents of the true faith seeking only to purge the Sangha of its corrupt contamination by wordly interests.[28] To this extent the fact that recent nationalist movements in both Burma and Ceylon have been interpreted, at least by some observers, as symptoms of a Buddhist revival is itself the continuation of a long tradition. Having said that, I should add that so far as Burma is concerned, the views which well-qualified observers hold on these matters are very divergent.[29]

I have already remarked that Ne Win seems to have hoped that his military regime, by bringing back to the Government of Burma the benefits of bureaucratic rationality which it had previously enjoyed under the British, would make possible an era of modern industrialism. Likewise, Ceylonese politicians have for years past put tremendous verbal emphasis upon the need for industrial development. Yet in neither country do the fine words ever seem to result in substantial deeds. No doubt the causes for this failure are very complex, yet one possible factor may be that there is something about the Ethic of Buddhism which is fundamentally at variance with the Spirit of Capitalism.

If Weber was right, then competitive capitalism finds its natural seed bed among people of cautious puritanical disposition who are savers rather than spenders, who prefer investment to conspicuous consumption, and who have confidence that they are the elect of God. But the practical (as distinct from scriptural) ethic of Theravada Buddhism is very much the converse of this. Each man is for himself alone, and there are no elect; an endless prospect of future lives of suffering is the common prospect of all. The standard pattern is to lead a wild gay life while you are young and become a sainted patriarch (*upásaka*) when you are old. Youth is a time of gambling and reckless speculation; maturity is a period of piety accompanied by the performance of works of merit. One approved form of merit earning is to expend accumulated resources on spectacular public works, including temples, bridges, and 'irrigation channels. Building a factory for the benefit of your personal descendants quite definitely does *not* fall into the category of works of merit.

As I have already remarked, in the early days of Ceylon's independence, under the influence of Prime Minister D. S. Senanayake, the Ceylon Government devoted nearly all its development resources to what were known as Peasant Colonization Schemes. In the days of Ceylon's Buddhist grandeur, prior to the thirteenth century, the Sinhalese Kingdom had been focused in the dry zone in what is now the North Central Province and had been based on spectacular irrigation works. In subsequent centuries much of this territory was abandoned to jungle, but the skeleton of the old irrigation system remained. Senanayake's plan was to reconstruct and extend the irrigated splendours of the twelfth century Kingdom and thus relieve the population pressure from the wet zone of the Southwest.

On the economic merits of this scheme there has been much dispute; on its political merits there can be no doubt whatever. In the context of the times it appealed strongly to nascent, Sinhalese, Buddhist nationalism. But what is usually overlooked is Senanayake's personal position. He was a member of the Goyigama (cultivator) caste, which, in Kandyan terms, is the highest caste. But Senanayake was not himself a Kandyan; he came from the Low Country and his caste status was notably lower than that of his kinsman S. W. R. Dias-Bandaranaike, and vastly lower than that of S. W. R. D.'s wife, who was by birth a Kandyan aristocrat of the highest rank. Senanayake's personal fortune had come from ownership of a graphite (plumbago) mine, a commercial undertaking with no flavor of merit. Thus for Senanayake, in his role as Prime Minister, to organize the construction of splendid irrigation works in precise imitation of the Great Sinhalese Kings of the legendary past was simultaneously a status climbing action in terms of the pecking order of caste ranking, and a superbly royal piece of Buddhist merit earning. To have devoted the same resources to the development of industry in the Colombo urban region might have greater long term advantages for Ceylon's economy but, from Senanayake's personal point of view, it could have had no merit at all. The question of how fast countries such as Ceylon and Burma can, will, or should industrialize is partly a matter of carrots and sticks.

Those who believe that there is a Law of Nature which declares that all underdeveloped countries will "progress" to a stage of industrialization tend to assume that all those who are so progressing must necessarily welcome the prospect with open arms. In other words, they assume that the basic Christian dogma of the coming millennium when all mankind shall live in peace and happiness in the New Jerusalem is shared by all the world. But this is not the case. A good Buddhist has no vision of a New Heaven and a New Earth; his ambitions are strictly personal and escapist; the most he is prepared to hope for is a future existence which is rather less unpleasant than this one.

When an ideology of the latter sort prevails, economic progress will come about only when it is the line of least resistance under pressure from uncomfortable events. And by uncomfortable I mean physically uncomfortable, not just economically precarious. For example, when judged by the criteria of the economists of the World Bank, the present state and future prospects of Ceylon are wholly deplorable and rapidly approaching crisis. Yet so far as I can judge, the average Ceylon peasant does not feel himself at all badly off. For the time being anyway, increased crop yields have eased the stresses of a rising population. So long as this situation continues there will be no sustained pressure on the politicians to act against the anti-capitalist biases of their Buddhist ethic.

The statisticians can see that Ceylon is shortly to be faced with a population problem of the most intractable kind, but this issue does not yet have acute political reality. The present political pressures are elsewhere. The semi-rebellions of 1958 and 1971 had independent origins, but both recruited their support from the same underprivileged class, the "educated" unemployed who are qualified for clerical office work but have never seen the inside of a factory and have come to believe that the work of a farm laborer is undignified.

This potentially valuable but neglected sector of the population demands employment which the government cannot provide. Because it has twice been proved that this is a sector of the population which is capable of being organized into a rebellious force, it is bound to be a focus of government attention for many years to come. Yet despite a good deal of public rhetoric, the educated unemployed do not, as yet, seem to constitute "a movement" or to share readily identifiable political objectives. Their random demands do not seem likely to generate any significant increase in the pace of modernization. What is more probable is that the threat to law and order which their activities present may encourage the establishment of yet one more military dictatorship.

The Burma situation seems to me very similar, but with the population pressure factor removed. In Burma there is still plenty of room for everyone. The climate is pleasant; nature is generous. Provided the gadgetry of modern technology is given low priority, a "reasonable" standard of life is available to everyone. A military government which provides a fair degree of law and order without an excess of tyranny and which allows the individual to pursue his private personal salvation is as much as can be hoped for. Ne Win does not put the revival of Buddhism high on his list of priorities, but his regime provides a practical context in which Buddhism can flourish. In Theravada Buddhism that is a very traditional state of affairs.[30]

Now let me revert briefly to some issues of general theory. A prime difficulty for all contemporary politicians in countries such as Burma and Ceylon is that circumstances make it essential that they should be "culturally bilingual." In order to operate in the sphere of international diplomacy or to participate in the benefits which may flow from the various agencies of the United Nations, the leader needs to play the role of a secular, cosmopolitan Westerner. Yet if he is to retain the allegiance of his homeland supporters he must demonstrate a nationalistic hatred of colonial oppression, and this implies a commitment to isolationism and local religious values. Thus the ambitious politician is constantly required to choose between alternative models of "correct" behavior. Four such alternatives are represented in the diagram shown below:

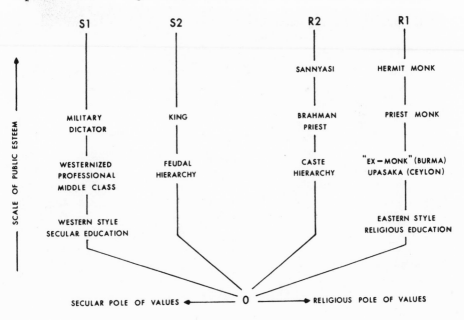

At the extremes the politician may expect to earn public esteem either by adherence to rational secular values which put emphasis on bureaucratic efficiency in the Colonialist mode (S.1), or by an approach to saintliness through an emphasis on nonrational religious values, the support of religious institutions, and the performance of works of merit (R.1). Channel S.1 calls for a Western-style University education, adherence of likeminded westernized elite, and public declarations concerning the importance of industrial development, modernization, efficiency, law and order, and so on. The crown of success is to achieve the status of a Colonial Governor and amounts, in effect, to a military dictatorship.

In the Burma-Ceylon context, Channel R.1 implies repeated public declarations in support of the Sangha, the bias of public expenditure towards traditionally recognized works of merit, and a personal life of austerity in accordance with the formal precepts appropriate to a lay devotee (upāsaka) or, in Burma, to an ex-monk. However, in the ideal type model, the ultimate goal of the successful devotee is to achieve sainthood through abstention from all secular affairs, a mode of existence which is radically incompatible with the active pursuit of a political career.

Between these two extremes we have the self-reciprocal channels S.2 and R.2. The model for S.2 is the traditional Buddhist kingship. The King is an arbitrary tyrant dispensing arbitrary justice and arbitrary benefits through a para-feudal hierarchy, but his ritual duties include not only the performance of works of merit and public support for the Sangha but also participation in "local" religious rites which have more in common with Hinduism than Buddhism (ploughing ceremonials and nat worship in Burma, the Kandyan perahera and Kataragama Deviyo festivals in Ceylon). These rituals not only imply respect for the values of caste hierarchy (R.2), but they also serve to link people with territory in a way that the pure ideology of Buddhism does not.

As model schema these three systems (S.1, R.1, and S.2/R.2) are mutually exclusive; in the context of operational politics they overlap. The case histories which I have cited make it quite plain that, at different stages of his career, one and the same individual may be driven to exploit the advantages of any one of my four "channels of esteem."

An analysis of this sort can at best provide a rough indication of the mechanism of a highly complex social process, but it may help to make comprehensible certain sequences of political action which might otherwise appear totally inconsistent. For example, the evidence suggests that Premier U Nu would have preferred to pursue his ambitions along channel R.1, but he found himself compelled by circumstances to pick up symbols from channels R.2, S.2, and S.1. Likewise, his compatriots Aung San and Ne Win might have preferred to follow channel S.1, but their actual performance often appears more appropriate to channels S.2, R.2, or R.1.

In South Asia in recent years, the most successful politicians have been those who were most adroit at exploiting such shifts of metaphor to their own advantage. The diagram suggests that, provided the charge of being "old fashioned" can be avoided, there may be advantages in keeping rather close to channel S.2. This may explain why it is that for the time being, both in India and Ceylon, the combination of aristocracy and feminine intuition has proved irresistible.

REFERENCES

1. D. E. Smith, *Religion and Politics in Burma* (Princeton: Princeton University Press, 1965), p. 118.

2. *Ibid.,* pp. 115-116; see also F. R. von der Mehden, *Religion and Nationalism in Southeast Asia* (Madison: University of Wisconsin Press, 1963), and H. Bechert, *Buddhismus, Staat und Gesellschaft in den Ländern des Theravada Buddhismus* (Schriften des Instituts für Asienkunde in Hamburg, Band XVII, Parts 1 and 2, 1966, 1967), Part 2, pp. 165-167.

3. Clifford Geertz, *Islam Observed* (New Haven: Yale University Press, 1968).

4. D. E. Smith, *Religion and Politics in Burma,* p. 23.

5. W. Rahula, *History of Buddhism in Ceylon* (Colombo: M. D. Gunasena and Co., 1956), p. 66.

6. *Culuvamsa,* trans. Wilhelm Steiger and M. Rickmers, Parts I and II. (Colombo: Ceylon Government Information Department, 1953), Part I, pp. 31-38.

7. But compare Tambiah's comments on the Burmese *thathanabaing* and related institutions in this issue of *Dædalus.*

8. M. E. Spiro, *Buddhism and Society* (New York: Harper and Row, 1970), p. 382.

9. E. M. Mendelson, "Buddhism and the Burmese Establishment," *Archives de Sociologies des Religions,* No. 17, pp. 85-95.

10. During the colonial phase Burma was a dependency of the Government of India rather than of Great Britain.

11. G. C. Mendis, *Ceylon Today and Yesterday,* 2nd ed. (Colombo: Associated Newspapers of Ceylon, 1963), pp. 170-171.

12. W. H. Wriggins, *Ceylon: Dilemmas of a New Nation* (Princeton: Princeton University Press, 1960), pp. 110-113; M. R. Singer, *The Emerging Elite: A Study of Political Leadership in Ceylon* (Cambridge, Mass., M.I.T. Press, 1964), pp. 14-17.

13. D. E. Smith, *Religion and Politics in Burma,* p. 177.

14. However, U Ba U in *My Burma* (New York: Taplinger Publishing Co., 1959), p. 170 maintains that in 1943 the Japanese had contemplated reestablishing a puppet Burmese monarchy with either the Prince of Pyinmana, a son of King Mindon, or a grandson of King Thibaw as King.

15. E. Sarkisyanz, *Buddhist Backgrounds of the Burmese Revolution* (The Hague: Martinus Nijhoff, 1965).

16. H. Bechert, *Buddhismus, Staat und Gesellschaft in den Ländern des Theravada Buddhismus,* Part 2, p. 166.

17. J. G. Scott and J. P. Hardiman, *Gazetteer of Upper Burma and the Shan States* (Rangoon: Government Printer, 1900), Part 1, vol. 2, p. 2.

18. Sir J. E. Tennent, *Ceylon,* 2 vols. (London: Longman, Green, Longman and Roberts, 1859), Vol. 2, p. 182.

19. See D. E. Smith, ed., *South Asian Politics and Religion* (Princeton: Princeton University Press, 1966), citations from 1969 paperback edition, p. 456, and D. E. Smith, *Religion and Politics in Burma,* p. 141. See also Sir Ivor Jennings, "Politics in Ceylon since 1952," *Pacific Affairs,* 27, p. 344.

20. D. E. Smith, ed., *South Asian Politics and Religion,* pp. 490-499.

21. H. Bechert, *Buddhismus, Staat und Gesellschaft in den Ländern des Theravada Buddhismus,* Part 1, pp. 342-345.

22. See F. N. Trager, *Burma, From Kingdom to Republic* (London: Pall Mall Press, 1966), pp. 59, 77-78.

23. See M. S. Collis, *Last and First in Burma (1941-48)* (London: Faber and Faber, 1956), pp. 267, 272-277.

24. See H. Bechert, *Buddhismus, Staat und Gesellschaft in den Ländern des Theravada Buddhismus,* Part 2, p. 132.

25. F. N. Trager, "Aung San of Burma" in *Asia III* (1965); also *Burma, From Kingdom to Republic,* pp. 55-90.

26. *Ibid.,* p. 56.

27. For Siam-Thailand, see H. G. Quaritch Wales, *Siamese State Ceremonies: Their History and Function* (London: Quaritch, 1931), pp. 31, 166, 156f. For Burma, see Father Sangermano, *The Burmese Empire a Hundred Years ago as described by Father Sangermano,* notes and introduction by John Jardine (Westminster, London: Archibald Constable, 1893), p. 76n. For Ceylon, see M. B. Ariyapala, *Society in Mediæval Ceylon* (Colombo: K. V. G. de Silva, 1956), p. 44ff.

28. Aung San's career provides an interesting negative case. Aung San did not personally aspire to be a "good Buddhist"; it was rather that his fame gave him the credit of "Good Buddhist" characteristics. When he became "General" (Bogyoke) Aung San he modeled himself on the Japanese Generals with whom he needed to associate; this, coupled with a naturally unostentatious temperament, gave him a reputation for exaggerated personal austerity: he was said to behave like a Buddhist virtuous Hero of ancient tradition.

29. See M. E. Spiro, *Buddhism and Society;* Sir Charles Crosthwaite, *The Pacification of Burma* (London: E. Arnold and Co., 1912); D. E. Smith, *Religion and Politics in Burma;* E. Sarkisyanz, *Buddhist Backgrounds of the Burmese Revolution.*

30. F. N. Trager, *Burma, From Kingdom to Republic,* pp. 210-211.

S. J. TAMBIAH

The Persistence and Transformation of Tradition in Southeast Asia, With Special Reference to Thailand

TRADITION IS a word much used by politician and scholar, conservative and radical, priest and rebel. It is used most of the time in an uncritical "ahistorical" sense to denote some kind of collective heritage that has supposedly been transmitted relatively unchanged from the past. By conceiving of tradition in this way, two things tend to be forgotten: that the past was, perhaps, as open and dynamic to the actors of that time as our own age appears to us; and that the norms, rules, and orientations of the past were not necessarily as consistent, unified, and coherent as we tend to imagine.

Deep-seated Dialectical Tensions in Theravada Buddhist Societies

The major point with which I want to begin this discussion is that there are, indeed, in Southeast Asian societies great continuities between the past and the present that are expressed in deep structure relations between politics and religion. These relations, however, are best viewed as constituting dialectical tensions or parameters rather than age-sanctified, unambiguous rules.

Take for instance Ceylon, Burma, and Thailand which together make up a meaningful belt by virtue of their sharing a common religion—Theravada Buddhism. Through the ages, there was communication and interchange between these countries in religious matters. But on first sight today, each country appears to differ significantly from the other. Ceylon appears to combine radical socialist politics with an official support for Buddhism; Burma on the other hand, combines a general's autocratic and bureaucratic rule with a nominal "secularism" that underplays Buddhism and is distrustful of its political use. Thailand stands on the extreme right; its revered (but relatively powerless) kingship is propped up by a powerful military clique which champions Buddhism as the state religion and as a sacred national heritage. These three countries, then, appear to mix politics and religion in different proportions to produce different compounds. Nevertheless, a few decades ago Ceylon was ruled by a relatively conservative party (UNP) which tried to keep Buddhism and politics apart or at least within bounds; in contrast, Burma a dozen years ago was enthusiastically behind U Nu, who tried to combine a fervent Buddhism with "democratic" and "socialist" politics; and Thailand, after the so-called revolution of 1932, responded at least for a brief spell to Pridi's socialist, secularist, democratic politics. In other words, the structure of the political system and its relation to Buddhism is not necessarily permanent at any time in these three countries. The patterns comprise temporary crystallizations; each society, it would seem, could change its pattern over time, but the patterns themselves constitute a limited set of possibilities. And these possibilities appear to relate to a deeper underlying and persisting set of dialectical tensions stemming from the historical relationship between Buddhism and the polity from the Asokan era in India, and subsequently from the various Buddhist kingdoms of South and Southeast Asia of Sinhalese, Mon, Burmese, and Thai extractions.

One of the most important features of these Theravada Buddhist polities is their active *consciousness of historical continuity*, a consciousness that was accentuated and burgeoned at the end of the colonial era and at the dawn of independence. This consciousness may have suffered eclipses and amnesias during various periods of decline, but at times of resurgence and expansion old literary texts and mythologies always provided the models for revival and lent an air of authenticity to the claim of continuity. Thus, one of the distinguishing features of Southeast Asian Buddhist politics was an understanding of history that conceived each country's national destiny to be the protection and guardianship of the religion. Yet, as I have said, this allegedly continuous tradition always contained paradoxes and dialectical tensions which may be expressed as parameters.

In discussing these parameters one should, perhaps, for the sake of clarity make a distinction between canonical Buddhism, which takes as its point of reference the Pali canon known as "Tripitaka" (three baskets), and historical Buddhism, which refers to later developments and accretions notably from the time of Emperor Asoka onwards. The tensions I discuss derive primarily from historical Buddhism, though certain seeds may be found in the canon itself.

The first parameter relates to the antithetical role of the monk: on the one hand, as world renouncer, the monk receives gifts and sustenance from laymen with no obligation to make a return; on the other hand, the monk has an obligation to reciprocate and give spiritual and humanitarian service to the laymen (and in certain circumstances, to become engaged in this-worldly activity while remaining detached and renouncing the fruits of action). This dichotomy is also reflected elsewhere: the monk's vocation of learning and the vocation of meditation, monks dwelling in towns and those living in the forest, and monks implicated in monastic organization and those who remain apart as hermits or ascetics.

An associated problem relates to the fact that a monk who has truly renounced lay life and has gone from home into homelessness should ideally never return to the world; but alternately, canonical Buddhism has always sanctioned a monk's giving up his robes without any stigma attached if he found it difficult to conform to the monk's regimen. In Ceylon there is, however, a social stigma attached to a monk returning to the world; perhaps this may be accounted for by the Indian-Hindu view that the process of a *sannyasin* renouncing caste society, becoming casteless and immune to caste rules, and therefore being unable to return to it subsequently has implications for Sinhalese society which also has castes.[1] But Burma and Thailand and Laos have gone in the opposite direction. For most of the youth in these countries, being ordained as novice or monk at the threshold of adulthood is a "rite of passage," a desirable spiritual and social accomplishment. Temporary monkhood is common, and even more importantly, monks who have spent some time in robes acquiring education, reputation, and skills, both spiritual and social, use them to advantage when they reenter lay society. (Increasingly, a similar trend is discernable in Ceylon with the founding of universities where monks are able to receive higher education on equal terms with laymen.)

Another paradox is that while the general norm is that a monk should keep away from politics and should not use his spiritual powers for political purposes—because a political monk does damage to the Sangha—yet the political monk emerges from time to time in Buddhist countries. In recent times, among the trio it is Ceylon and Burma that have generated and stimulated the political monk, while Thailand has tended to control or squash him. Perhaps the explanation lies in the impact of colonial rule on the former and its absence in Thailand. We shall return to this later, but here let us note that in Burma during British rule monks and ex-monks emerged as leaders of rebellions (for example, the Saya San revolt) against an alien ruler who had "disestablished" Buddhism. Moreover in the post-independence era, given democratic politics and the weak political control exercised over monks by a popularly elected government, the activist political monk has flourished in Burma and Ceylon, particularly in urban areas (although these activists are numerically only a minority of the total monk population). In Thailand, however, where Buddhism is the state religion, where traditional autocracy remains secure in the form of a military government, where kingship itself is preserved as a revered institution, the explicitly political activist monk is not allowed to emerge, and if he does, is likely to be treated harshly when he is felt to be a threat to the secular power.[2] However, educated and activistic elite monks in contemporary Thailand are, as we shall see later, seeking a positive role for themselves within the present political and ecclesiastical dispensation and are redefining the role of monks in society in new directions.

Curiously, the question of "orthodoxy" in the behavior of monks relates in Buddhist countries today not so much to the propagation of heretical doctrines as to the breaking of rules of conduct and etiquette as laid down in the *vinaya* code. In the history of Buddhism there have been, of course, major sectarian splits on doctrinal matters, but more characteristically, schisms within the Sangha have arisen on questions of "discipline" relating to details of ritual, etiquette, and conduct, such as methods of ordination, of wearing the robe, or laxness of behavior regarding the handling of money or sexual morality. The ancient kings supposedly wielded the right to "purify" the Sangha, and in Ceylon, Burma, and Thailand this cleaning of the stables had more to do with the worldliness or laxness of monks than with their heretical beliefs. A possible explanation may be phrased in these terms: Buddhism draws a firm distinction between the path of the monk and that of the layman; the monk's pursuit of salvation is ideally so "individualized" and removed from worldly pursuits that it is difficult to set limits in matters of philosophical doctrine relating to the salvation quest, while what needs to be guarded and can be guarded against is the possible degeneration of the monk's conduct toward the householder's worldly way of life.

We are now in a position to explore the paradoxes built into the relation between Buddhism as religion and the polity as the political domain.

The Asokan mythology is well-entrenched in the Buddhist countries of Southeast Asia, particularly the formula that the king is the patron and protector of the religion, that he must of necessity be a Buddhist himself, and that such a king is an embodiment of *dharma*. In Ceylon, these elements were further elaborated into the ideology that the identity of Sinhalese society was a Buddhist identity, its national consciousness indissolubly linked with Buddhism, and that it was a special historic task entrusted to the Sinhalese to defend the religion against its enemies. As is well known, the Mahavamsa, composed by monks, is the great religious *cum* political dynastic chronicle of the Sinhalese. But the same idea of a special "national" destiny linked with religion and protected by righteous kings, themselves Buddhas-to-be, was included in the traditions of the Mon, Burmese, Thai, and Laotian kingdoms as well.

In Ceylon, this doctrine of identifying state and society with Buddhism created difficulties in the post-colonial era when the larger society included non-Buddhist and non-Sinhalese speaking minorities. The ideology leads to an intolerant dogma that excludes other religions and languages from equal membership within the polity. While in Ceylon the Sinhalese have practiced this dogma against a group equal to themselves in culture and civilization, in Burma the same intolerant, exclusionary attitudes were focused on the hill tribes considered to be "inferior" to the Burmese. And Thailand in recent years has demonstrated the same intolerance toward its hill tribes, particularly the Meo who have suffered from military action against them. Moreover, both Burma and Thailand are not averse to training the same guns on Moslem minorities, whether their ethnic origins are the same as or different from the Buddhist majority.

This constant strain to identify the religion with the state and the Buddhist state, in turn, with a Buddhist society creates perpetual internal cleavages of a sort that are absent in Hindu India (except when that society collides headlong with a militant, excluding religion like Islam). Traditionally, Hinduism did not formulate its identity through king or state, but through the caste system which comprises society. Hinduism has always tended to encompass its minorities and to incorporate and hierarchize them; I am not suggesting, however, that "dominant" groups in India do not economically exploit tribal groups or take political and military action against them if they are considered intractable. Only that the grounds for doing so are not justified in religious terms. But Buddhism, which especially in its militant phases has associated itself with a political definition of its competence, tends to exclude and eliminate its "aliens" and its minorities rather than try to incorporate them. While India has successfully withstood all attempts in modern times to conjoin state and religion, Ceylon, Burma, and Thailand find it difficult to keep at bay the demands that Buddhism be declared the official and privileged religion of the state.

One remarkable feature of the Buddhist mix may be mentioned *en passant*. In the post-independence era not only has Buddhism been a strong ingredient of Sinhalese, Burmese, and Thai nationalism, but indeed most politicians, even the ardent reformers and modernizers, have felt the imperative need to ally themselves with the revival of Buddhism and to declare their political aims as being consistent with Buddhism. How are the politicians of Buddhist countries—conservatives and radicals—able to achieve this, while in Islamic countries where religion makes similar political demands, radical reformers sometimes feel it necessary to attack and disown a "conservative" Islam? My answer is that it is precisely because Islam legislates on matters social, familial, and jural that reformers feel the need to blast it away when it opposes their remedies, whereas it is precisely because Buddhism is imprecise and scarcely legislates on matters of lay social ethics that it can act as an umbrella of political identity at the widest level without fear of creating internal cleavages among the believers.

Despite these historic, persisting identifications of religion with political authority and state, there exists also a basic distinction that ideally the Sangha (the monastic order) and the political authority are separate domains. In theory, the Sangha experiences immunity in its internal matters and even in relation to its property and endowments. Nevertheless, these boundaries are never preserved in practice. We have noted already that the king was granted the right to "purify" the religion by taking forceful action against monasteries and monks not living according to the *vinaya* rules and thereby bringing the religion into disrepute.

The counterpart of this incursion by the ruler into religion is that kings have always needed the Sangha and its eminent monks to legitimate their authority. Thus, there is no doubt that in ancient Ceylon during the Anuradhapura period kings played the political game of supporting one or the other of the three *nikayas*—the Mahavihara, the Abhayagiri, and the Jetavana—in order to strengthen their power. Schisms within the Sangha were not unrelated to the vagaries of dynastic politics, especially when rebellions were endemic, successions rapid, and usurpers frequent. It is also clear that the requirements for legitimation of the current king were closely allied with purifications of the Sangha and with initiating new ordinations (*upasampada*) of monks. A king of Tamil origin, Kirti Sri Rajasimha, sought legitimation through similar means in the eighteenth century. And even in the last few decades, various Prime Ministers of Ceylon, Burma, and Thailand have wooed the Sangha for support and legitimation of their position. Thus, despite the formal separation of Sangha and ruler their activities interpenetrate and their fortunes oscillate according to the state of play. In our own times, politicians find that the felt necessity to "revive" and support Buddhism not only activates demands among enthusiasts for making Buddhism the state religion, but also spawns politically active monks. Yet the dangers inherent in these trends again force governments to politically neutralize the monks and to declare the Sangha's remoteness from the affairs of this world. The oscillation is endemic and repetitive and a conspicuous feature of contemporary politics.

We next come to the dialectical tension faced by a lay politician who is a self-proclaimed Buddhist with regard to the problem of violence and the use of force in political action. This tension was already built into the ancient formula that the king was both a wheel-rolling *cakkravartin* (universal emperor) and a *bodhisattva* (Buddha-to-be). The doctrinal resolution in historical Buddhism was that the king was a righteous ruler, an embodiment of *dharma,* and the fountainhead of justice. This avoided any contradiction between the activities of ruling and the practice of morality, between indulgence in politics and the religious pursuit.

In actual fact, however, political effectiveness and the practice of morality were never achieved concurrently by great men. Kings must be good killers before they can turn to piety and good works. Asoka's alleged conversion and his pious pillar edicts were subsequent to the victorious wars which made possible the largest empire India had known until the arrival of the British. Dutha Gamini, the Sinhalese hero, indulged in successful violence and blood-spilling in his defeat of the Tamils before he could build his monuments and accumulate his credit of merit. Formerly, therefore, kings made the passage from violence to piety; today this pattern is still visible among ordinary folk who, after a boisterous and robust youth, may become pious *upasaka* in their old age, withdrawing from the world and practicing the precepts.

Interestingly enough, especially in modern times, the opposite passage is also possible and politically feasible—first to be a monk and then later to become actively engaged with this world. For notable examples we should turn to Burma and Thailand where ex-monks have become successful men of the world—high civil servants, politicians, teachers, and even businessmen. More interestingly, U Nu of Burma recharged his moral batteries by periodically retreating for a short time into meditation and temporary monkhood before returning to active phases of politics. In Thailand, the king himself temporarily donned the monk's robe, a gesture that gave him the stamp of maturity. And less dramatically, Sinhalese politicians from Bandaranayake to lesser men have felt that their political performance would be aided by public acts of piety and good works, thus demonstrating that for a layman there was a feedback from religious activity to this-worldly success. Thus, we see in these examples varying quantities in the mix between morality and politics, *ahimsa* and force—shifts from one state to the other and sometimes an elusive balance between the two.

The final dialectical theme I would like to discuss is the traditional coexistence of divine kingship and political insurrection—at first sight, two unlikely bedfellows. The kings of Southeast Asia not only gave themselves the title of Bodhisattva and acted as the keepers of the Buddha's relics as regalia validating kingship, but also employed court brahmins to purify and divinize them, to make them earthly Indras and Shivas. Indeed, their palaces were made the center of the universe. Hence it is all the more bizarre that in reality a king's position was unstable. The heads of kings rolled frequently because succession rules were vague, rebellions endemic, and the overall political scaffolding fragile, expanding and contracting with the military fortunes of the ruler and his rivals. One might say that it is precisely because the recruitment of kings was contentious that whoever ascended the throne subsequently sought to be legitimated by the Buddhist Sangha and divinized by court functionaries. The political weakness is not unconnected to the ritual elaboration. Given this historical precedent, *coups d'état*, political assassinations, the toppling of governments in present-day politics, and the counter theme of divinizing successful politicians dead or alive should not altogether appear incongruous. U Nu was considered by many Burmese as a saint and as the long-awaited messianic ruler, Maitriya, because it was alleged he practiced *ahimsa* and benevolent politics. But he was toppled and now lives in banishment. Bandaranaike was considered by some as Diyasena, the king who would initiate the new Buddhist era, but he was assassinated by a monk and has subsequently been deified as a Bandara guardian deity.

Notwithstanding the traditions of divinization and bodhisattvaship, there is also in Buddhist countries another mythological tradition which advocates a social contract and utilitarian theory of kingship. The *Dhammathat* literature of Burma, the *Thamasat* of Thailand—both being derived from the Indian precedent of legal treatises (*dharmasastra*)—and the parallel text called the *Nitinighanduva* in Ceylon contain a Buddhist version of the origins of society (which in many ways inverts the Hindu version contained in the *Laws of Manu*). According to this view, the progressive degeneracy of man created the need for government which, in turn, led to the election by men of the first King Mahasammata. Moreover, this elective theory of kingship is counterbalanced by asserting at the same time that Mahasammata was a virtuous man, an embodiment of *dharma* and destined to become a Buddha; and that it was as his minister that the sage Manu discovered the perfect law. Thus, we see how a secular theory of government is balanced against the charismatic properties of kingship, thereby creating a polarity which can accommodate different kinds of empirical events.

Tradition and Its Transformation in Thailand

Having hitherto explored certain tradition-based, dialectical themes relating to politics and religion which appear to have persisted over time as continuities in the Buddhist countries of Southeast Asia, I must now transform the model by suggesting how the direction in which Ceylon, Burma, and Thailand have moved in recent times is vitally affected by the nature of their contact with Western powers. If I have previously taken a perspective of persistence, I should now make a correction by taking into account dynamic inputs which have led to irreversible and sometimes unique changes.

In the rest of this paper I shall focus primarily on Thailand. Since Ceylon and Burma are covered in greater detail by Edmund Leach, I shall allude to them hereafter only in a brief comparative manner in order to highlight the distinctive features of the Thai situation.

The Western Impact on Thailand

It is said that the great divide between Ceylon, Burma (and Cambodia) on the one hand, and Thailand on the other is their different experience of the Western impact in Asia: subjection to or relief from colonial domination by the Western imperial powers. This difference in historical experience perhaps also determines the difference in their contemporary political postures. Ceylon and Burma, subject to British colonial rule until the late 1940's, have undergone a period of politics characterized by militant Buddhism spearheaded by Buddhist monks, and of social upheavals with a strong "revivalist" and—at least in ideology—"socialist" or "democratic" tinge. Ceylon has today gone farthest in its socialist politics, whereas Burma has replaced U Nu's brand of democratic socialism with a military dictatorship which considers itself on the side of socialism and against

Western capitalistic imperialism. Significantly, Ne Win's government published, after the takeover, a document called *The Burmese Road to Socialism*.

Thailand's political stance is dramatically different.[3] Since the short-lived *coup d'état* of 1932, which made the monarchy constitutional and initiated an abortive democratic system, Thailand has been ruled by a succession of military-police cliques. On the one hand, these governments have been frankly totalitarian, sometimes even trigger-happy, and in international politics firmly in the American camp; on the other hand, they have staunchly supported, exploited, and manipulated the institutions of kingship and Buddhist religion in order to maintain themselves in power and to evoke political loyalty and conformity. It would, however, be wrong and altogether to miss the point not to realize that the present political system in Thailand—capped by a revered (though politically clipped) monarchy, legitimated by a ritualistically robust Buddhism, and controlled by army and police generals—enjoys by and large the "support" of the large mass of citizens who recognize themselves as Thai. The three million or so local Chinese cannot be assumed as automatically supporting the military government, though they have made their accommodation to it.[4] The peasantry are, of course, devoted to Buddhism and to kingship; although their interaction with Thai bureaucracy is remote, there is by and large no resistance to the government, except among certain elements in the border regions. These dissidents are one of three groups: peasants victimized by the police and the bureaucracy, fugitives from justice, and a small number of politically committed "communist insurgents." While the support of the rural peasantry is largely passive, that of the relatively large bureaucracy manned by educated Thais is more direct and politically the more important for purposes of power maintenance.

It is this seemingly unique character of the Thai polity and its political orientations (when compared to the political configuration of other Asian countries) that should be remembered in trying to understand modern developments. The unravelling of the underlying features has, I believe, lessons to teach us, lessons wider in application than to Thailand alone. For it seems to me that Thailand today portrays features which would find their analogues and parallels in contemporary Ceylon and Burma had these societies not been subject to colonial rule by European powers and had they been allowed to continue into modern times with their traditional political systems characterized by kingship, supporting Buddhism and in turn being supported by it, and operating through a "patrimonial" or "feudal" administrative structure in which hierarchical status was all important.[5]

Although I have said that the colonial experience divides Ceylon and Burma from Thailand, it is necessary to qualify and refine this point in two ways. The first is what I have demonstrated earlier in this article, that since Sinhala Ceylon and Burma (excluding the tribes) were Buddhist polities before the Western impact, deeply entrenched traditional features persist in these societies, features which are also clearly recognizable as living traditions in the present Thai system. In all three countries, there are strong similarities imprinted on their contemporary sociopolitical systems: the high evaluation of administrative or governmental positions, the superiority accorded to politics over economics, the encompassing importance of hierarchical status in bureaucracies, the strong belief that Buddhism and the state are deeply intertwined and that it is the responsibility of the state to protect the religion, if not to declare it as the established state religion.

The second refinement relates to the Western impact on Thailand.[6] Although Thailand was not subjugated by the British or French (or other competing Western powers), the sheer threat posed by these countries, especially during the reigns of King Mongkut and King Chulalongkorn in the second half of the nineteenth century, with Britain positioned in the West and South in Burma and Malaya, and the French even more belligerantly poised in the East in Cambodia and Laos (French Indo-China), necessarily evoked a response.

It is true, of course, that although Thailand was not politically subjugated and ruled by a Western power, the economy that developed was basically "colonial." The exploitation of teak forests, the mining of tin, the export of rice were activities that fitted into the typical imperial economic pattern as surely as those of Indo-China, or Burma, or Malaya.

Nevertheless, it must be firmly recognized that the fact that the Thais continued to rule themselves through their traditional political machinery made a vital difference to the subsequent shape and temper of the country. In lieu of actual territorial conquest, the demands by Western powers for lifting trade barriers and the granting of extra-territorial privileges because Thailand was too "primitive" to guarantee the safety and well-being of European subjects drove the Thai royalty, the princes, and some of the noble families toward a "modernization" imposed from the top. This is exemplified by the building of communications networks—roads, railways, the telegraph and postal services, the revamping and refashioning of an administrative system consisting of ministries and departments as well as a territorial grid, the expansion of education, and training and recruitment of personnel to man the bureaucracies. A feature that is less well appreciated because of its long term consequences is that King Chulalongkorn and his successors modernized and expanded the armed forces (the army and navy) in order to meet the colonial threat. And thereby hangs a tale: the army increasingly became an independent "power" group in the political system; it opened its ranks to newly educated elements of the population outside the aristocracy and the old nobility; and ever since the 1930's it has seized the political functions previously wielded by the king. Subsequent events simply connived at making the armed forces the most important power group in the society—especially in the aftermath of World War II when the United States has fed and armed the growing military giant to further its own anti-communist politics in Asia. The Thai generals, pursuing a pro-United States policy, are deeply entrenched in the society, carrying out periodic *coups* (euphemistically called "revolutions") from within in order to further strengthen themselves.

What I should particularly like to highlight here is that, rather than considering the Western impact on Thailand as having produced discontinuities and dramatic changes in the Thai polity, it is more revealing to view it as having reinforced and accentuated in certain significant aspects both its overt and latent structural features. The king remains today as a politico-religious symbolic entity, but the actual political role in all its authoritarian aspects is wielded by the army and the bureaucratic elite. The hierarchical administrative structure of officials during the monarchical era has now simply been enlarged into an extensive bureaucracy which, in true traditional style, is by and large loyal and acquiescent to the powers that be. For the traditional definition is that officials exist to implement the ruler's injunctions. And the contemporary attitude is that the bureaucracy is charged with maintaining law and order and with furthering the achievement of stability and continuity of society. Thus, in Thailand both the political powerwielders and its largely conformist bureaucracy are ranged on the same side and tend to think not only of "insurgents," but also of any elected parliament scrutinizing, criticizing, and delaying their activities as rocking the boat and as inimical to public order. In other words, "democracy" and "mass participation in government" as conceived by the Westerner is simply not in accord with the past or present Thai social structure (and therefore also with Thai temperament and attitudes).

I particularly have in mind here the recent *coup d'état* staged in Thailand in early November (1971). There were several official reasons given by the National Executive Council for this "revolution": the increasing communist threat, especially in Laos where the enemy has built two roads to the Thai border; the irresponsibility and extremeness of many elected members of the Legislative Asssembly who hold up governmental projects, especially by delaying the passing of the Budget; increasing crime, student unrest, and labor strikes; the problem of dealing with a China newly admitted to the United Nations, and the problematic nature of the local Chinese population whose political affiliations are suspect. I have questioned several Thai government officials, teachers, and professionals; all approve, without much demur, of the military action in the interests of suppressing alleged political radicalism and civil crimes and of maintaining order. It is of crucial importance to appreciate this general orientation of the Thai political order in any comparative study of post-traditional societies in Southeast Asia. However, it would be fallacious to infer that the present framework of the Thai polity cannot generate dynamic trends and transformations from within, although no doubt it sets limits to the kind of changes that are considered acceptable.

In the remainder of this essay I shall describe certain transformations taking place today in Thailand that relate intimately to one of its most sensitive and "sacred" cultural traditions: the tenets of Buddhism and the place of Buddhist monks in society. I shall deal with ideological formulations made by contemporary elite scholar monks, formulations which on the one hand are a response to contemporary needs and tasks, and on the other seek their authority in the pristine canonical texts. In a sense these monks can be regarded as "modernizers" or "innovators" in that they are attempting to find new permutations of old codes, or to make new connections between old (ambiguous) tenets, or even to transform them. This ideological drive and its associated programs of positive this-worldly action on the part of Thai monks I shall therefore call *transformation based on tradition*.

Ideological Transformation Based on Tradition

The canonical texts of Buddhism (like the Bible of Christianity or the core texts of any other religion) are complex and rich in meaning, and by the same token sometimes "ambiguous" or capable of different levels of interpretation. The Thai monk-ideologists of today most definitely find authority for their interpretations in the canonical texts; their interpretations certainly differ in some crucial aspects from those given in the past primarily by Western interpreters of Buddhism. I shall deal with the character of the doctrinal interpretations by contemporary Thai scholar monks by first discussing some of the ideas of Thailand's most renowned religious thinker, Buddhadasa Bhikkhu, who is famous for his sermons, writings, and religious practices at Suan Mokh (the park of liberation) in South Thailand.

Buddhadasa (though influenced by Zen Buddhism) is scrupulously and rigorously orthodox in one objective: the aim of the Buddhist quest, as he never tires of telling us, is "complete freedom from selfhood" (*anatta*) and the attainment of "emptiness" (*sunnata*), which is beyond both good and bad action (*karma*). "To train oneself not to cling to anything with the feeling of 'I' or 'mine,' that is the highest system of spiritual culture."[7] His interpretations are compelling because they stem from one basic thrust: it is the world *here and now* that is relevant. This fundamental point has many ramifications and resonances. Not only does it call for action here and now as being productive, but it also "interiorizes" inside man's mind the Buddhist cosmology by declaring that heavens and hells, rebirth (*samsara*) and liberation (*nirvana*), are not outside us as events or places but inside as internal states and experiences. Central to this exposition is the flat assertion that the language of the common man is misleading and vastly different from the language of the dhamma.

Thus the ordinary man conceives the four woeful states (apaya) realistically and materially as outside him, attained after death, as hell (naraka), as the realms of beasts, of the hungry ghosts (peta), and of the frightened ghosts (asura). But in Dhammic language the woeful states are experienced here and now: "The hungry ghosts of Dhamma language are purely mental states. Ambition based on craving, worry based on craving—to be afflicted with these is to be born a hungry ghost." 'If one is afraid, one is simultaneously born an asura."[8] "Whenever greed, anger and delusion cause us to be excited and heated, then we become creatures in the hell-like samsara."[9] Again, in dealing with the paired concepts of heaven and hell, he declares that while in everyday language they are realms outside to be attained after death, nevertheless "the heaven and hell of Dhamma language are to be found in the mind and may be attained any time at all depending on one's mental make-up."[10]

Moving even more daringly, Buddhadasa does the same thing with the concept of Nirvana. Expounding that there are different levels of Nirvana, he says: "Nirvana is attained at any moment that the mind becomes free from compounding. Freedom from compounding, at any moment, is nirvana. Permanent cessation of compounding is full nirvana."[11] (Compounding means grasping and clinging with attachment.) And finally, he pushes this insight to the ultimate limit when, in a lecture titled "In Samsara Exists Nibbana," he postulates the contemporariness of samsara and nibbana: "since there exists both suffering and the cessation of suffering within our living body, it is inevitable [that] the whirlpool of samsara and nibbana are there, and the Lord Buddha has already declared the truth".[12]

What Buddhadasa's ideas forcefully refute and deny is the fatalism, the postponement of action, the unreality of this world, and therefore the apathy toward it attributed to Buddhism by stereotype commentators. He is, in fact, saying that the world here and now, our own present time, our experienced mental states comprise the stage for urgent and immediate action in the form of Buddhist practice. Perhaps an ever more important ideological assertion is that the quest for Nirvana does not mean abnegation and renunciation of action in this world: the ideal is that man should act in this world with metta, with loving kindness and compassion, not for his own selfish gain but for the collective good. The ideal man does not renounce action, only the fruits of action for himself. Finally, it is clear that Buddhadasa (as do many other Thai scholar monks) totally rejects the view that Buddhism is "pessimistic" and "misanthropic" and stands for a devaluation of this world.

A transition or tranformation from this position to an even more activistic orientation to the world is provided by various scholar monks concerned with the provision of higher religious *cum* secular education for monks. Their main aim is that monks should recover their educational roles in society which they have lost in modern times. It is argued that monks, by virtue of being disinterested persons who have renounced politics and property, can provide effective leadership not only in the practice of morality, but also in stimulating social and economic development.

In Bangkok, there are quite a few of these vigorous scholar-monks and educational administrators who have preserved themselves from total involvement with the performance of religious merit rituals, or with the pursuit of ecclesiastical titles and office so as to direct their energies to activities they think worthwhile. I shall take as my example Phra Sri Wisudhimoli (previously Phra Prayudh Payutto), who is Assistant Secretary General at Mahachulalongkorn University, a university for monks.[13]

Phra Sri's views of the need for monks to play a positive role in modern society rests on the basic proposition that, since monks are materially dependent on the laity, they have a duty to make a return. He argues that there is doctrinal basis for this idea because the Buddha is supposed to have said: "The monks should always reflect that our existence depends on other people."[14] Traditionally the service rendered by monks to society was not only helping laymen to free themselves from suffering by the practice of kindness and mercy, but was also related to the imparting of education in monastery schools. This role which has been lost in recent times must be recovered, argues Phra Sri.

Phra Sri says that it was during the last 70-80 years that the monks have lost their previous roles and status as a result of the impact of Western civilization and the modernization of Thailand. Secular schools, hospitals, courts of law, recreational facilities—all took away the previous functions of the *wat*. Equally disastrous was the monks' recalcitrance to accept change and to familiarize themselves with the new circumstances. The result was the alienation of lay society from monks, who were considered intellectually old-fashioned and found wanting in relation to the new prestigious knowledge. The monks' traditional *pariyattitham* studies and their system of knowledge were felt to be useless for daily life. Nevertheless, there was a time, even during this period of Western impact, when King Chulalongkorn entrusted elementary education to monks and also established for them two institutions of higher learning. In the long run, however, secular schools replaced wat schools.

It is rightly emphasized by Phra Sri that today, when so many of the young monks are strongly disposed to pursue knowledge, the problem is scarcely that of motivating them to learn but of giving them sufficient and adequate education. Traditional ecclesiastical education in the *dhamma* and in the Pali language would not suffice either because there is a heavy demand for supplementation by secular subjects. The monks and novices of today most definitely want to learn *than wicha log* (worldly subjects). The realization of this need by active scholar monks and educators explains the enthusiastic functioning (despite inadequate finance and facilities) of the two universities for monks (Mahachulalongkorn and Mahamakut), of teacher training institutions, and of many wat-run adult schools in Bangkok and Thonburi imparting secondary, secular education to monks and novices.

There is a keen appreciation among the monks themselves that the gradual decrease in numbers being ordained as regular novices and monks (for a longer period than merely one *phansa* or lent), and the increasing tendency for educated monks and novices to disrobe and enter lay society can be stemmed only by the two-fold policy of making monastic education varied, relevant, and interesting—by including "worldly subjects"—and of giving active roles to educated monks so that they can find fulfillment.

In the light of this, we can appreciate another of Phra Sri's basic propositions, that it is "the duty of a monk to study and practice." This principle entails for the monk three kinds of transactions with laymen: the imparting of education (*kaan suksa*), the propagation of *dhamma* (*kaan poey pa*), and the rendering of assistance (*kaan soeng kraw*), which includes giving moral advice, performing rituals, and providing leadership in social welfare and development work in rural areas.

Thus, through these activities it is hoped that monks will recover their traditional roles. They are, it is claimed, especially suited to educate and to stimulate development precisely because they have renounced politics and are not concerned with interfering in administrative matters. Moreover, having also renounced private property, monks become inexpensive extension agents to employ, for their personal needs are simple and the time available to them ample.

Missionary Monks (Dhammathud) and Community Development

Given these activistic ideological orientations, it is not surprising that in recent years monks have become involved in various community development and "missionizing" programs, variously called Dhammathud, Dhammacarick, and Dhammapatana. These programs relate to the hill tribes and to the politically "sensitive" and economically least developed border regions, especially in the Northeast, North, and South. (The *Dhammathud* program also includes sending missions of monks to Malaysia, Indonesia, Europe, and America, in order to propagate Buddhism there.)

Once again, the ideological legitimation for this thrust is found in impeccable doctrinal texts. Many contemporary doctrinally-sophisticated monks would refer to Buddha's admonition to the first group of monks he sent out to spread the teaching: "Go you forth, O Bhikkhus . . . to preach the divine life for the benefit and happiness of the world, including gods and men." (Mahavagga, Vinaya Pitaka) Or again, the Catukkanipata, Anguttara Nikaya reports that: "The Dhamma and Vinaya of the Tathagata is present in the world for the happiness of the world including gods and men."

Thus Colonel Pin Mutukan, the Director General of the Religious Affairs Department (1970) and keen promoter of the *dhammathud* program, exhorted monks to engage in missionary work,[15] just as the Buddha's first act after enlightenment was to go forth and convert five disciples. He criticized the present-day custom whereby monks believe that the right conduct is to await an invitation by laymen (*nimon*) to preach. As in early Buddhism, monks should go out to wats, houses, the jungle, fields, and prisons and teach the dhamma *even if the recipient does not believe in it or does not want it.* (This nicely justified monks teaching the Buddhist "morality" to the "primitive" hill tribes.)

The Dhammathud Program in Thailand

The program of sending out missionary-monks to the border provinces was first begun in 1964 when monks from Bangkok were sent to the Northeast to propagate Buddhism. Subsequently monks were sent out to the South. The program was first conceived at a political level and encouraged by the officials in the Religious Affairs Department; the fact that it was planned in the metropolis explains why it took the form of sending monks from Bangkok to the provinces.

By 1965, the program had matured to seven groups of monks totalling 751 individuals; in 1969 the number of groups had swollen to nine with 1,816 participating monks. Although it was originally sponsored by the Department of Religious Affairs, in its second year the program was officially taken under the wing of the Mahathera Samakhom (the Supreme Ecclesiastical Council of the Sangha). Each of the nine groups was allotted a particular part of the country and put in the charge of an eminent monk with ecclesiastical rank. Very high ranking ecclesiastical monks, members of the Supreme Council, were appointed Leader and Deputy Leaders,[16] and as may be expected, the majority of these high ranking leaders had their seats in the capital city.[17]

Bangkok monks go out to the provinces, and for the short space of some two to three months (usually between March and June), they travel from village to village in the company of local monks, by foot, car, or bus, giving sermons and inculcating values of good citizenship and loyalty. These peripatetic monks are expected to teach the Dhamma and to impart instruction about the correct forms of ritual, worship, and meditation practice. In the area of social welfare and national development, they preach on the need for people to practice restraint in consumption, to observe proper sanitary conditions, and to improve their health.

Although it is difficult to estimate the practical results of the *dhammathud* program,[18] it is clear that it has a usefulness: it is, indeed, a very cheap program of propagation and propaganda, because the monks are merely paid their travel expenses and no wages. Apart from the accruing religious benefits, the monks serve the valuable political function not only of relaying the wishes of the government to the people, but also and more importantly, of channeling upwards the grievances of the isolated villages, such as the inadequacy of schools and roads, or the uncivil behavior of civil servants and police officers. Thus, one report by monks did not mince words when it declared: "The problems of the people which the Government should solve urgently are transport, security, illness, and the conduct of some civil servants. Another problem is securing reasonable prices for agricultural products."[19]

Finally, it is clear that either explicitly in the case of some groups or implicitly in the case of others, the *dhammathud* program has the objective of stemming communism and of drumming up loyalty to Religion and King, to the Nation, and by extension to the Government. Monks I have interviewed report making these exhortations, and the statements of other groups show that counter-insurgency was explicitly on their minds.[20] Insofar as monks do propagate these values, they will not be easily ignored or disregarded by virtue of the respect and regard they enjoy in the society.

The Community Development Program sponsored by Mahachulalongkorn and Mahamakut Universities is better conceived, more serious in intent, and constitutes a direct response from within the ranks of educated monks to the need for them to play a more positive role in society. I shall report on this program from the perspective of Mahachulalongkorn.

The Mahachulalongkorn project is two-pronged. One program sends out to the provinces for a working period of one or two years monk-volunteers who have completed at least five years service and have graduated from the University. Before departure they are usually given a short course on development work. These graduate-volunteers are detailed to work under the ecclesiastical governors of provinces (*chaokhana changwad*) doing what is requested of them but usually teaching in monastic schools. They are also expected ideally to stimulate local monks to form social work centers for the promotion of community development.

It is evident that this program has, apart from the benefits derived by the recipients of their service, the function of satisfying the achievement needs of educated monks, of giving them fulfilling roles so that they can use their education creatively, both in religious and secular subjects, and, important for the Sangha, of postponing by at least two years the possibility of their derobing to join lay society and perhaps finding in it a more rewarding occupational niche. Roughly eighty graduate monks are sent out each year, and since their period of service is usually about one year (upon its completion they usually return to Bangkok to teach at the University, or go to India for further study at Benares, Nalanda, and other universities, or decide to derobe), the total number in the field at any one time does not differ from the annual number despatched. The Asia Foundation, which has enthusiastically supported the Mahachula program, gives the graduate monks serving in the field an honorarium (of a few hundred baht) to take care of travel, food, and other expenses.

The second part of the project does the converse: for a period of usually two months, it brings to Bangkok suitable volunteer monks from the provinces for intensive training and then returns them to their old wats and villages so that they can initiate community development projects.[21] In the program which began in November 1971, lectures were being given in Rural Development, First Aid, Meditation Practice, Credit Societies, Ecology and Environment, Buddhism and the Modern Man, Comparative Religion, History of Buddhism, and Administrative Work of the Monastery Secretary (lekha wat). The lecturers included monks, a medical doctor, a journalist, a publisher, and an official from the Ministry of Justice. There were fifty-nine monks from forty provinces being trained at Mahachulalongkorn in 1972, while in previous years the number was around forty.

The intention is, when these monks return to the provinces, that they will initiate development work on a long term basis; thus, it is realized that to do this work they should be made aware of the villagers' physical, social, and economic needs and given some idea of how they can be met. The program also aims at giving these monks information about the basic public laws and government policies, so that they can be not only suitable mediators between villagers, government officials, and agencies, but also informed advocates of national development, if not effective initiators of welfare projects.

In some instances at least, this program appears to have borne better fruit than the dhammathud program discussed earlier, if only for the simple fact that its relatively long-term and more systematic character permits cumulative achievement. Social service programs have also been activated at certain provincial Buddhist centers, mostly located in Northeast Thailand, which train local monks to initiate village development projects.[22] To what extent are these programs "political" in nature? The dhammathud program has a more obvious political coloring than that of the university, which is more concerned with community development than with intensifying national political integration through religious cum political progaganda. While in the narrow sense the university program may be "non-political," yet it is clear that in its own prospectus the university declares its concern with national well-being and its willingness to work with relevant government units. Also to be remembered is that a number of the members of the project's advisory committee, and indeed the project's patrons, are eminent ecclesiastical dignitaries already involved with *dhammathud* work. And the advisory committee's lay representatives are directors-general of various government departments: they are, in other words, high government officials. Such interlocking membership shows the linkage between the monks' universities, the ecclesiastical hierarchy, and the secular administration.[23] The interlocking with government agencies and personnel is much more direct in the hill tribes *dhammacarick* program, which sends both monks and officials to propagate Buddhism to the "heathen," and is also seen in the Wat Phra Singh project in the North.

In the long run, the result of the monks' development work would be to draw the Sangha, especially the eccesiastical hierarchy, into closer relations with the government hierarchy and officials, both at the central and the regional levels. The possibility of the Bangkok-based upper reaches of the ecclesiastical hierarchy working closely with government Ministries and Departments, which are also centralized in Bangkok, is easily comprehended. At the provincial level, the ecclesiastical governors and their district heads would also increasingly, if unsystematically, be drawn into contact with the secular governors, *nai amphurs* (district officers), and other officials. Indeed, some of the reports of the *dhammathud* groups clearly request that government officials work more closely with them in order to ensure success and that government officials helping in the monks' programs be given special recognition. All these developments could lead to a firmer cross-linkage and a closer integration at all levels between the ecclesiastical framework and the political structure than has hitherto been obtained (especially at the lower levels of the hierarchy in the rural areas). It should also be noted that for some years the government has promoted rural development programs, the most spectacular being the "accelerated rural development" (ARD) program undertaken in so-called "sensitive" areas. In this wider perspective, the monks' development activities constitute only a band in the total spectrum.

The monks' dissemination of Buddhism among the hill tribes—irrespective of whether these tribes desire it or not—is part of a wider governmental action to incorporate and domesticate the "politically sensitive" tribes into the Thai polity. Monks with whom I have conversed talk blithely of going to the hill tribes to teach them the *dhamma* and morality, completely unaware of the fact that these non-Thai minorities may have their own valid cultures and moralities. But this insensitivity, which in the past characterized the approach of many Christian missionaries, is also a characteristic of historical Theravada Buddhism itself. However, the reasons behind the obtuseness are different in the two cases. Most Sinhalese and the vast majority of Burmese and Thai can only conceptualize their identity and their nationhood in terms of their adherence to Buddhism; thus Burmese Buddhism *cum* Nationhood has, in the recent past, expressed itself not only in terms of intolerance of the hill tribes' religions and cultures, but also in terms of denying elementary religious rights to minorities like the Muslims.[24] Recently, Sinhalese Buddhist attitudes to minorities bore a similar character in that Buddhism helped to delineate nationhood and ethnicity. The Thai concept of nationhood and polity also most conspicuously reflects the inherent and intrinsic role of Buddhism. Thus, "Buddhist Nationalism" in its political and cultural dimensions dictates the policies whereby minorities—especially those considered politically and culturally inferior—are "nationalized" and "domesticated," or if they resist, simply eliminated.

The Social Infrastructure of Monks' Activism

An analytical question poses itself regarding the kind of social infrastructural processes that can be seen as generating or, if this is too strong a word, as linked with the activistic ideology of Thai monks at the present time. The infrastructural basis is the modern Sangha's role as an educational network, providing the channels for geographical and social mobility and for the intellectual aspirations of an important segment of the population—the poor peasants. Historically, the Sangha has always played this role,[25] but in modern times it is intensified to a degree never previously known.

The monastic network provides education for poor rural boys to whom secular education is not conveniently accessible or whose families cannot afford the expense of secular, secondary, higher education. From an educational perspective, the monastic system can be portrayed as a network connecting village wat (possessing elementary *pariyattitham* schools) with district and, more importantly, provincial wat centers (usually the seats of provincial ecclesiastical heads) which have education facilities that can better prepare students for *nagtham* and the lower levels of *parien* examinations. These provincial centers, in turn, are linked to the multitude of wat in Bangkok, many of which have even superior pali schools and can therefore not only prepare monks and novices for higher pali exams, but also prepare them for entry into the universities. They also serve as residential bases from which monks and novices can attend other wat-based "adult" schools, teaching secular subjects. B.A. degrees in Buddhism, Education, or Social Science can be secured from the two universities at the top of the ladder. The other adult schools prepare monks and novices for the Ministry of Education's secular, primary and secondary level examinations and, subsequently, for teacher training certificates or diplomas.

What should be emphasized is that today the monastic network has a vital educational function for poor rural boys; that the most talented and motivated of these boys find their way to the capital city as novices or monks; and that in the contemporary circumstances they are not satisfied with a purely traditional religious education but most devoutly want to acquire knowledge of secular subjects (*wicha log*).

It follows inevitably that these talented monks, religiously disciplined and increasingly better informed in modern secular knowledge, should want to play an active role in this world if they remain in robes. The current ideological stress on the "this-worldly" and "here and now" relevance of Buddhism, and the current programs of community development in which young educated monks wish to participate are manifestations of an underlying educational explosion among the religious.

If the committed scholar monks and ecclesiastical authorities do not find fulfilling roles for young educated monks and novices, they will be tempted, once they have finished their education, to derobe in even larger numbers than before in order to find satisfying occupations in lay society. In my view such a process is not to be deplored; these provincial youth discarding the monk's garb after securing education have neither exploited nor demeaned their faith. Most have been assiduous observers of the *vinaya* rules, and when they leave they do make a contribution to lay society, and newer and younger educational cohorts will succeed them.

A curious feature results from all this. The Buddhist Sangha, an institution revered as much as the monarchy and perhaps more widely, is manned, essentially, by rural males originating from farming families. Urban society increasingly produces fewer and fewer regular monks, though it still provides temporary monks for a single lent of three months, or for a shorter duration. The poorest region of Thailand, the Northeast, produces not only the largest number of monks and novices, but also the largest regional contingent of monks and novices residing in Bangkok-Thonburi. Thus we are faced with the splendid paradox that if the Northeast today is the seedbed of the largest number of political "insurgents," it is also the foremost bastion of the Buddhist faith and the source of the religious legitimation of the Bangkok-based, political and administrative authority.[26]

From this primarily rural recruitment of the country's monks and novices can be deduced a political fact: by virtue of being rural and of farming stock, the religious are predisposed in Thailand to be largely conservative and orthodox, with a willingness to accept constituted political authority and to work with it rather than question it, let alone attack it. In a sense it is true that most of the religious, like their rural kinsmen (*yaad phi naung*), are "apolitical," removed from politics, and therefore not oriented to participating in its processes. (It is interesting that, although Burmese monks have in recent times a more dynamic tradition of political participation, often against the government, Melford E. Spiro still characterizes the majority of Burmese monks as conservative and orthodox for the same reason I have given.[27])

It is precisely because the vast majority of Bangkok monks are of rural origin that the plan to send educated, energetic, young monks on *dhammathud* or community development work back to their own villages or provinces makes this kind of program in one way brilliant and strategically feasible. Not only will monks be going to their home provinces, but they are also returning as successful, urban-sophisticated "scholars" with the title of *pramaha* for pali proficiency (which is in short supply in the rural areas), and even possibly with a B.A. degree or some level of teacher training. Hence establishing rapport among the rural population would not normally constitute a difficulty, and, by virtue of their achievements, they may even be accepted as opinion leaders and teachers (*achaan*) capable of showing the way.

But this kind of advantage is countered by a certain disadvantage: while monks can, indeed, efficiently perform educational and counseling roles relating to personal and family problems, in addition to their usual role of preaching the *dhamma* and performing rituals, it is questionable whether they can effectively lead and sponsor on a long-term basis community development projects which require highly trained professional skills (in both technical and communication engineering). Of course, their participation in these activities in cooperation with secular experts and lay professionals is another matter, and their inclusion in such partnerships may be productive.

Be that as it may, one should be realistic about the degree to which monks, whose basic preoccupation is the "spiritual task" of ethical study and practice, have the organization and the capacity to shoulder country-wide plans of development and welfare. Here history can give us a warning, if not teach us a lesson. In the 1890's, in King Chulalongkorn's reign, the princely monk Vachirayarn and Prince Damrong, the Minister of Interior, sought to push through elementary education in the provinces by using the monastic schools and monks as the vehicles and agents. The program was successful for a few years, but it is instructive that Vachirayarn threw in the sponge and asked that the Sangha be relieved of the onerous educational task, because the Sangha was becoming "over-bureaucratized" and involved with government machinery, because the load was too heavy for the monastic system to carry, and also, perhaps, because monks were not in the long run the best transmitters of secular knowledge.[28]

The Political Coloring of Burmese and Sinhalese Monks

The orientations of Thai monks differ from those of their Burmese and Sinhalese contemporaries in two main respects. In Ceylon and Burma, while resorting to modern mass methods for disseminating propaganda, the monks at the same time rejected Western culture and knowledge in the course of their revivalism and their demand for the restoration of an idealized past. This was part and parcel of the rejection of Western colonialism and of Western cultural values and customs, which were seen as having destroyed or degraded indigenous forms. Thailand, lacking this kind of direct traumatic colonial supremacy, is in many ways today more open to Western influence. This is clearly reflected in the orientations and aspirations of the monks: theirs is not a rejection but an active adaptation to the West—at least in regard to their thirst for Western secular knowledge and their borrowing of certain organizational techniques. Precisely because there has been a historical continuity and their past is alive in their present, Thai monks do not self-consciously cry for the revival of the past.

The second major difference between the monks relates to their political orientations. The Thai monks by and large accept the existing political authority as valid, and in their recent activistic phase have desired to act in support of the political authority, or at least to act within the confines of the established system. Furthermore, the Thai Sangha today, more or less in line with conditions that prevailed in the past when the central authority was strong, is also firmly controlled by the political rulers as regards their freedom to engage in political activity. Once again this situation is heir to a historical continuity: at least since the establishment of the strong Chakkri dynasty, from 1782 onwards, monks have kept free of political activity.

The situation is dramatically different in Burma and Ceylon. There, too, the orthodox historical pattern was that the Sangha legitimated and supported strong monarchies (which also, by definition, were strong patrons of the Sangha). But the virtual "disestablishment" of Buddhism in the colonial era and the consequent atrophy of any hierarchical ecclesiastical authority exerting control over the monks and monasteries gave rise in Burma to flux, schisms, the formation of new fraternities, monastic disputes, and the relaxation of monastic discipline. Indeed, the domination by a Western colonial power activated Buddhist monks into a tradition of political action often in defiance of the constituted government, a tradition which they carried with them well into the post-independence era.

The Burmese religious tale during British times is instructive.[29] Before the British conquest, Burma had a certain ecclesiastical structure and organization: the king appointed the thathanabaing (sangharaja), the head of the Sangha, who in turn appointed regional (gainggyoks) and other ecclesiastical officers. (Thailand established a similar hierarchy in the mid-nineteenth century, and an especially strong one in 1902 by King Chulalongkorn's Sangha Act.) Government officers appointed by the king enforced the thathanabaing's authority to settle monastic property disputes and to maintain discipline within the Sangha.

The chief factor causing increasing entropy in the Burmese religious sphere was the British practice of "religious neutrality"; this was actually a policy of vacillation and progressive withdrawal of support for the ecclesiastical authorities which produced atomization and lack of orderly relations within the Sangha, and between the monks and the political authority. The erosion first began in 1852 when, after the conquest of Lower Burma, no ecclesiastical authority was recognized for this area, since the religious head was in the still unconquered Upper Burma with his seat in Mandalay. After the conquest of Upper Burma in 1886, the British, fearing that the Sangha and its monks were a potential center of resistance to British control, failed to make the *thathanabaing*'s jurisdiction effective. After 1895 his office was not filled for eight years, and in 1938 the office lapsed altogether. In the meantime, his authority had no legality in Lower Burma which refused to be ruled by any ecclesiastical authority. And throughout the country the politicization of monks and their engagement in militant, anti-colonial, nationalist politics, accompanied by the breaking of many *vinaya* rules, drew from the British a tardy attempt to revive the authority of monks of senior (*sayadaw*) status. Even here British policy proved to be inconsistent, for in 1935 the Rangoon High Court ruled that the hierarchy set up in Upper Burma, including the authority of the *thathanabaing*, had "no constitutional or legal status, and are in the same position as any other religious body not established by the State."[30]

Thus the British lack of support for the traditional Buddhist ecclesiastical structure resulted in the weakening of the Sangha, a serious decay in internal order, and a powerful increase in political activity. D. E. Smith succinctly states the argument:

In India neither Hinduism nor Islam ever developed an ecclesiastical structure; their strength lay in the socio-religious institutions (caste, Islamic law) which regulated every aspect of day-to-day life. The vitality of Buddhism in Burma (as in other Theravada Buddhist countries), however, was largely dependent on the ecclesiastical structure which maintained the unity and discipline of the monkhood. Any religion in which ecclesiastical organization plays such an important role is vulnerable to an uncongenial political environment.[31]

The politicization of the monks and the weakened, atomistic nature of Sangha organization have persisted into the post-independence period, even during the U Nu era of state promotion of Buddhism and euphoric Buddhist revival manifested by the holding of the Sixth Great Buddhist Council (1954-56), by the achievements of the Buddha Sasana Council in translating Buddhist texts, by the propagation of Buddhism among the hill tribes (*dhamma-duta*), and by the popularizing of meditation. It is these programs which, in turn, have influenced Thai Buddhism. However, in the midst of this religious resurgence, Burmese monks have successfully resisted any semblance of political control and regulation: they have refused the registration of monks, rejected the Ecclesiastical Courts Act of 1949 which was devised to settle monastic disputes and breaches of discipline, and they have turned down the proposal to create a Sangha Assembly to regulate Sangha Affairs on the grounds that it was mooted by the secular authority. Mass meetings, militant action, open confrontations with U Nu—the politician who came nearest to their conception of the traditional ruler—and anti-Moslem riots have all contributed to the military takeover by Ne Win.

Ceylon's story is similar in essentials, if different in details. It can only be briefly referred to here. At a time when the traditional Kandyan Kingdom did not have a unified ecclesiastical hierarchy, there was a royal attempt, no doubt based on precedent,[32] especially in the eighteenth century, to centralize control of monastic affairs in two chapters—Malvatte and Asgiriya. But, more importantly, the British disestablishment of Buddhism was accompanied by their progressive reluctance to support monastic offices, adjudicate monastic land rights, and sponsor politicoreligious rituals, which were traditional functions of the king. The shifting of the political and economic center of gravity to the Southwestern lowlands and coastal areas led to the creation there of new fraternities, to a Buddhist revival among the urban bourgeoisie, and to increasing participation of monks in political activity. This activity intensified after independence, when the revival of Buddhism and the Sinhala language and culture, and their elevation to their rightful place became the slogans of democratic politics. And the contemporary Sinhalese monks, especially the members of the affluent land-endowed Siyam Nikaya, reject any plan for centralized control and unified ecclesiastical authority because they will be deprived of their economic privileges.

In contradistinction to Thailand, it seems inevitable that not only would many monks in Ceylon and Burma, especially those that are urban-based, become political activists, but also that ideologists in these countries would make attempts to fuse Buddhism with some kind of doctrine of "democratic socialism." For what Burma and Ceylon inherited at the end of British rule was a parliamentary structure for the enactment of politics through "democratic processes." This structure necessarily directs politicians in search of votes to try to champion Buddhist nationalism on the one hand, and democratic/socialist policies on the other. It is understandable, since the Buddhist religion is an important ingredient of the Burmese or Sinhalese concept of nation, that as politics becomes more democratic it would, at least during a certain initial phase, inevitably become more religious-minded before it becomes more secular. That politicians should therefore seek an ideological mix called "Buddhist socialism" should not surprise us.[33]

Some Perspectives on Post-Traditional Societies

Felix Gilbert, writing in the Spring 1971 issue of *Daedalus*,[34] commented that a profound change in historical outlook has taken place because of the decline of European power and the consequent rise to importance of non-European peoples.

The historical process is no longer seen as a continuum. The notion of the continuity of the historical process was Europe-centred; it was the story of a development that began in the ancient world and the Mediterranean area, spread over the whole of Europe creating various nations with a common legacy, and issued in the domination of the world by the European nations.

The student of South and Southeast Asian societies has not merely a simple-minded Europo-centric view of world history to correct.. In many ways the European colonial impact on Asia was as much discontinuous in its effect on native societies as was the previous influence of longer-lived, pulsating Indian and Chinese empires on the smaller inbetween societies situated from Burma to Indonesia. All these impacts changed the face of the host societies. Moreover, India and China themselves were, in their turn, subject to waves of conquest and new influences.

It is precisely because of this archaeological layering that it is possible to make several statements which add up to a complex whole. It is clear, for instance, that there are deep-seated continuities in the form of structures and dialectical orientations that have persisted through the period of Western impact into the present in all Asian societies. It is also clear that the Western impact, while introducing dynamic change, cannot be regarded as *uniquely* discontinuous in its effect on the colonies and satellite countries. For one thing, these same countries had experienced other major impacts before the arrival of Europeans, and for another, it is possible to demonstrate that whatever differential changes they experienced in modern times Ceylon, Burma, and Thailand can still be placed in a wider frame which encompasses certain of their important particularities and distinctive features.

Thailand is a conspicuous example of the persistence of traditional features—of historical continuities that modify modernization—and also of transformations based on tradition. Although there is much that is similar among Ceylon, Burma, and Thailand, I must also concede that the European colonization of Ceylon and Burma has radically affected and perhaps introduced irreversible changes regarding the twin axes of traditional kingship and monastic organization, and the consequent direction of politics, both among monks and laymen. Thailand, by comparison, despite its experience of modernization shows a greater continuity of structure with the traditional Buddhist polity that was historically common to all three countries.

Thus, against the large backdrop of historical continuities, it is unquestionably true to say that it is recent, changing, political and economic circumstances that account for the different political and religious ideologies prevailing in Burma and Ceylon on the one hand, and Thailand on the other. But note again that the primary issues which engage the peoples of these countries relate to definitions of and relations between religion, nationhood, state, and minorities—which can be traced back to persisting deep-rooted orientations.

I must emphasize that we should guard against a simpleminded view which gives *value orientations* the dominant place in the understanding of behavior. For often the view that value orientations generate behavior goes hand in hand with a profoundly ahistorical perspective that these orientations have some kind of unchanging existence and comprise clear, unambiguous rules of action from time immemorial.

Such a static view is patently unhelpful in studying contemporary events in Southeast Asia. Even if we start with the Buddhist canonical texts as the unchanging and historically given set of doctrines, we find that this fund of ideas can be differently interpreted *within limits* to justify different courses of political and religious action. Moreover, we have noted in detail that several deep-seated and persisting orientations in Southeast Asia (as perhaps elsewhere) are more meaningfully viewed as parameters, dialectical tensions, and even paradoxes. Thus it comes about that the "Buddhist socialism" of Burma is a different crystallization from the Buddhist *dhammathud* activism of Thailand. And in both countries the this-worldly role formulated for monks diverges from the monk's behavior deduced by Max Weber, that Buddhism represented a pessimistic devaluation of this world, indeed a "flight from the world," and was therefore incapable of generating an "inner-worldly" asceticism. Weber at least deduced from the canonical texts features of historical behavior (which were in many ways concordant with his interpretations). But there is much less justification for contemporary scholars to parrot the Weberian formulations as applicable to later times. For since the canonical doctrines and subsequent commentaries and accretions are rich and, therefore, capable of different readings to fit changed events or to stimulate new courses of action, we cannot be sure that for *inherent* reasons Buddhism is incapable of a rational, this-worldly orientation.

REFERENCES

1. The situation in Ceylon is somewhat complex: while the *nikayas* or sects of monks—notably Siyam Nikaya and Amarapura—recruit by caste, curiously a layman pays reverence to the robe, whatever caste the wearer may actually belong to. In this sense the monk's vocation supersedes caste.

2. The contrast between the fortunes of two monks in Ceylon and Thailand in recent times is instructive. In Ceylon, Buddharakita became a power in the land in the

late 1950's until he overplayed his hand and became implicated in the murder of Prime Minister Bandaranaike. In Thailand, Pimmolatham, an able monk high up in the ecclesiastical hierarchy, was summarily derobed and jailed by Prime Minister Sarit in the early 1960's on truly shadowy grounds. The political accusations leveled against him were never proven, but the disciplinary action was decisive.

3. For lack of knowledge I shall not deal with Cambodia, which appears to support my hypothesis. Under Sihanouk Cambodia took a "neutralist" position, more in sympathy with China and Russia than with the United States. Sihanouk renounced his "kingship" in favor of a more participatory political system—a gesture that compares remarkably with Thailand's absorption with the monarchy as a symbol of identity and political stability.

4. See G. William Skinner, *Leadership and Power in the Chinese Community of Thailand* (Ithaca: Cornell University Press, 1958) for the pattern of relations between the Thai government and the Chinese.

5. See Akin Rabibhadana: *The Organization of Thai Society in the Early Bangkok Period, 1782-1873*, Data Paper No. 74, Southeast Asia Program, Cornell University, for a description of Thai political structure and orientations in the nineteenth century.

6. W. F. Vella, *The Impact of the West on Government in Thailand* (Berkeley: University of California Press, 1955).

7. *Exchanging Dhamma while Fighting,* Mutual Understanding Between Religions, Series No. 10 (Bangkok, 1969), pp. 32-33.

8. *Two Kinds of Language (Phasan Khon and Pasaa Dham).*

9. *In Samsara Exists Nibbana,* Mutual Understanding Between Religions, Series No. 12 (Bangkok, 1970).

10. *Ibid.,* pp. 23-24.

11. *Why Were We Born,* Mutual Understanding Between Religions, Series No. 11 (Bangkok, 1971).

12. *In Samsara Exists Nibbana.*

13. Some of his ideas are stated in these two essays: "Problems, Status, Duties of the Sangha in Modern Society," *Visakha Puja, BE 2511* (The Buddhist Association of Thailand, 1968); and "Monks' Roles in Contemporary Thai Society" (in Thai), *Buddha Sasana Gah Samakhom Thai Prachuban* [Buddhism and Contemporary Thai Society], (Siam Samakhom: Bangkok, 1970).

14. See the Khuddaka Nikaya. Other references cited are the Sigalavoda Sutta in which monks and laymen are exhorted to render service to each other; also Bahukara Sutta, Anguttara Nikaya.

15. "Dhammathud Development," *Phra Dhammathud,* 1 (1968); this is a magazine printed in Thai and edited by monks.

16. In 1971 the Maekor Phra Dhammathud was Somdej Prawannarat, Abbot of the Wat Chetupon, and his two deputies were Phra Ubali Kunoopatjaan, abbot of Wat Cakkrawad (and also head of Group 6), and Somdej Phramahaweerawong (also head of Group 5).

17. In 1968 six of the nine groups were led by monks from Bangkok-Thonburi. An important exception is Group 4 headed by the abbot of Wat Phra Singh in Chiengmai.

18. The annual reports of the various Dhammathud groups tend to show arithmetic inflation; thus, for instance, in 1968 all nine groups claimed to have instructed some 67,000 provincial monks and novices, 47,000 government officials, 16,000 workers, 19,000 prisoners, and half a million students; they also claim to have instructed 1,295,000 members of the public at mass meetings, and elicited the declaration by 168,000 individuals that they were Buddhists (this last, referred to as "Buddhamamakan," is strangely reminiscent of the mass conversions claimed in the old days by Catholic priests in India and Ceylon). *Annual Report of the Department of Religious Affairs*, 1968.

19. *A Summary of Phrathammathud Work Within the Country in 1969*, prepared by the Department of Religious Affairs.

20. For example, Group 6 reported in 1969 estimates of Communists in the Northeast in Nakorn Panom, Ubol, and Buriram and warned that if the Government did not remedy shortcomings the Communists would gain ground. Group 4, however, warned: "The Phrathammathud should not often mention or talk about the terrorists, for accusation is not the monk's habit. Moreover accusations will be dangerous to Dhammathud themselves." Group 9 asserted with uncomplicated enthusiasm, "when teaching people, emphasis should be placed on the gratitude people owe to the nation, religion, and the King, including the land in which they live and which gives them peace and happiness." *Ibid*.

21. The University authorities send out letters to the ecclesiastical governors of selected provinces to send volunteers who have completed at least five years of service, who have reached at least any of the Pali or Nagtham grades (Pali grades range from 3-9, and Nagtham from 1-3: Thri, Tho and Ek), and who are not over fifty years of age.

22. For example, an evaluation report sent from the Surin center for 1970 claims the building of roads, wells, and latrines in certain provinces. Ubol is said to have the first of these provincial centers; another such center appears to exist in Loey. All of these locations are in the Northeast.

No discussion of provincial achievements in the sphere of community development led by monks is complete without mention of the *dhamma patana* mission organized by Wat Phra Singh in Chiengmai. The mission sends teams composed of teachers and students of monastic schools, students from Chiengmai University and Agricultural College, government officials, and lay assistants. In 1967, 10 teams composed of five to six members each were sent to various districts in the North, and their report for that year of work, including the building or repairing of roads, footpaths, small bridges, latrines, wells, school buildings, and equipment, is quite impressive. These comments are based on reports provided me by Mr. Klausner of the Asia Foundation, Bangkok. These social service programs are in part financed by the Asia Foundation, which appears to be the largest donor and sponsor.

23. The university project gained, in 1971, the "official" stamp of approval and patronage of the Supreme Council of the Sangha and the lay Department of Religious Affairs. This official recognition is expressed in terms of the request that this year's provincial trainees be also taught the methods of *dhammathud* missionary work—a request that gives recognition without changing the content of the training course.

24. D. E. Smith, *Religion and Politics in Burma* (Princeton: Princeton University Press, 1965).

25. See, for example, D. K. Wyatt, "The Buddhist Monkhood as an Avenue of Social Mobility in Traditional Thai Society," *Sinlapakon*, 5, No. 1 (1966), pp. 41-49.

26. The following statistics are illustrative: The Northeast with roughly ¼ of the country's population had in 1968 50 per cent of the country's wats, 32 per cent of the monks, and 48 per cent of the novices. The monastic educational statistics for 1968 are also revealing: the Northeastern provinces are said to have contained 41 per cent of the country's religious teachers in monastic schools (*khru pariyatham*), 41 per cent of the *dhamma* students (*nagrian tham*), and 38 per cent of the pali students (*nagrian pali*). If you add to this the Northeastern monks based in Bangkok and Thonburi the numbers will increase. A survey taken in 1968 revealed that 58 per cent of the students at Mahachulalongkorn University for monks came from the Northeast.

27. Melford E. Spiro, *Buddhism and Society, A Great Tradition and Its Burmese Vicissitudes* (New York: Harper and Row, 1970).

28. See D. K. Wyatt, *The Politics of Reform in Thailand: Education in the Reign of King Chulalongkorn* (New Haven: Yale University Press, 1968).

29. For a full account of the developments in Burma in the colonial era, see D. E. Smith, *Religion and Politics in Burma*.

30. *Ibid.*, p. 56.

31. *Ibid.*, p. 43.

32. For example, the purification and unification of the Sangha that Parakrama Bahu I is said to have achieved.

33. See E. Sarkisyanz, *Buddhist Backgrounds to the Burmese Revolution* (The Hague: Martinus Nijhoff, 1965), for a sympathetic treatment of Burmese ideological formulations.

34. Felix Gilbert, "Post Scriptum," *Dædalus*, 100, No. 2 (Spring 1971).

HEINZ BECHERT

Sangha, State, Society, "Nation": Persistence of Traditions in "Post-Traditional" Buddhist Societies

BUDDHISM IN Ceylon and in four countries of mainland Southeast Asia— Burma, Thailand, Cambodia, and Laos—is described by the term "Theravada Buddhism." Although Theravada Buddhism, a dogma based on the canonical scriptures in Pali, is a rather conservative form of Buddhism, we can observe a marked difference between earlier and more modern states in its development.

I propose a threefold distinction of "canonical," "traditional," and "modern" Buddhism. "Canonical" Buddhism (*Urbuddhismus*) is the Buddhism found in the *tripitaka*, the canonical scriptures in Pali. These scriptures are of Indian origin. Thus, they represent the particular form of Indian Buddhism on which later Ceylonese and Southeast Asian Buddhism is based. Though there are differences between teachings and conceptions found in earlier strata and those found in later strata of these scriptures, we can describe "canonical" Buddhism as a rather coherent system of religious and philosophical teachings that includes a systematized set of rules and regulations for the behavior of the members of the Sangha, namely, the monastic communities. "Traditional" Buddhism is the totality of beliefs and practices of Buddhists in the periods after the final codification of the canonical scriptures and before the beginnings of the modern period. In the Theravada countries, "traditional" Buddhism is characterized by its integration in the sociocultural system as the "national" religion and by the emergence of formalized state-Sangha relations. "Modern" Buddhism is a common designation of all forms of Buddhism that have developed under the impact of the changes which have taken place in the modern period; these include "modernistic" forms of Buddhism as well as "traditionalist" responses to the challenge of outside influences.

For an analysis of the modern developments, the patterns of Sangha-state and of Sangha-society relations in the earlier forms of Buddhism must be considered. The Sangha in the early period was a community of ascetics avoiding any form of direct involvement in the affairs of state and society.

The charisma of the Buddhist saint was connected with his detachment from the world. Surely, the Buddha advised kings and ministers on the application of moral and religious precepts in political life, but never on practical politics. The relations existing between Sangha and state were designed to minimize potential Sangha-state friction and to keep the Sangha independent from the state. Interference of the Sangha in political matters would have been against the established rules of the monastic order. The order belonged to "the four directions": it was by definition universal and supranational. The Sangha did not have any "guardian" central body which could supervise the way in which the word of the Buddha was to be interpreted or the way in which Buddhists should cope with problems on the basis of the Buddha's word found in the scriptural evidence. The only accepted authority was the word of the Buddha, later on supplemented by the classical commentaries said to be based on an uninterrupted lineage of teachers leading back to the Buddha himself. Thus, the early Sangha had no organizational structure that could counteract the forces of fragmentation.

When the Sangha had grown up into an influential factor in social life, its original conception no longer applied to the facts, but it was never formally invalidated. From the rather unclear traditions concerning the early Buddhist councils, we can conjecture that the kings of that period were not entirely indifferent to some of the internal developments of the Sangha, particularly to schisms that threatened the religious peace of the country. However, the first monarch to act in a way that led to the establishment of formalized state-Sangha relations was the great King Ashoka. We know from his so-called "schism edict," preserved in three inscriptions, that he had purged the Sangha and given orders to his "mahamatras" or state officials to control the observance of the edict. Many Sanghas had split into factions as a result of controversies on the rules of monastic discipline and their application. The existence of considerable monastic property from donations made it attractive for individuals who did not have the least intention of observing the rules to enter the Sangha. To remove this unfortunate state of affairs, it was necessary either to bring all the monks of a divided Sangha into harmony again or to expel those monks who were not willing to live and act according to the rules of Vinaya. Such an action by power of state was henceforth called a "Sasana reform"—a purge of the monastic institutions of the Buddhist religion.[1]

It was also in the course of the missionary activities carried out by order of King Ashoka that the Buddhist religion was embraced by the contemporary king of Ceylon, Devanampiyatissa. Buddhism in the particular form of Theravada (which Ceylon imported from India) has since remained the religion of the Sinhalese in an unbroken tradition. The concept of the responsibility of the state for the well-being of the Sangha, resulting in a duty to act, if necessary, in the interest of the purity of the Sangha, became an important element of the traditional Sinhalese state ideology.[2] A justification for the interference of the state into internal matters of the Sangha was derived from the traditions concerning the already mentioned Sasana reform enacted by Ashoka, the ideal Buddhist king of the past. In a long process, the relations between Sangha and the state were more and more formalized. State officials acted to control the large-scale properties of the monasteries; the kings passed laws concerning the interpretation of the monastic rules and the organizational structure of the Sangha. Although these rules are said to have been formulated by monastic assemblies on the invitation of the kings, it is rather clear from the introductions of those texts that it was the king who finally decided on important matters, though within the framework of the established rules and traditions of the monastic order.[3]

This integration of the Sangha in the structure of the state completely changed the original function and position of the Sangha. Certainly, there were still meditating monks retired from any contact with the outside world. However, the majority of the monks had to fulfill a number of obligations within society: they acted as the literati preserving a great part of literature and higher studies, including historical and other non-religious writings. The monks taught the fundamentals of education to the villagers. It was because of them that the Theravada countries still had a higher literacy rate than European countries like England in the beginning of the nineteenth century. Further, the monks served the spiritual needs of the community in many ways. Donations to the Sangha provided high merit leading to a better rebirth. The wealth of the great monasteries did not, however, induce monks to live a life of austerity fitting for a Buddhist monk; it had a rather contradictory effect, which called for public control of these properties in the interest of the Sasana.

The formalized and hierarchical Sangha structure which was built up in the mediaeval Buddhist states of Ceylon, Burma, Siam, and in the Khmer kingdom for the control of the Sangha also had an important advantage for the state: it gave the state the means to prevent political activity by the Sangha. When the Sangha grew larger and larger in the course of time, it also grew into a potential factor in politics, having a direct connection with the rural masses. Its organization had much more continuity than did that of the state. Thus, the enforcement of the old rule that the Sangha had no right to exercise any political influence was of vital importance for the state power. Accounts by visitors to the kingdoms of Ceylon, Burma, and Siam invariably mention the political abstinence of the Sangha in concordance with the canonical law.

We must not forget, however, that certain elements of the religious life remained outside the organizational structure of the Buddhist states. There were always, mainly in periods of crisis, chiliastic movements fostering expectations that a "world-emperor" (Cakravartin), preceding the appearance of the next Buddha, would establish a universal empire, and similar beliefs. Such movements could lead to rebellions. Groups of hermits living outside the established Sangha organizations repeatedly questioned the validity of the tradition of the monks' ordination. A number of other non-orthodox movements also existed on the verge of the Buddhist communities. These groups were often persecuted, but some of their traditions have survived and seen a revival in recent times.

Some elements of political ideology in the "official" system of traditional Theravada were not in full agreement with the teachings embodied in the Buddhist scriptures. The most conspicuous of these concepts is that of "Buddhist nationalism" which first emerged in Ceylon. The Dipavamsa ("Chronicle of the Island"), written in the fourth century or the first half of the fifth century, and the Mahavamsa ("Great Chronicle"), which was composed around 500 A.D., embody a particular ideology of state-Sangha relations and the belief that the Sinhalese nation has a unique role for the preservation of the Buddhist religion. The chronicles mention personal visits made by the Buddha to the island of Ceylon and a prophecy that Ceylon would be the "island of the dharma," the center of the Buddha's religion. The descendants of Vijaya, the founding father of the Sinhalese nation, are said to become the future preservers of the Buddhist religion. In this and other chronicle narrations, a complete system of political ideology is provided, and the basic idea is that of the unity of nation and religion. The culminating point of the chronicle, namely, the account of the life and deeds of King Dutthagamani, is the most striking example of the principle of this unity of the Sinhalese nation and the Buddhist religion. In this chapter of the "Great Chronicle," even the basic principles of Buddhist religion are subordinate to this leading notion. The Sinhalese nation was thus one of the first nations to create an ideology of national identity based on the unity of language, culture, and religion.[4] Though their notion was not applicable to other Buddhist nations, certain elements were copied, particularly in Burma. We can, therefore, describe "Buddhist nationalism" as a component of the way of thinking of traditional or precolonial and premodern Theravada Buddhist societies.

Another constituent of Buddhist political and social thinking is the ideal of the welfare state. As is well-known, important elements of a welfare state orientation are found in King Ashoka's inscriptions. Ashoka was described as the ideal monarch or the "model king" in all later works composed in Theravada countries, and many kings claimed in their inscriptions and other documents that they followed his example. It was, of course, not the tolerant Ashoka and his non-confessional "dharma" concept that influenced the thinking of later periods. His inscriptions had long been forgotten when they were rediscovered and deciphered in the nineteenth and twentieth centuries. Buddhists in Theravada countries knew Ashoka only through the particular way his activities were depicted in the commentaries and chronicles of Pali literature. His concept of a welfare state, however, was never forgotten.[5] It was not so much in spite of the fact that the political reality was far from this ideal model, but rather because of the conflict of ideal and real that these notions had so much resonance in the traditional society of Buddhist countries.

The actual exercise of political power in the premodern Buddhist states was, in most periods, more governed by the traditions of worldly statecraft than by the traditions of Buddhist state ideology. Secular statecraft in Indian tradition was always power-oriented. It has found its classical expression in the Arthashastra, the compendium of politics attributed to Kautalya. This tradition has counterbalanced the idealistic traditions of Buddhist state theory.

In spite of the integration of the Sangha in the political structure and the acceptance of Buddhism as the state religion, traditional Buddhism has never completely renounced the distinction between the mundane and the supramundane spheres. The Sasana—the Buddhist religion and its institutions—is exclusively concerned with the supramundane sphere; its objective is salvation and nothing else. Though this sphere was extended and the state, being the protector of the Sasana, was partially included among the entities legitimized by the Buddhist religion, quite a number of activities which we would classify as "religious" remained outside the scope of the Sasana and thus lacked Buddhist legitimation. A number of ceremonies, such as a king's consecration, fertility rites, and the cult of the gods, were considered mundane affairs in which the Buddhist monks were not expected to take part. Such rites were performed by court Brahmins or by other groups of priests, but not by monks.

Buddhist political thinking in Theravada countries is a very complex structure which cannot be explained in terms of Buddhist traditions alone, but must be understood as a comprehensive system of Buddhist and non-Buddhist practices and beliefs that has emerged in the course of many centuries. The basically Mahayanic concept that identified a king with a Bodhisattva (a future Buddha)[6] deserves particular mention, because it meant a legitimation of power by a supposed "posthumous" sainthood without binding the ruler to the rules of saintly conduct. This type of legitimation was revived in the recent movement of political Buddhism and applied to a number of famous personalities, such as the Anagarika Dharmapala, S. W. R. D. Bandaranaike, U Nu, and others. Non-Buddhist fertility cults are reflected in the tradition of the charisma of kings.[7] Hindu thinking is also in evidence.

Basic changes were effected in the Buddhist countries by the impact of colonialism. It was first in Ceylon and in Burma that the Sangha was "disestablished," the traditional ties between state and Sangha being disconnected. Although it was a rather slow process in the "Kandyan provinces" of Ceylon—the former Sinhalese kingdom where the British crown had promised to continue the protection of Buddhist institutions in the treaty of 1815[8]—the disestablishment was enforced in Burma immediately after annexation.[9] In this way the monastic institutions became disconnected units of a more or less private character. The well-intentioned creation of a system of control of the monasteries by lay trustees, provided for in the Buddhist Temporalities Ordinance issued by the Government of Ceylon in 1889, did not work because the necessary infrastructure of effective bodies of self-government did not exist.[10]

The results of this "disestablishment" of the Sangha were disastrous for the monastic discipline. The ecclesiastic jurisdiction broke down completely. In this way, the colonial regime made possible what the ancient Buddhist regimes had always tried to prevent, namely, a completely independent Sangha with all its traditional influence and resources remaining intact. The Sangha thus became a powerful factor of mass politicization in Ceylon and in Burma. There was still, however, the canonical injunction against political activities by the monks. The Buddhist public accepted political activity of the Sangha as legitimate only in periods of crisis when the survival of Buddhism itself was considered to be at stake.[11] Such situations arose in Burma in 1917 and in Ceylon in 1956 and, to a lesser degree, on some other occasions.[12]

In Thailand and in Cambodia we observe a rather different course of development. Here, the traditional system of state-Sangha relations was not destroyed; it was organizationally modernized. The state remained in control of the larger monastic properties and supervised ecclesiastic jurisdiction and appointments in the hierarchy. The crisis of modernization did not, therefore, result in a marked increase of political activity by Buddhist monks in these countries.

As a reaction against the disintegration of the Sangha in colonial Ceylon and Burma, reform movements inside the Sangha sprung up. The early reform movements still made use of the traditional hierarchical structures of the Order. In Ceylon, the earliest of these reformist sections of the Sangha was established in 1802 by the reintroduction of an ordination lineage from Burma. Its organization followed the model of the Sangha structure of mediaeval Ceylon in all detail. The same can be said of most of the later reformist nikayas or "sects" of Ceylonese and Burmese Sangha. Here, old organizational models were used in a new setting, in a situation in which state control over the Sangha no longer existed. These new Sangha organizations had, therefore, the task before them of avoiding the breakdown of discipline without the help of state interference in their autonomous structures. It can be said that at least a number of the new nikayas have been successful and have thereby made an important contribution toward modernizing a traditional organizational model. On the other hand, the concept behind these activities was completely traditional. In the rather large number of tracts dealing with the controversies of the nikayas in matters of monastic discipline and hierarchy, we do not find any "modernistic" concepts. The arguments are invariably taken from the earlier works of vinaya literature, particularly from the canonical and commentarial texts in Pali.

Buddhist modernism developed only after 1870, Ceylon being the first country where this kind of movement came into existence. The emergence of the modernistic ideology was a slow process. The earliest documents of the modern Buddhist revival are the vadas—public controversies between Buddhists and Christian missionaries. However, the most famous of these public controversies, that between Migettuvatte Gunananda Thera and two Wesleyan missionaries, held in 1873 in Panadura, cannot be called a document of Buddhist modernism in the narrow sense of the concept, though it foreshadows some of the characteristic attitudes of Buddhist modernism.[13]

Buddhist modernism is characterized by the emphasis laid on rationalist elements in Buddhist teachings, by the belief that the teachings of Buddhism and those of modern science are not only in conformity but identical, by the tacit elimination of the traditional cosmology, and by a reinterpretation of the objective of the Buddhist religion in terms of social reform and the building of a better world. To quote Professor G. P. Malalasekera, one of the leading personalities of Buddhist modernism and cofounder of the World Fellowship of Buddhists:

When Asia, after having lain dormant for nearly five centuries, is once more taking its due place in the world and bids fair to be the leader of the new age it is significant that Buddhism, which, more than any other force, was responsible for the great civilisations and great cultural influences of that continent, should also be coming back to its rightful place. The Buddha was the first great scientist to appear among men. That Buddha discovered what scientists have only now discovered, that there is nothing called matter or mind existing separately in this world but they are the result of forces which continually cause them to come into operation and that they dissolved and came into operation again. Buddhism seeks the meaning of life in life itself. In this search, life is ennobled. Life becomes an external and a fulfilled Now. Truth is not a relevation but a discovery. The human person has to realise itself as the subject of knowledge, as socially responsible and as artistically creative.[14]

Buddhism is now described as the "religion of optimism and activity." Problems of the world must be solved by application of Buddhist tenets in all fields of human life. Buddhist modernism consequently does away with the old separation of the supramundane and mundane spheres.[15]

Legitimation for the new understanding of Buddhism was sought from the canonic scriptures as well as from traditional Buddhism; the ideology of the latter was partially and selectively revived. It was, of course, reinterpreted in the light of the new understanding of the objectives of religious activity. Certain references to political questions in the scriptures are now interpreted as the Buddha's guidelines for political life, and the old structure of the Sangha is described as a model for a democratic state. Not only the Ashokan state, as depicted in chronicles and inscriptions, but also

an idealistic description of the Buddhist kingdoms in pre-colonial times—
which has not much in common with historical facts—is being used for the
legitimation of change intended by Buddhist modernists.[16]

It is clear that the modernists had to compromise with traditionalist
forces. The modernists who had given the initial impulses to the movement
had belonged to the highly educated and modernized urban elite, but the
Buddhist revival could only succeed as a political force if the rural masses
were activated. The rural population and the large majority of the monks,
however, were still guided by non-modern ways of thinking. This situation
is responsible for many of the contradictions found in the writings of Buddhist modernists.

Besides the problems caused by the diversity in educational standards
of the Buddhist leaders, there are several dichotomies in Buddhist tradition
which must be taken into consideration in order to correctly analyze the
particular forms into which traditional codes have evolved in post-traditional Buddhist societies. On the one hand, there are state responsibility
and state control of the Sangha legitimized by the tradition of Sasana reform; on the other hand, there is the concept of an independent Sangha
forbidding any state interference into its internal matters. The delicate
balance of these two concepts worked out in the old Buddhist monarchies
was no longer applicable in a modern secular state with a republican constitution. Several attempts at a reform of the Sangha in Ceylon and in
Burma have failed, and the attempts made in these countries to install
Buddhism as the state religion have resulted in considerable political tension and even in disturbances.[17] The state religion issue is still very much
alive in Ceylon. We can, however, safely predict that the only possible
solution to the problem in a modern society will be the establishment, as an
autonomous body, of the Buddhist religious community.

One of the central issues which has led to the necessity of discussing reform measures for the Sangha is the existence of large-scale monastic properties. Particularly in Ceylon, monastic "landlordism" has been an important
force for many centuries. It has not only led to a deep involvement of economic interests by family and caste groups in the administration of Sangha
property, but also to outside influences on the appointment of the head
monks ("chief incumbents" of the monasteries) in control of these properties. The monks are, therefore, not at all as equal as they should be according to the original constitution of the Sangha; there are many rich
monks leading a life which has nothing in common with that of an ascetic.
On the other hand, there are poor monks who do not participate in the income of the wealthy monasteries. It is clear that the issue of redistribution
of monastic income is a controversial issue for both monks and laity.

A number of other dichotomies which were at least partially balanced
in the traditional system became contradictory in the context of a post-
traditional society: the antithesis of Buddhist universalism and Buddhist

nationalism; the antithesis of the Sangha as a purely religious community and the Sangha as the defender of national tradition; and the antithesis of the side-by-side existence of a juridic understanding of the structure and membership in the Sangha, as suggested in the original "canonic" teachings of the Buddha, and of the charismatic role of the Sangha with the concept of its sacredness that cannot be explained rationally. In modern Buddhism we observe, in addition to this, the antithesis of the prohibition of political activity by monks and the desirability of such activity in the interests of the national independence movement.

For a correct understanding of the particular forms of continuity of traditional modes in Buddhist countries, we must also consider the importance of regional or national differences between the Buddhist countries. It may suffice to note a few examples. The function of the monks differs to a considerable degree in Ceylon, Burma, and Thailand. The systems of education have developed differently in these countries. Whereas in Burma and Thailand, Buddhism and Buddhist monks play a key role in the process of national integration in border areas, there is no scope for conversion of the Tamil minority in Ceylon. Membership in the Sangha for limited periods —a conspicuous feature of Burmese and Thai Buddhism that has contributed to the spread of knowledge about details of Buddhist dogma in the male lay population—is completely out of the question in Ceylon, where membership in the Sangha is practically always a decision for a lifetime. Consequently, there is a charismatic appeal to ex-monks in Burma and Thailand, if they have entered and left the Sangha in an orderly manner, whereas an ex-monk is a social outcast in Ceylon. The cults of the gods are much more integrated in a rather syncretistic system of Buddhist and non-Buddhist beliefs in Ceylon than they are in Burma or Thailand, whereas "messianic Buddhism" and similar non-orthodox forms of Buddhism play a much greater role in the Southeast Asian countries than they do in Ceylon.

Traditional codes can be used in a modern or post-traditional context in quite different ways: on the one hand, the Buddhist saint—and the monk should be equated with the saint in the ideal case—is supposed to act outside society and politics; on the other hand, however, the charisma of the yellow robe can be used as a political asset, and the merit accumulated during former membership in the Sangha helps a Burmese politician more in gaining popularity than does any political activity. The Bodhisattva ideal, which is essentially of otherworldly character like any other basically Buddhist concept, was used for political purposes again and again—for example, by U Nu in his political agitation in 1960 and 1961.

Post-traditional society in the Buddhist countries must be explained in the particular context of continuity in the individual countries. However, the foregoing remarks will have shown that there are important common features of the Theravada countries and also that Buddhist religious traditions are basically "open to change."

REFERENCES

1. There were several misinterpretations of the edict and the relevant portions in the Ceylonese chronicles. An interpretation is given by H. Bechert, "Aśokas 'Schismenedikt' und der Begriff Sanghabheda," *Wiener Zeitschrift für die Kunde Südund Ostasiens,* 5 (1961), 18-52.

2. Wilhelm Geiger, *Culture of Ceylon in Mediaeval Times* (Wiesbaden: Harrassowitz, 1960), pp. 203-206.

3. Relevant texts from Ceylon were published and translated by Nandasena Ratnapala, *The Katikavatas, Laws of the Buddhist Order of Ceylon from the Twelfth Century to the Eighteenth Century* (Müchen: Münchener Studien zur Sprachwissenschaft, 1971).

4. See H. Bechert, "Zum Ursprung der Geschichtsschreibung im indischen Kulturbereich," Nachrichten der Akademie der Wissenschaften in Göttingen, Phil.-hist. Kl., 1969, No. 2; See also "The Beginning of Buddhist Historiography in Ceylon," *Journal of the Bihar Research Society* (forthcoming).

5. See E. Sarkisyanz, *Buddhist Backgrounds of the Burmese Revolution* (The Hague: Martinus Nijhoff, 1965).

6. For the influence of the Bodhisattva ideal in Burmese Buddhist political tradition, see *ibid.,* pp. 43-48.

7. *Ibid.,* pp. 49-53.

8. H. Bechert, *Buddhismus, Staat und Gesellschaft in den Ländern des Theravada-Buddhismus,* vol. 1 (Frankfurt: Schriften des Instituts für Asienkunde in Hamburg, 1966), pp. 230-236; K. M. de Silva, "Buddhism and the British Government in Ceylon," *Ceylon Historical Journal,* 10 (1960-61), 91-159.

9. See Bechert, *Buddhismus, Staat und Gesellschaft,* vol. 2 (1967), pp. 16-21, 41-44.

10. *Ibid.,* vol. 1, pp. 236-240.

11. See H. Bechert, "Theravada Buddhism and Mass Politics," in D. E. Smith, ed., *Religion and Political Modernization* (New Haven: Yale University Press, forthcoming).

12. For the factual information concerning the political activity of Buddhist monks see Bechert, *Buddhismus, Staat und Gesellschaft,* vols. 1-2.

13. The text of this controversy was published in an English translation by James Martin Peebles, *Buddhism and Christianity in Discussion Face to Face, or, an Oral Debate between Rev. Migettuwatte and Rev. D. Silva held at Pantura, Ceylon* (Battle Creek, Michigan, 1873).

14. G. P. Malalasekera, "Buddhism Seeks Meaning of Life in Life Itself," *The Buddhist,* 29 (1958-59), 178f.

15. In this connection the symbolism of the "Buddha on the market place" becomes understandable. See Gananath Obeyesekera, "Religious Symbolism and Political Change in Ceylon," in Bardwell L. Smith, ed., *The Two Wheels of Dhamma* (Chambersburg, Pa.: American Academy of Religion, 1972), pp. 58-78.

16. A detailed discussion of Buddhist modernism is found in Bechert, *Buddhismus, Staat und Gesellschaft,* vol. 1, pp. 37-108.

17. For detailed accounts of these developments before 1964, see *ibid.*, vol. 1, pp. 267-300; vol. 2, pp. 54-86. See also Donald Eugene Smith, *Religion and Politics in Burma* (Princeton, N.J.: Princeton University Press, 1965), and Smith, ed., *South Asian Politics and Religion* (Princeton, N.J.: Princeton University Press, 1966), pp. 489-546.

J. C. HEESTERMAN

India and the Inner Conflict of Tradition

EVER SINCE English utilitarians or evangelicals and Indian reformers set out to modernize India, the problem of misunderstood tradition and miscarrying modernization has been with us. It may, therefore, not be out of place to take a point of view that may enable us to understand the meaning and function of tradition, not in order to oppose it once more to modernity but rather in order to arrive eventually at an integrated view.

To begin with we may view tradition as the way society formulates and deals with the basic problems of human existence. In other words, it is the way in which society comes to terms with the insoluble problem of life and death, including such life and death matters as food and water in a world of scarcity.[1] In this respect, of course, it is not different from modernity. Since the fundamental problem is truly insoluble it has to be attacked, formulated, and dealt with each time anew under a different aspect. Tradition is, therefore, and has to be bound up with the ever-shifting present. Hence the irritating flexibility and fluidity of tradition.

This can be clearly seen in customary law and its procedures, such as the much-vaunted simplicity of village or panchayat justice. The point is not so much its rustic simplicity—in fact its procedures are often far from clear to the unwary observer—but its basis in the intuitive understanding that the participants in the face-to-face society have of the web of social relations and each other's place in it. This intuitive knowledge makes it possible to do without objective rules, precedent, and case construction and yet arrive at decisions (or stalemates) that are acceptable to the participants. But the results from case to case will often be far from lucid to the outsider, let alone easily comparable. For customary law and its proceedings are not concerned primarily with the objective truth of the matter but with the subjective truth of the persons involved which will differ from situation to situation. Obviously, the worst thing that can happen to customary law is codification. And the same goes for the sometimes hair-raising complications of rights in the soil, the division of its produce, and even of weights and measures,[2] complications that hardly seem to bother

97

the local participants but only come out when the revenue administration wants to describe and fix them in an objective and systematic fashion.

However, tradition cannot be only flexible and situational. For its essential mission is still to deal in a structured way with the insoluble life-death problem in all its situational manifestations. It must, therefore, also offer a plan or order independent of and above the actual situation. It is this transcendent order that provides man with the fixed orientation for legitimizing his actions in the middle of situational flux. In other words, tradition has to be both immanent in the actual situation so as to keep up with shifting reality and transcendent so as to fulfill its orientating and legitimizing function. Thus, we can understand the paradoxical but traditionally common idea that transcendent law is all the time there, suspended as it were in midair, and that it can be "found" by agonistic procedures, verbal or otherwise.[3] Here also seems to lie the meaning of the urge for consensus. In this way truth and law are at the same time transcendent and immanent in society. Obviously this is a tour de force, but it can work as long as truth and law are not explicitly codified.

This is not different in the case of the Indian concept of *dharma*. The well-known difficulty to define and translate this term is the result of its being caught on the horns of the same dilemma. *Dharma* is the transcendent lodestar and as such is removed from the pressures of man's daily affairs. Or in L. Dumont's adaption of Thiers' phrase about the constitutional monarch, "le dharma règne de haut sans avoir, ce qui lui serait fatal, à gouverner."[4] It is therefore based on the Veda, the *shruti*, even though the connection between Veda and *dharma* is in reality nonexistent; on the other hand *dharma* has to be relevant for an ordinary man in society who does eat meat, marries his cross-cousin, interacts closely with people exhibiting different degrees of impurity, and generally has to act contrary to the tenets of *dharma*. In short, *dharma* has to take custom into account. Indeed *ācāra*, custom, is considered an important source of *dharma*, and the task of determining what is the right custom falls on the assembly, the *pariṣad*. Of course this *pariṣad* should be composed of educated and virtuous men, who by definition will be conversant with the Veda, however little relevance the Veda may have for the matter in hand. In theory the circle is conveniently closed and everything is as it should be.[5] But the reference to the council or assembly is no less significant, and in the final analysis the *dharma* texts cannot but concede that no blame is attached to the man who simply follows the customs of his community even if they are contrary to the *dharma*.[6] But neither will such a man arrive at the transcendent solution of the life-death problem for, even after his death, he will remain bound to his community in following births.

Here I think we arrive at the hard core of tradition, namely its inner conflict. Tradition is determined by the particular form in which it expresses the conflict between its immanence in society and its transcendent aspiration of solving the fundamental problem of human existence. Although this view of tradition as a paradox does not look very promising, it may offer us a vantage point for our understanding of social and cultural processes. Instead of having to explain away the obvious rifts and fissures so as to arrive at a harmonious and coherent pattern, we may exploit the essentially fractured picture for a dynamic view of society and culture as organized around an inner conflict.

Let me try to illustrate this with reference to Indian civilization. The task has been greatly facilitated by L. Dumont's fundamental work on caste and hierarchy,[7] although I shall have to differ from his main thesis on the place of hierarchy. Briefly then, we find here two diagonally opposed principles of organization, the one based on hierarchical interdependence and the other on separation and independence, represented respectively by the king (or the dominant caste) and the brahmin. A practical illustration of this situation may be found in A. C. Mayer's study of a village in Central India.[8] The dominant rajputs (literally, "king's sons") of the village who entertain, notwithstanding their royal pretensions, commensal relations with a group of definitely lower "allied" castes—an arrangement that also seems to help them to maintain their dominance through their retinue of "allies"—clearly exhibit a pattern of hierarchical interdependence and reciprocity. On the other hand there are the vegetarian khatis (farmers) and a few artisan castes that tend to restrict their relations, each to his own caste. These castes can be said to "opt out" of the system of interdependence and to stress their independence. Their "opting out" is equally reflected in the distinct though far from rare oddity that whereas some higher castes may accept their food, they themselves refuse to return the compliment, thereby demonstrating their disregard of interdependence. In other words, they follow a brahminic pattern also reflected in a simple, unostentatious life style as against the "royal" style of the rajputs, whose extensive relations require generous hospitality.

Yet the typically brahminized khatis and other castes following the same pattern are placed by the consensus of the informants fairly low on the ranking scale, below the rajputs and their allies. From the point of view of brahminic values as the touchstone of hierarchy, the fact that the meat eating and generally unbrahminic rajputs and their "allied" servants are credited with a higher rank is distinctly embarrassing. Professor Dumont observes that "here to all appearances the principle of the pure and the impure is in abeyance," a circumstance which he feels to be fairly unique. He then argues that "this is the point at which . . . power participates in purity, although the latter negates it in theory; or in other words, this is the point at which the solidarity between the first two varnas reveals itself." The solution, however, does not seem to require this somewhat awkward explanation. The trouble is not so much with the reported facts, but with the unitary theory of an all-encompassing ideology of hierarchy which forces us to underplay the real contradictions. Since Professor Dumont recognizes these contradictions which he analyzes so clearly, one wonders why he did not exploit them for his theoretical work instead of relegating them to a secondary level. For if we start by taking them seriously, it becomes at once clear that we are confronted—as the villager is—with two opposite and irreconcilable principles of organization, the one stressing interdependence, the other independence. The relevant point is, then, not so much the unexplainable low rank of the brahminized caste but rather that this ranking, in fact, runs aground on their brahminical separateness and independence, which are reflected in their opting out of the regular system of food and drink exchanges. Professor Mayer, therefore, has to put them in his table of castes in a separate block not under but next to the rajputs and their allies, while the other castes follow under the rajputs.

Lest it be thought that the situation in this village is an exception with regard to the overall system, it may be worthwhile to consider for a moment the strikingly parallel right-left division of castes known from South India. This well-known but so far rather hazy phenomenon has recently been studied by Brenda F. Beck.[9] The right-hand division appears to be composed of the dominant peasants such as the Gaundar, who "are known in legend, ritual and even by title as the 'kings of the area,'" and the service castes directly dependent on them. They form a closely knit complex resembling each other in ritual matters and entertaining an elaborate system of exchanges. The left-hand division is made up of vegetarian, brahmin-emulating castes which exhibit various degrees of independence from the "kings" of the area because of their outside contacts through trade and marketable skills. As against the coherence of the kinglike group and its "dependers"—constituting, as Miss Beck puts it, the "in" group of "allied" castes[10]—the left-hand castes are far more diverse and exclusive, not least among themselves. They do not form a coherent bloc but a plurality of separate, mutually independent units. Consequently, the ranking that is fairly simple and clear-cut within the right-hand bloc tends to be vague if not irrelevant with the left-hand castes. For in the left-hand division the higher castes do not mediate power and prestige for the lower ones as is the case in the right-hand bloc.[11] So here, too, we find an essentially dichotomous picture held together not by an integrating hierarchy of values but by the conflict between the two principles of hierarchical interdependence on the one hand, and of separation and independence on the other. This case, moreover, is the more interesting because it points up the systematic nature of the dichotomy.

Actual hierarchy, then, seems to be based on real relations such as become apparent in the acceptance of food and drink, and these relations are tied up with the distribution of power and focused on rights in the soil, which are managed by the "kings." On the other hand, where the brahminic "way out" is followed, not relations but isolation becomes the keyword and hierarchy consequently breaks down. But it would be wrong to see the two principles simply as two different traditions. For notwithstanding their obvious irreconcilability, the brahminic ideal of separateness and independence is still recognized as the ultimately valid one. Thus Mayer's rajputs, when they maintain close relations with the lower "allied castes," are far from denying the ultimate validity of the brahminic ideal that would require them to keep themselves apart. Their excuse is that they need servants with whom they have to keep close contacts;[12] in other words, as mediators of power and prestige they can not help having to live in a world made up of relations. Equally, the fact that the brahmin is deemed to be above the right-left dichotomy means the recognition of the ideal he stands for as the ultimately valid one.

So the brahmin and the total independence he represents cap the dichotomous system, signifying that it is still felt to be one, albeit contradictory, whole. But this does not create a system of hierarchial interdependence, for such a system can only be given reality in actual relations. The brahmin ideal, however, rejects all relations in favor of absolute independence. It can, therefore, only be an outside reference point for each separate group and cannot relate them to each other, either vertically or horizontally.

Nor does this ideal reference point resolve the conflict on the higher level of an all-encompassing ideology. For the brahminical rejection of relations obviously can not be reconciled with the system of relations that society is based on, nor can it encompass them. The "kingly" order immanent in social relations and the transcendent brahminical order are irreconcilably opposed to each other. This unresolved conflict is the form Indian tradition has developed to express and deal with the insoluble problem with which all tradition is essentially concerned. For, as the oldest ritual texts already make clear, society is felt to be based on the alternation of life and death, and consequently participation in society's web of relations is felt to be tantamount to continual involvement with death. The radical way to escape from this situation was resolutely to turn one's back to society and thereby to overcome death.[13] That this is an impossibility is hardly relevant. The point is that tradition can only deal with the insoluble by being itself an unresolved conflict.

We may then recognize the pivot of Indian tradition in the irreconcilability of "brahmin" and "king," who yet are dependent on each other. For the king will need the transcendent legitimation that only the brahmin can give. But the brahmin, however much he may need the king's material support, can not enter into relations with the king for this would involve him in the world of interdependence—a situation that would be fatal to the brahmin's transcendence,[14] in the same way that "governing" would be fatal to *dharma*.

What relevance can the foregoing considerations have for modernity? The first thing to note is that there hardly seems to be room for a conflict between tradition and modernity. For whatever room there is has already been taken up by the unresolved conflict of tradition itself. Modernity, then, would seem to find its predestined place within tradition's own, essentially broken, and contradictory framework.

The indubitable fact of the alienness of modernity introduced by a colonial government seems to be heavily overrated as a source of difficulties. For such a view is ultimately based on the romantic belief in the closed and monolithic character of a civilization as an autonomous organism. That this is not only a belief that as such is beyond proof or disproof, but rank superstition is sufficiently clear—even the most superficial reading on Indian civilization can demonstrate this—and should not detain us here.

The essential point is that the alien and the modern offer new ways to deal with the long-standing, unresolved conflict and as such are more often than not eagerly welcomed. For modernity is, if anything, dedicated to the devaluing or even the breaking up of primordial groups which it wants to replace with suprapersonal, universalistic groupings. As we saw already, this tendency is at the heart of the traditional conflict between "kingly" interdependence and brahminic independence, Thus, for instance, the "joint-family" has been idealized out of recognition as a badge of cultural identity coming straight out of hoary tradition. Obviously "jointness" may serve as an adequate device where other means of securing labor on the one hand and subsistence on the other are lacking. Nevertheless, brahminical theory prefers the division of the father's estate by the surviving sons,[15] as it usually favors the individual over the collectivity.[16] It is therefore not surprising that modernization, even when clearly derived from the West, and "brahminization" (or "sanskritization") are often seen to tie in easily with each other.[17] In this way modernity—in a sense already "transcendent" by the fact of its alienness—comes to partake of the transcendent legitimation that brahminic theory possesses.

Viewed in this way modernity would seem to add only a few new possibilities to the old conflict while the latter remains the same, so that when everything is said and done nothing has changed. Though this view may be helpful in laying the ghost of the overworked tradition-modernity fight, it is not sufficient. For it would come down to yet another assertion of India's perennial unchangeability grinding all innovation to meaningless dust. On the contrary, it should be asked whether the obvious changes that have been wrought over the last hundred or two hundred years are only of a superficial nature without any significant impact on the overall structure. Or in other words, whether the inner conflict on which Indian civilization is built did not change in form and content.

Perhaps the effect of change can nowhere be seen in a clearer way than in the socio-political sphere; at least it is best documented here.[18] As a convenient starting point we may take the traditional empire, such as that of the Mughals. This, like other traditional empires, was a rambling collection of smaller and bigger local centers enjoying various degrees of power and influence over their surroundings and continually competing with each other for local or regional predominance. By far the biggest center was for a long time the Mughal power situated in the strategic Delhi-Agra area. But even so it was, for all its power and prestige, in fact, no more than one power, albeit a preponderant one, among others. In order to realize its claims it had to continually ally itself with the local powers, which, of course, expected more than only immaterial benefits for their cooperation. In other words, the empire lacked the independent power and resources to fully realize its claims, and the price for the necessary cooperation of the local powers further weakened the imperial resources. In order to strengthen its resource base the empire had to resort to conquest and expansion. But these also required substantial, initial investments for obtaining the necessary support, and it has been shown that with the conquest of the Deccan in the second half of the seventeenth century, when the empire reached its greatest expansion, the cost of conquest became so heavy as to be fatal. For conquest meant a cumbersome process of winning over the holders of local influence by distributing imperial resources, including crown lands, before any benefit could be reaped.[19] Thus the empire naturally and irrevocably shriveled again into a local sphere of influence or "little kingdom" at the mercy of new would-be empire builders such as the Marathas, the Afghans, and eventually the British.

In fact the Mughal empire reflects on an enlarged scale the cycle of the segmentary polity. Such a polity continually alternates between total dispersion of power among the segments that balance each other in an ever shifting pattern of rivalry and alliance, and the effort on the part of particular segments to rise above the mêlée, centralize part of the power available, level down the other segments, and replace them with an administration apparatus.[20] In the case of total dispersion there is a potentially unending concatenation of smaller and greater centers interconnecting wide areas. Such a situation seems to be reflected in the geographical extension of "a regional network of hypergamy which links dispersed and often socially disparate groups within a generalized marital exchange pattern," as has been observed for the North Indian rajputs.[21] The poor man's solution to empire, one is tempted to conclude. Its strength is exactly the dispersion of power so that it can in no one place be attacked and finally broken, while at the same time the continual open or latent conflict between the segments is managed through diffusion without the need for any easily overstrained central institution.

This situation of dispersed power is, of course, not a static one. Out of the flux of shifting rivalry and cooperation new centers steadily arise and

new power concentrations are attempted. When such centers are successful they break out of the concatenation of overlapping units. But by the
same token their area of influence will be limited, for the wide-ranging
horizontal ties on which the concatenation is based have to be broken.
Now, even if such a center or segment manages to reduce the surrounding
ones and to replace them with an administrative apparatus, the allegiance
of the people who man the apparatus must be secured. In other words, the
carefully extracted resources that should be concentrated in the hands of
the ruler have to be redistributed. As we saw already in the case of the
Mughal empire, expansion offers no solution for it only heightens the need
for distribution. Since, moreover, resources are for the greatest part tied up
with the soil and its agricultural produce, the simplest if not the only way
of distribution is to parcel out the rights in the soil itself and the power
that goes with them. Total clusters of rights—not single, specific ones—have
to be parceled out and the dispersion of power is restored once again, if it
has indeed ever stopped being dispersed.

Under these circumstances there can hardly be any form of organization
except one that is almost exclusively based on comprehensive personal relations. For, since even the source of power—the rights in the soil and its
produce—is diffused throughout, power can not be broken down in separate, specific functions but is parceled out in total, undifferentiated packages. The participants in the network can only be differentiated as to the
greater or lesser amount of power—and this too may be fluctuating—but
not as to the kind of power. The ruler is, therefore, no more than a *primus
inter pares;* his functionaries are in fact his co-sharers in the realm, and
there is practically no room for specific impersonal relations as a basis of
the polity.

This is strikingly illustrated in the ancient Indian text on statecraft, the
Arthaśāstra, which presents a compelling picture of a centralized bureaucratic state. But on closer inspection the realities show through the cracks.
The numerous government departments are not connected by lines of command, delegation and communication. They are all separate units on the
same level and any control or coordination, it seems, has to be personally
secured by the ruler. Likewise, the officers of state are presented as a corps
of ranked functionaries enjoying fixed salaries; however, at the same time
they seem to be co-sharers with the king.[22] A similarly ambivalent view is
given of the state: on the one hand one can easily take the text's description of the state in the sense of a monolithically coherent unit; yet, when
considered in the context of the theory of the "circle" of kings—the text's
schematization of the segmentary concatenation of centers—the state comes
to look curiously fluid and open-ended. For when in the context of the "circle" the elements or factors of the state are enumerated, they include not
only the internal elements but also external ones such as the ally and even

the enemy. Segmentation does not stop at the boundaries of the state but permeates it. The state seems to be ready at any moment to dissolve in the "circle."

The interesting point is that the text allows us to clearly discern the realities and their limitations, while at the same time enunciating an ideal state of affairs trascending by far the actual possibilities. But both viewpoints are blended into one whole. It is the same contradictory double point of vision we noticed already as the basis of tradition. On the one hand the unavoidable reality of the "little kingdom" and the segmentary order had to be accounted for, while on the other a way out towards an ideal state of affairs transcending the fluidity of the actual situation had to be formulated so as to offer a fixed reference point for legitimation.

This double point of vision seems to be connected with the two principles of social organization. Most prominent of course is the segmentary organization centered on the distribution of rights in the soil and its produce —in short, the "kingly" model. But an equally important form of organization seems usually to be overlooked in the context of state formation, probably because it operates in the margin of and threatens the "kingly" organization. I am referring to the war band in its different forms, a subject that would merit a separate study. Here only a few points can be referred to that are relevant in connection with state formation. The first point, then, is that, in contradistinction to the segmentary "kingly" organization, membership of the war band is not based on ascription but freely recruited on the basis of individual allegiance to a single successful leader.

An old and well-documented illustration of this phenomenon may be found in the ancient Indian *vrātya* bands described in the ritual texts.[23] In that context they form a problem because they do not fit into the well-ordered and rational system of ritual expounded by these texts. From the point of view of the inner conflict of tradition their occurrence in this context is not so strange. Two points are of particular interest. In the first place, the *vrātya* band is not simply a contrapuntal feature deviating from the normal system, for it clearly ties in with practical needs. Its activities center around transhuming and raiding expeditions necessitated by the scarcity during the lean season. Thus we are told that such bands set out in autumn after the monsoon harvest in search of food for their men and cattle and return before the next monsoon. The second point is that the *vrātya*, for all his "heterodoxy," is still the starting point for the brahminical model of withdrawal and renunciation. In this connection it does not seem fortuitous that in South India left-hand groups were involved in the clearing and settlement of previously forested areas and that "warriors" were generally members of the left division.[24] Here we can observe the connection with the problem of state formation, especially when we take into consideration the transformation of South Indian polity into a warrior-dominated and warfare-oriented one in the thirteenth and fourteenth centuries.[25]

Probably the best studied material regarding this function of the war band is that of the ancient Germanic peoples. Authors of ancient Rome had also noticed the difference between the polycephalous (or acephalous) organizations of the settled tribes and the war band's uniting of individual members from different tribes under a successful leader. It is especially this type of organization, based on the association of different ethnic elements under a single leadership, the conquest of land, and the establishment of overlordships in new areas, that seems to have determined to a great extent the essence of medieval kingship.[26]

Of course, such developments are only possible when advantage can be taken of adjoining rich areas and their resources, such as Roman Gallia. Similarly, the Mughal empire started with exactly such a predatory war band led by the founder of the dynasty, Babur. On a smaller scale, dacoity seems to play the same role in rajput state formation.[27] The critical point in such developments is, however, the moment of success, for by itself the war band does not create new resources but only causes a reshuffle. It may be of interest to note that in early medieval Europe, as in the Mughal case, the principle of a non-ascriptive contractual bond with the ruler that also governed the original war band lived on in the organization of the polity—in Europe as feudalism, in India as the jagir system. But the end result remained the same: segmentation. For the main part of the resources remains tied up with the soil. This in turn means, as already argued, a reversal to segmentation and the parceling out of total packages of rights and power. Thus the Mughal empire could only exist as a "Personalverband" based on personal relations.

Yet such traditional empires are at the same time characterized by an orientation to a suprapersonal and durable unity in which power is regulated by rationally organized bureaucratic agencies on the basis of impersonal principles of justice. In short, it is oriented towards a transcendent legitimation that it tries to translate into reality.

The prime example is, perhaps, the third century B.C. Maurya empire whose ruler Asoka went to the unusual length of posting the tenets of the transcendent Buddhist-inspired *dharma* on rocks and pillars throughout his empire so as the galvanize, as it were, his wide-spread domains into a universalistic, suprapersonal unity. There are, however, no indications that the empire was much more than a segmentary concatenation that perhaps derived some extra strength and resources from its command of important trade routes—the same routes along which the famous inscriptions were placed. But the woefully inadequate reality content of the universal *dharma* as the foundation of the empire becomes apparent when Asoka claims to have achieved the final victory of the imperial *dharma* by sending missions propagating the *dharma* to the courts of all rulers known to him—missions that went perfectly unnoticed except for their elaborate mention in his own inscriptions. In the same way we can understand the Mughal Aurangzeb's effort to establish an Islamic polity, as well as the failure to achieve it. The traditional empire, then, fluctuates in the middle space between two diametrically opponent poles: on the one hand the total dispersion of power throughout a segmentary and fluid concatenation where the political is completely merged into the social order; on the other the far-out ideal of a universalistic polity where power is made independent from the social order and is administered according to fixed, transcendent rules.[28] The latter pole is in the literal sense transcendent in that it is beyond the limitations of actual society and can therefore possess ultimate legitimating force. It can only be imagined in an extra-societal, never-never world such as Asoka's *dharma* empire, the *'umma* or universal brotherhood of all believers as the ideal Islamic polity,[29] or the universitas christiana. It certainly has a strong attraction but its mobilizing potential has to be spent outside or, at best, in the fringe of society which is, in Indian terms, in the sphere of world renunciation. If the pattern of dispersed power may be considered the poor man's solution to empire, the extra-societal transcendent ideal may be called the poor man's dream of empire.

Against the backdrop of the traditional empire we may now try to understand the change that modernity has brought about in the inner conflict of Indian tradition as it is reflected in the socio-political sphere. This change, then, bears on the relationship between reality and the legitimating ideal or, in specifically Indian terms, between the "kingly" and the brahminical, renunciatory order.

As argued, the lack of resources blocked the way towards a change in this relationship. The first requirement for modernity to be effective would therefore seem to be a new base of resources free from commitments to the traditional arrangements. In itself, however, this is not sufficient, for nothing prevents these resources from also being absorbed in the traditional way. Thus, for instance, the extra resources obtained by a successful war (or rather, raiding activities) easily melt away in the existing channels of distribution without causing any structural change. Or, as the *Arthaśāstra* revealingly puts it, the conqueror should give all his allies their dues from the war loot, even if he should lose by it, for in this way he will be agreeable to the "circle of kings."[30] What modernity therefore has to be based on, apart from a new resource base, is a new pattern of distribution, a pattern no longer governed by the ramification of personal relations but by an impersonal code of principles and rules. This means that the realm of politics and the stuff it is made of—power and resources—must be set apart and safeguarded against the demands of the traditional order.

It would seem that it is precisely this that the first carrier of modernity in India, the British Indian Government, achieved to a remarkable, previously unknown degree. It is, of course, the old but traditionally unattainable ideal. What made its success possible was the simple fact that British rule

over India was part of an expanding world power that had its center outside India and drew its main strength from its dominant position in world
trade backed up by a growing industry. Though it needed India in different ways, it was not solely dependent on India's agrarian resources. It
could, therefore, afford to stay away from involvement in Indian society.
In fact it could not only afford to do so, it simply had to work hard to establish and maintain this privileged position. For the first decades of the East
India Company's rule over Bengal had clearly shown that its resources and
power were not safe from the danger of being drained away. Whatever the
philosophy behind the code of rules and regulations of 1795, including the
"Permanent Settlement" of the land-revenue in Bengal, its aim was unmistakably to disengage the government from involvement in the local and
regional segmentary order. The government's resources and power, including the use of force, were reserved and administered according to an ever-
expanding rational system of impersonal regulations.

Obviously this was no simple matter. The problem before the colonial
government was to strike a balance, from situation to situation and from
crisis to crisis, between the need for withdrawal and the pressures for involvement. But the pattern was set. The distributive demands that kept
being made on the center in various ways from various quarters were no
longer met on their own terms but by the formulation and application of
objective rules that bored ever deeper down towards the grass roots level.
Though in this way the contacts between the modern and traditional orders
grew immensely, there could be no integration, far less an overall impact of
modernity on the traditional dispensation. For the very *modus operandi* of
modernity precluded such a comprehensive impact. It was devised to deal
with specific cases in specific ways according to specific rules, so as not to
have to deal with total situations and comprehensive relations. In this perspective a local magnate was not a comprehensive leader of his men but
exclusively a legal landowner. Only as such could he have his interests
looked after by the government.[31] But this meant also that the specific impingements of modernity—though often dramatic for the persons involved—
were met by the comprehensiveness of the traditional order that diffused
the effects of modern impingements, closed the ranks, and eventually, after
a reshuffle, remained the same.

This dual dispensation had the great advantage of giving an unknown
measure of reality to the dream of a universalistic order. But its failure was
that it could not come to grips with the comprehensiveness and diffuseness
of the traditional order. It could only refuse full access to the center's
power so that the traditional order could not gain strength at the expense
of the center; the most that the center's reservation of power could achieve
with regard to the "little kingdom" was to freeze it and thereby reduce its
peculiar efficacy which lies in its fluidity. But in this way no fundamental
change could be brought about in the traditional order.

Of course the division was never watertight, nor could it be. The government could not operate in a vacuum and there had, therefore, to be considerable "leakages." Thus, there were groups that derived a measure of power and influence through their connection with the government and especially through positions in its extensive bureaucracy.[32] More importantly, however, the simple fact of India's becoming part of an expanding commercial empire with access to the world market made for the development of another independent resource base—or rather a plurality of small ones—in the hands of groups of landlords, cultivators, and commercial enterpreneurs.[33] Such groups easily outgrew the reduced circumstances of the "little kingdom," and even though they were in no position to compete directly with the government their demands on the center were hard to ignore. The always precarious balance of the dual dispensation became more and more threatened and eventually had to be completely overhauled.

Here the traditional inner conflict presented itself in a new form brought about by the partial and unintegrated realization of modernity. Briefly, the problem was—and is—that modernity operates on the assumption, or rather the fiction, that society consists of an arbitrary collection of isolated individuals, while the unity of the whole is not realized through immediate relations of hierarchical interdependence but mediated by abstract, impersonal rules and principles. This, as we saw, is not new. What is new is the resource base that makes it possible to give the idea a substantial degree of reality. In order to achieve this degree of reality modernity requires a "horizontal" pattern of distribution connecting the individuals who only in this way are able to realize their independence from the "vertical" relations embedding them in the "little kingdom."

Now perfectly "horizontal" distribution, even if all resources would be spent on it, is an impossibility. The very fact of distribution is bound to create inequalities, for even the most perfect set of rules has still to be operated by people who perform the distribution at different stages and levels and are thereby placed in positions of unequal power. In this way the system would easily slip back into the segmentary "little kingdom" concatenation and modernity would lose its reality content. In the final analysis the problem is again insoluble, but it can be managed in new ways; the "horizontal" and "vertical" orders must be allowed to interpenetrate. Obviously, a colonial government can not allow this interpenetration to come about, since it would irredeemably impair its position. When it comes to that point it can only react by total withdrawal, as indeed happened. The problem can only be managed by a national polity, for only a national polity can take the risks implied by the interpenetration of the "horizontal" and "vertical" orders. Such a polity, prepared slowly over the previous century or so, came into being in the interbellum period in the form of the Indian National Congress.

It has been customary to explain the success of the single most important figure in this process, Gandhi, by pointing to his expert wielding of traditional religious symbols and ideas, but this is only half the truth. Gandhi, apart from the symbols that had also been used by others, was a renouncer personifying in his relation to the sociopolitical world the inner conflict of tradition. This also qualified him to deal with the conflict in its modern form, but as such he played a totally unprecedented role. As has recently been pointed out, "the reason, over and above the use of religion in politics, why Gandhi was able to initiate national movements with such conspicuous success was because he recognized the social pluralism of India and exploited the traditional loyalties of different sections of society to draw them into political agitations."[34] If I am allowed to paraphrase this statement I would say that he managed to attend to the organization of both the "vertical" demands of the segmentary order and the conflicting need for "horizontal" unity. That the actions aiming at horizontal unity and therefore centered on universal moral issues were far less successful and showed a far lower degree of control than his earlier, locally restricted ones which focused on material grievances[35] was to be expected. Given that horizontal, no less than vertical, unity must be sustained by distribution and that access to the center's power and resources was as yet barred, the measure of reality he gave to horizontal, national unity, if only during the short span of a nationwide agitation, was a totally new phenomenon.

Equally remarkable and instructive are the limits of horizontal, national unity that became painfully clear at the same time. The unity of the nation is apparently not bounded by ethnic, linguistic, or geographical criteria nor even by the extent of existing or potential channels of distribution. The final criterion would seem to be the recognition of a specific formulation of transcendent authority and legitimation. For the Hindu this was clearly and unequivocally the renunciatory ideal. It was this ideal that was not only referred to but effectively embodied by Gandhi, who thereby could arbitrate conflict and guarantee ultimate unity. Here, of course, Hindus and Muslims had eventually to part company. As long as horizontal unity was only an idea beyond the reach of reality, it had no direct impact. Once it was given reality it had to have practical consequences, however painful.

This parenthesis on the limits of horizontal, national unity also shows us something of the precarious and explosive situation that arises from the blending of the vertical and horizontal orders into one reality. Everything then depends on the development of an institutional framework for dealing with this situation. Here probably lies Gandhi's greatest achievement, namely in the remolding of the Indian National Congress so that it could fulfill this function. For Gandhi did not simply give it a moral inspiration which usually faded once the particular action was over, but he played a dominant role in the different phases of its reorganization during the interbellum period.[36] Its remarkable success lay in its capacity to accommodate both the segmentary local and regional demands and the precarious reality of horizontal unity. This means, however, that Congress had to be the arena of the resulting tensions and conflicts to the point of becoming identified with these conflicts and consequently being threatened with breakdown. However, so far no other organization has been able to take over its function. Even though the demise of the Congress has been predicted again and again and even pronounced after the general elections of 1967, it showed its resilience—a resilience that paradoxically seems to be based on its conflictive nature— by its comeback two years later, and it is still there as the indispensable arena of conflict and national unity. Whatever the fate of India's political system in general and of the Congress in particular—as argued, it is inherently precarious—the main point is that India has been remarkably successful in setting up the institutional framework for dealing with the traditional conflict in its modern reincarnation.

To conclude: successful modernity does not mean the supersession of tradition or the superimposition on it of a different order. It means that the inner conflict of tradition is now fought within the confines of an expanded reality that transcends the limits of the "little kingdom" so as to include ultimate authority and legitimation themselves. Authority and legitimation are no longer transcendent and safe in an ultramundane sphere but part of reality—and therefore constantly called into question. In contradistinction to tradition, modernity must valorize change because the authority of its code of abstract rules and principles no longer transcends reality. Modernity has not solved the inner conflict of tradition, nor can it ever do so. But it has fundamentally changed it by carrying it over into the sphere of a single explosive reality.

REFERENCES

1. For the constant threat of scarcity and starvation, see W. Rau, *Staat und Gesellschaft im alten Indien* (Wiesbaden: O. Harrassowitz, 1957), p. 31.

2. W. C. Neale, "Reciprocity and Redistribution," in K. Polanyi, C. M. Arensberg, H. W. Pearson, eds., *Trade and Market in Early Empires* (Glencoe, Ill.: Free Press, 1957), pp. 218-236; also, same, in R. E. Frykenberg, ed., *Land Control and Social Structure in Indian History* (Madison: University of Wisconsin Press, 1969), p. 5.

3. O. Brunner, "Vom Gottesgenadentum zum monarchischen Prinzip," *Das Königtum* (Darmstadt: Mainau Vorträge, 1956), p. 289 on "der urtümliche Glauben dass die Entscheidung der Waffen 'Gott und das Recht' offenbare." In the same way we can understand the feudal obligation of consilium binding both the lord and his men. On the origin of the Nāstika, *Wiener Zeitschrift für die Kunde Süd- und Ostasiens*, 12-13 (1968-69), pp. 171-185.

112   J. C. HEESTERMAN

4. L. Dumont, *Homo Hierarchicus* (Paris: Gallimard, 1967), p. 107.

5. R. Lingat, *Les Sources du droit dans le système traditionel de l'Inde* (Paris: Mouton, 1967), pp. 29-32.

6. R. Lingat, "Time and the Dharma," *Contributions to Indian Sociology*, 6 (1965), p. 13.

7. L. Dumont, *Homo Hierarchicus*, trans. M. Sainsbury (London: Weidenfeld and Nicolson, 1970).

8. A. C. Mayer, *Caste and Kinship in Central India* (Berkeley: University of California Press, 1960), pp. 33-47; also same, *South West Journal of Anthropology* 14, pp. 407-427. Mayer's findings are also discussed by Dumont, *Homo Hierarchicus*, para. 36.

9. Brenda F. Beck, "The Right-Left Division of South Indian Society," *Journal of Asian Studies*, 29, No. 4 (August 1970), pp. 779-798.

10. Miss Beck's use of the latter term seems to echo Mayer's concept of "allied castes."

11. See Miss Beck's graph, where we find right-hand castes neatly ranked in an almost vertical row, while the left hand castes are typically scattered and their rankings consequently vague. Thus, for instance, the left-hand merchant (no. 7) is, as may be expected, slightly higher than the artisan from the same division (no. 9). Yet the latter one scores higher as regards brahminical conformity.

12. A. C. Mayer, *Caste and Kinship in Central India*, p. 37.

13. For a detailed discussion of this theme, see "Brahmin, Ritual and Renouncer," *Wiener Zeitschrift für die Kunde Süd- und Ostasiens*, 8 (1964), pp. 1-31; also, in the same publication, "The Case of the Severed Head," 11 (1967), pp. 21-43.

14. See "Priesthood and the Brahmin," *Contributions to Indian Sociology*, 5, pp. 46-49.

15. *Mānava Dharmaśāstra*, 9.111.

16. The earliest manifestation of brahminical individualism is the insistence on the single sacrificer, who has the ritual performed for his own benefit, and the prohibition of collective sacrifices as a social event. *Sacra publica* are conspicuous by their absence and even the royal consecration is represented as a single sacrificer affair. But from the texts it transpires with sufficient clarity that this onesided stress on individualism represented a daring innovation on the part of the systematizers of the ritual, which most probably was never fully put into practice. For next to it the non-systematized ritual continued in full force.

17. M. N. Srinivas, *Caste in Modern India and Other Essays* (Bombay: Asia Publishing House, 1962), chaps. 1 and 2; on the modernity of brahminical law, see L. I. and S. H. Rudolph, *The Modernity of Tradition* (Chicago: University of Chicago Press, 1967), pp. 269-279.

18. It would, of course, be equally possible to study change by focusing on the cultural sphere. The pivotal point would then have to be the development of the concept of "Hinduism" and its content which, coming up in the thirties of the last century in English literature on India and expressing nothing more than an ill-assorted complex of social and religious customs, rites and beliefs, both popular and scriptural, develop into a world religion, expressing the awareness of a new universalistic identity on the part of educated Indians.

19. M. Athar Ali, *The Mughal Mobility under Aurangzeb* (London, 1966), p. 173.

20. R. G. Fox, *Kin, Clan, Raja, and Rule* (Berkeley: University of California Press, 1971). The author discerns five stages of a development cycle moving from a segmentary lineage system through stratification to the break-through of ruling elements that "rip through the genealogical cover which had tied their political activities to the expansive familism of the group" (p. 159). Finally the system reverts again to the first stage. Though the analysis refers to the kinship-based rajput polity, the two main points of the cycle, dispersion and concentration of power, are generally relevant. We may think also of Leach's analysis of the transition between the Kachin and Shan types of polity in *Political Systems of Highland Burma* (Boston: Beacon Press, 1965).

21. R. G. Fox, *Kin, Clan, Raja, and Rule*, p. 170.

22. See "Kautalya and the Ancient Indian State," *Wiener Zeitschrift für die Kunde Süd-und Ostasiens*, 15 (1971), pp. 5-22.

23. See "Vrātya and Sacrifice," *Indo-Iranian Journal*, 6 (1962), pp. 1-37.

24. Brenda F. Beck, "The Right-Left Division of South Indian Society," p. 780.

25. B. Stein, "Integration of the Agrarian System of South India," in R. E. Frykenberg, ed., *Land Control*, p. 188 ff.

26. W. Schlesinger, "Das Heerkönigtum," *Das Königtum* (Darmstadt: Marinau Vorträge, 1967), pp. 105-143.

27. S. N. Gordon, "Scarf and Sword," *Indian Economic and Social History Review*, 6 (1969), pp. 403-29; see also D. H. A. Kolff, *Sannyasi-Trader-Soldiers*, and Gordon's comment, *Ibid.*, 8 (1971), pp. 213-220.

28. Another way of describing this bifurcation would be in terms of the divorce of power and authority, the latter being beyond reach in the transcendent extrasocial sphere. See "Power and Authority in Indian Tradition," contribution to seminar on tradition and politics at the S.O.A.S., London, 1-3 July 1969 (to be published).

29. It is perhaps not just accidental that the prophet left no instructions as to the community's form of government.

30. *Kautilīya Arthaśāstra*, ed. Kangle, 7.5.49.

31. F. R. Metcalf, "From Raja to Landlord and British Land Policy," in R. E. Frykenberg, *Land Control*, pp. 123-141 and 143-162.; P. D. Reeves, "Landlords and Party Politics" in D. A. Low, ed., *Soundings in Modern South Asian History* (Berkeley: University of California Press, 1968), pp. 261-282.

32. For a case in point, see R. E. Frykenberg's study of local influence and central authority, *Guntur District, 1788-1848* (Oxford: Clarendon Press, 1965).

33. With regard to India's economic history in the nineteenth century the seminal suggestions of M. D. Morris are particularly interesting; see M. D. Morris, ed., *Indian Economy in the Nineteenth Century: A Symposium* (Delhi, 1969).

34. R. Kumar, "The Political Process in India," *South Asia*, 1 (August 1971), p. 97.

35. *Ibid.*, p. 101.

36. Gandhi's role in the reorganization of the Congress comes out clearly in D. Rothermund, "Constitutional Reform versus National Agitation," *Journal of Asian Studies*, 21, pp. 505-521.

ASHIS NANDY

The Making and Unmaking of Political Cultures in India

Culture and Political Culture

ALL SOCIETIES have traditions, but only a few have traditions which are central, overpowering, and vital. These are the traditional societies, the whipping boys of students of political development. But there is a particular brand of traditional society that is known to others—and to itself—by variegated civilizations it represents. In these societies, the traditions are not merely dominant and living, but they are also sufficiently pliable, sufficiently complex, and sufficiently self-confident to accommodate, without being threatened, to the society's efforts to redesign its identity. Unlike other traditional societies, these have traditions that are not supplanted by modern structures; instead, they are given new meanings. Speaking anthropomorphically, these societies are not only difficult to surprise or threaten, but they are also almost impervious to external change. Their very cultural autonomy forces them to carry alone, even at the nadir of their strength and dynamism, both the immense burdens and advantages of their histories. We shall call them historical societies.[1]

Two other characteristics frequently reinforce the distinctive identities of these historical societies. First, their territories are often bounded by major historical civilizations.[2] Not only do countries such as India and China have within them a number of cultural strains, but there is also a fairly large number of carriers of the Indian and Chinese cultures existing outside the boundaries of these states. Still, China and India remain, by and large, the "natural" geographical bastions of the Chinese and Indian cultures. According to certain theorists, they live by an awareness of this fact; according to others, they are doomed by it. Second, these societies often have a dominent group of literati who articulate the great traditions of the civilization and give them unusually great prominence in their politics. The mandarin may have been officially reduced to a cipher by the redbook-reading activists, but he lives in the minds of the new rulers themselves. The Brahmin today may have lost the battle of competitive mass politics,

115

but Brahminic norms survive at many levels, even in the increasingly dominant, non-Brahminic sectors, whose self-interest no longer demands conformity to these norms. Because the elites flamboyantly articulate their "high" culture, using its symbols to seek justification for their acts and ideas, at least in their public lives, the common framework for political action also gives prominence to the dominant traditions of the society.

In India, both of these characteristics have helped hide the subtle, diverse modes of change in the relationship between culture and politics. Three methodological developments have contributed to this. First, empirical political theory is very much a product of a small sector of the Western world: necessarily, it is highly dependent on the written word, on contacts with those individuals conversant in Western language, and on the norms of Western social·sciences. These men are often members of the same strata that have sustained the great traditions of the society. Large sections of Indian society, on the other hand, though intensively studied at the micro level, are still partly alien to these Western methods and their exponents. This great intimacy between the discipline of comparative politics and the representatives of the great traditions has largely fostered the concept of a one-to-one relationship between political culture and the major motifs in the society's cultural past. In the process, it has also validated a historicist perspective of the political system and underrated the importance of autonomous changes in the political sphere.

Second, in certain phases of political development, the dominant culture of the Indian society *did* determine most of its politics. During these phases, because the critical elite maintained and expressed this culture, the great traditions effected much of the variation in the society's political culture. There was, therefore, a natural pressure to better understand the dominant culture and to give it an importance which, at another time in history, might seem totally out of proportion.

Third, the more influential empirical theories seem to conceptualize political culture as either a set of subjective orientations to politics—a political belief-value system—or as a grouping of modal personality features linking the traditions and politics of a community.[3] In societies where, in each generation, new and discontinuous relationships are being established between subjective orientations to politics, experiences of socialization, and historical traditions, unless one takes into account the mechanics of these changing relationships, one can only speak of the culture of politics as an ephemeral cluster of attitudes.

To develop a more adequate approach, one must recognize on the one hand, that political culture is as much a conscious or unconscious reorganizing and reshaping as is any other facet of a people's culture, and on the other, that these modifications reflect the society's own priorities and adaptive needs, its struggle to learn from its own history whenever possible and to free itself from that history whenever necessary.[4]

Political Culture as Choice

At certain times in its political history, a people chooses to remember different features of its past and to emphasize different elements of its culture. One characteristic of a protean civilization such as India's is that it has many pasts; depending on the needs of each age, the nation brings a particular past into its consciousness. There is much variation within a certain tradition—for example, from the intense, earnest pacifism of Gandhi, with its extremely limited application of the principle of unavoidable violence, to the apparently sanctimonious pacifism of Nehru, combining a universalist humanism with national self-interest, to modern self-confident nationalism, which clearly sees pacifism and nonalignment as instruments of state policy. In this respect, cultural history is projection: one reads into it or takes out of it according to present-day needs.

What aspects of its historical civilization has Indian society been forced to emphasize—or deemphasize—while building a modern political community? Which subcultures, with what type of traditional skills and idioms, have been given salience by the changing political needs of the community? These two questions mark a theoretical vantage ground from which one may look at the contemporary culture of Indian politics as not simply a summation of the society's self-defined political values, but also as incorporating phase-adequate modalities of reaching, changing, or rejecting these values. The focus of interest, then, becomes the manner in which the values and the modalities have been structured into temporary gestalts by the typical problems faced by Indian politics at each phase of its development.[5]

From such a theoretical vantage ground, it also becomes clear that some of the major concerns of past ages are fast losing their relevance for contemporary India, while others, which have been "recessive" in earlier phases, are acquiring a new importance.[6] This process of selection has involved the society's unique orientation to politicization and political participation. We may conceive of this orientation as including five inter-related features; each of them has ensured the flexibility of the nation's political culture.

The first of these features of the "Indian System" is the traditional concept of politics as an amoral, ruthless statecraft, or a dispassionate pursuit of self-interest to which many of the norms of the nonpolitical sphere do not apply.[7] The long period during which high politics in India remained the prerogative of alien rulers further confirmed the image of politics as far removed from day-to-day mores and folkways. Second, Indian society was organized more around its culture than around its politics.[8] Since politics was marginal to the Indian's self-image, the traditional culture providing the scaffolding of the Indian identity, the society accepted political changes without being excessively defensive, without feeling that its very existence was being challenged, and with the confidence—justified or not—that politics touched only its less important self.

Third, the concept of dh*rma* or piety prompted the society to consider different spheres of life as different systems of ethics;[9] it was taken for granted that the values governing politics would be largely inconsistent with those governing other areas of life. At critical moments, therefore, the anomic forces released by political changes did not percolate into other areas. When the political sector became threateningly disjunctive, or began to negate some of the major assumptions of the society, the traditional lifestyle still was not dramatically disoriented. It is this segmentalization which allowed Indian society to incorporate the new and the original, by containing them within small compartmentalized areas of behavior.[10] Fourth, like the Sinic and the Islamic, Indian civilization considered other cultures inferior; unlike the Sinic and the Islamic, however, this attitude did not extend to the political sphere. Therefore, learning statecraft from others was never precluded, and exogenous political ideas never seemed diabolical instruments of subversion.

Finally, though Indian society was organized around its culture, this culture lacked an authoritative center; notwithstanding a priestly caste, there was not even an organized religion. At various times, this has promoted different types of functional relationships between politics on the one hand, and certain primordial groups and elements of the great tradition on the other. For instance, early in the nineteenth century, when politics most needed some knowledge of indigenous metaphysics, an ability to search for a meaningful relationship between native elites and colonial rulers, and a capacity to redefine the concept of participation in the till-then alien culture of the emerging modern sector, and certain caste-specific skills (for example, Brahminic skills) operating within institutionally more open regional subcultures (for example, Bengal), became functional to political participation. At a later time, these same skills and subcultural backgrounds became useless, and even liabilities. The sacred texts have also been used selectively by different groups at different times: the first generation of modernist reformers depended heavily on the Vedas and Upanishads; later, Gandhi and the nativists mainly drew support from the less universalist Geeta. These readjustments are one of the main reasons why politics in India often seems to underwrite the traditional cultural and social divisions, but the point to remember is that the political process has always underwritten different, and frequently antipodal subcultures or strata at various times.

It is, perhaps, this particular combination of cultural forces which has reversed the relationship between society and politics in India and given the culture of Indian politics its distinctiveness. Dominant models of political sociology define the "culture of politics" to be a function of social, cultural, and psychological processes. In a country where, today, a major political goal of the elites is to alter Indian social institutions, cultural life, and shared personality traits, the relationship between politics and society becomes much more complicated. It demands that one must, at each historical phase, reexamine this relationship to see which sector of life has become the current pace-setter. Recently in India, the political elites, supported by the state's authority, have played this role, which forces of economic and scientific change played in the eighteenth and nineteenth centuries in Europe, and which the communication system, youth, and university cultures are increasingly playing in technologically developed polities.

Power, Authority, and Dissent

A society has not only a unique organization of power, but also a unique concept of power. Contrary to popular belief, concern with power was never low in the value system of traditional India; if anything, themes of power were ubiquitous in the modal life style. The uniqueness of the traditional Indian concept of power lay in its strong "private" connotations.[11] Though rulers and ruling classes were traditionally recognized as legitimately wielding authority, the concept of this authority was ill-defined and diffused. There was little philosophical debate on issues such as the limits to political power, its role in society, and the duties and functions of those engaged in politics.[12] Moreover, not only did different spheres of action have different authority systems, but these areas were also divided by counterweighing authorities. The individual was largely free to choose his authority and follow his own beliefs, rather than to try and actualize collective values.[13] Naturally, the most respected form of power was self-control, particularly regulation of one's instinctual and materialistic self. The idea of an indigenous, central, public authority exercising political power could not be linked to the traditional ethos, because of the Hindu society's tenuous relationship, since the Middle Ages, with a succession of alien political orders, and because of the large-scale Hindu withdrawal from high politics. This situation had led to a further privatization of the concept of power. Thus, power increasingly came to mean power over self, and authority was primarily defined as the authority of traditions and of sacred texts. The former involved the delegitimization of any "external" power that could only be attained through competition and activities in the natural world; the latter involved acceptance of the authority of those who already held it, and rejection of the concept of achieving or challenging authority from outside. The two attitudes were closely related.[14]

This concept of power has two contradictory implications. On the one hand, the absence of any moral legitimacy for an ambition to rule makes having political power a somewhat illegitimate possession. This explains the pressure on the rulers to indulge in, or articulate the themes of conspicuous asceticism and self-sacrifice, and to vend even the most trivial politics as part of a grand moral design—as if power over one's own self (Gandhi called it self-control), the moral self dominating the self-seeking, instinctual self, legitimizes one's political power.[15] On the other hand, politics is also recognized as amoral statecraft, outside the compass of everyday living; although political leaders are expected to assume a self-righteous tone, there is also a certain cynicism about their moralism.[16] It is, perhaps, this conception of politics and politicians which Gandhi tried to counter by his "moral politics."

What, then, are the cultural checks against absolutism? What are the main sources of dissent or defiance? These are difficult questions to answer in a society where dissent has always been neutralized by absorbing it into the mainstream, where the most creative response has not been to establish an alternative power structure but to shift the locus of consensus within the existing authority system, where self-examination by the dominant center has always been preferred to the substitution of ideas by the dissenting periphery, and where the dominant tradition is ultimately that of "dissent through authority."[17]

The tradition in India, therefore, was to alter the dominant culture from within, by showing dissent to be a part of orthodoxy or by reinterpreting orthodoxy in terms of the needs of dissent. This was especially true of ideological deviations or innovations, the type of challenge the society repeatedly faced and became experienced in handling, until the British *raj* changed the nature of ideological dissent by coupling it with large-scale changes in the subsistence systems of society. New political ideas have always been acceptable in India, welcomed as a different aspect of a larger indivisible truth, and incorporated into the polity. Even when certain political polarities were not reconcilable within politics, they could at least be accommodated within the larger cultural framework.[18] Indian society has also never considered any political credo as competing with its own version of universalism;[19] instead, it has tried to soften the impact of these doctrines by reinterpreting them in particularist terms. Hindu tolerance is a particularist tolerance. Whereas other cultures depend on institutions to protect dissenters, defining the terms of conformity or orthodoxy narrowly, Hinduism is institutionally rigid, but interprets its conventions so broadly and allows the individual such a large choice within the orthodoxy that it is impossible to be a dissenter unless one is a dedicated and doctrinaire nonconformist.

The creative significance of this attitude toward ideological dissent is obvious, but there is a catch. Although abstract idea systems have been so attractive to the Indian mind, the hard choices required for their practical application have generally not interested the best minds in India. In fact, a slight contempt has attached to ideas that "work" or that can be operationalized or tested. Simultaneously, because ideas tend to lack immediate action parameters, new ideas are easily integrated with those that exist into an institutional consensus, and even into a millennial consensus. As a result, activism and commitment in the public sphere tend to lack prestige and fail to invoke commitment: there are few inner pressures to actualize one's ideas and ideals.[20]

The society's monistic metaphysic has influenced the articulation of dissent in yet another way. Charismatic leaders are expected to represent not only the majority of people, but also *all* people. Thus, to some extent, the anti-establishment must be reflected by the legitimate wielders of power.[21] Nehru and Indira Gandhi symbolize something more than the axial authority; they also represent the opposition in their fight against what they and others see as the retrograde pillars of the establishment within the government. This, however, has frequently reduced opposition to a game, albeit a deadly and serious one, played by permissible rules. Opposition from outside the consensual system does not seem opposition at all, but an attack on the "true dissenters": the power holders themselves.

Politics and Intellectuals

A nation is an idea. In the beginning of the nineteenth century, it was the intellectual elite—Brahminic, urban-centered, and pro-British—who made current the idea of an Indian polity; India as a political community was, in one sense, their discovery. Thus it is not surprising that intellectuals remained the main actors in Indian politics until a few decades ago.[22]

These men first believed that the idea of India, and of Indianness, must include a new integrated cultural identity. They spent the first half of the nineteenth century trying to create a different basis for political processes by redefining the Indians' shared cultural self to make it compatible with modern concepts of citizenship. This was, of course, a red herring in a historical society organized around its shared culture. Because it was a more peripheral sector of life, perhaps it would have been easier for politics to align itself with the existing culture; or, in a compartmentalizing society, this search for congruence might even have been unnecessary. The intellectuals' failure to understand the situation confined their impact to the small, urbanized, Western educated, upper caste groups to whom the economic and social changes initiated by the *raj* offered an entirely new life style.[23]

This attempt to alter the elements of the shared cultural identity soon created an inward-looking defensiveness, efforts to protect self-esteem, and a controversy over the extent to which the Indian political identity could be defined while, at the same time, rejecting Westernization. Borrowing from the West continued, but only covertly and only when it could be justified as a resurrection of India's past. One factor alone remained un-changed: the politics of cultural self-affirmation continued to underwrite existing modes of political participation and leadership. Because the debates centered on the revival of India's past, its sacred texts, and its dominant religious core, the reformers of political culture remained those who were, traditionally, its best interpreters, who enjoyed the inherited right and knew how, through their socialization and education, to be interpreters: the Brahminic cognoscenti.

Not surprisingly, as soon as the semblance of participatory politics evolved in India, the culture of Indian politics became aggressively anti-intellectual. Gandhian anti-intellectualism, for example, was basically an attempt to shift the center of political culture from liberal universalism and reinterpretations of Sanskritic texts to the hitherto peripheral, non-Brahminic cultures of the new participants in politics.[24] These little traditions did not require frequent reassessment to be made modern; they were intrinsically "modern," if not in content, at least in the manner in which the content was handled.

Making a virtue of many of those elements of Indian culture which had seemed liabilities to former modernizers, the Gandhian movement was implacably anti-materialist, to a certain extent deliberately totalist, and single-mindedly hostile to anything more particularist or less universalist than the nation. The non-Sanskritic traditions that it emphasized and used as sources for its activist, pragmatic ethics rendered any deep, abiding concern with metaphysics redundant.[25]

After independence, notwithstanding Nehru's half-hearted attempts to find intellectuals a place in politics, "intellectualism" as a political theme has become even more dominated by competitive politics.[26] This has not only contributed to the institutionalization of politics as a vocation with a tradition of its own, but has also led to a dangerous underestimation of the importance of intellectual assessment of policies, of "educated" statecraft, of political information processing, and of "informed guesses."[27] A more populist political culture, the growing belief in pragmatic activism, and the traditional separation of statecraft from intellectual activity sustained this attitude toward intellectuals. Politicians are still unwilling to recognize that political decision-making must involve a new awareness and use of knowledge, in a world where information and communications systems already perform the pace-setter role, which was filled by economic entrepreneurship in the nineteenth century and imperialism in the eighteenth century. The challenge to the Indian political system now lies in beginning to induct intellectuals into the decision-making centers on an entirely new basis: neither as Brahminic interpreters of the new politics, nor as ornaments of the system, but as professional technocrats. There are some indications that this is actually occurring.

Politics and Social Hierarchy

To the extent that politics manipulates and changes the distribution of power, political competition in India has come to mean the process through which the traditional hierarchies have been rendered more fluid and open, allowing the individual to alter his position in society, irrespective of his niche in the traditional order. Although the plural nature of the society has frequently induced the underlining of primordial collectivities as a basis for mass political mobilization, these politicized groups have been forced to compete on the basis of equality, not on the basis of their hierarchical status. In this respect, the traditional hierarchical order has been irrevocably damaged.[28]

But political relevance is not only attached to the occupants of hierarchical positions or the criteria of hierarchical status, but also includes the extent to which the principle of hierarchy permeates a political culture. Indian culture traditionally applied the concept of hierarchy to more aspects of life than did many other cultures.[29] One result of politicization in India has been that, whereas the criteria and incumbents have dramatically changed because of political competition and, particularly, electoral mobilization, the principle of hierarchy has spread into the new areas of the expanding modern sector.

It is as if the cultural tendency to hierarchize has found in political power a new criterion for social status. Thus the new politics and its bureaucracy have increasingly attracted power and status motivated individuals, and, in the process, have rendered subsidiary other "limited status systems"—traditional, as well as modern. Men operating within special status hierarchies, which should be at least partially autonomous from the central hierarchy (such as certain professions), tend to undervalue their own jobs and try to rise in "general" status. An appointment as an inconsequential political or bureaucratic functionary often seems more important to a man than recognition amongst his peers in his own area of specialization; the most creative intellectuals have often been lost in government departments, frozen at their respective levels of unimportance; influential positions within the educational system have attracted gifted scholars away from creative work; and bureaucrats have continued to dominate decision-making, even in highly specialized professions. Worst of all, the self-esteem of men not wielding political power has been more and more crushed.

It is paradoxical that while politicians have always played a creative role, by mobilizing and politicizing the peripheries of the society, by partially demolishing the traditional status system, and by undermining the earlier elitist social leadership, in the process they have also consolidated their power as a group and have increasingly become legitimate occupants of the apex of a new hierarchy. Today, any activity outside the sphere of power politics has become low-status. Although the simultaneous valuation of political activity as amoral and politicians as unscrupulous partially counters this trend, one of India's major tasks in the future will be to take certain sectors out of the political hierarchy, and to decelerate the tendency of all hierarchical systems to be dominated by the "new class" of politicians. The society's success in this area will ultimately determine how well it will be able to build strong multiple centers of excellence.

An accidental by-product of the new hierarchy is that India has managed to avoid the experience of many societies—including some highly developed ones—where politics struggles for autonomy from other sectors, such as big business and the military. The influence of feudal elements, of big business, and of the army is remarkably limited in Indian society; with the increase in political knowledge and the destruction of vote banks, it is even less effective. The politician in India now reigns supreme. In fact, by constantly stressing nonpolitical determination of politics, certain forms of radicalism have merely been encouraging political inaction.

However, its autonomy from other sectors has not released Indian politics from the stranglehold of its own adjunct: the governmental bureaucracy. The culture of Indian bureaucracy represents the society's attempt to "hierarchize away" or neutralize the new, the disruptive, and the noxious. The traditional style of containing chaos and fragmentation in India was to fit all contradictions within a new hierarchy compatible with the old order. The nation's pseudo-modern bureaucracy embodies this style. The most radical and modern policies, therefore, tend to be translated by the bureaucracy into posts, rules, and procedures; even attempts to reform the bureaucracy merely generate new bureaucratic structures.

Public Ethics

More than a shared set of political notions, it is the continuing effort to forge a common framework for these norms that has given the culture of Indian politics its distinctiveness. This blueprint of public ethics would have to fit with the needs of a competitive, achievement-oriented, plural system, and with a public life increasingly dominated by secondary-groups: in sum, with the requirements of modern citizenship. Perhaps, in a society where the network linking the dominant principles of indigenous culture with the cultures of its rulers was poor, and where politics had always remained outside the traditional ethical system, the search for a common ethics was bound to be initiated. There were several reasons why this common ethics was necessary. On the other hand, the image of politics as amoral was strengthened by an indigenous peasant culture that was provincial, seclusive, and strictly limited in its access to areas of governmental functioning: in such a culture, there were few opportunities to participate in sectors that required knowledge of public ethics. Thus the common man's subjective orientation to the public sphere was characterized by distrust and a certain cynicism.[30] Second, Indian socializing processes tended to equip the growing individual with ethical criteria that were especially congruent with tradition-directedness, and with efficient functioning in a primordial, interpersonal setting; any other criteria would not only have been meaningless, but also dysfunctional. Finally, even the attachment to traditional norms was weak in Indian society. Both the concepts of *maya* (illusion) and *anashakti* (detachment) extended to the norms themselves. In addition, there was no well-defined concept of evil in the traditional worldview. What, therefore, permitted change also discouraged any commitment to changes.

One of the first tasks which India's political modernizers set for themselves in the nineteenth century was to create a new ethics for public life and for impersonal political relationships. The need became more intense as politicization increased, and the elite politics of small, face-to-face, regional groupings gave way to the politics of mass participation, party building, and large-scale political organizations. Predictably, not only did these reform movements emphasize previously overlooked aspects of the Dharmashastras which had only become functional in the new social context, but they also ensured that the discovery of a new ethics remain a Brahminic pursuit.[31] All the major reform movements involved a large measure of Sanskritization, were elitist if not in principle at least in practice, and were infected with the then-current political theme of social service for the masses.[32] These movements also shared an ambivalence toward British colonialism: on the one hand, their leaders maintained excellent rapport with the government; on the other hand, their systems were either modeled around or were systematized protests against the religion, culture, politics, and administrative behavior of the Westerners. No wonder mass politics ultimately killed the reform movements.

The attempts to set up norms of public behavior within the frame of Sanskritic traditions ended with Gandhi. Gandhian politics transcended the Brahminic norms to seek a basis for public ethics in the folk cultures of India. In the process, he unshackled the Indian political culture from both the Brahminic tradition and from imported Western liberalism, between which there had developed such a fine fit. In searching for norms outside the arena within which the government, the liberal reformers, and the earlier nationalists were operating, Gandhi was, perhaps, only representing the trend of larger historical forces. By the time he entered politics, the reform movements had already been frozen by the changing meaning of reform, which had come to mean the colonial government as the ultimate arbiter in social matters.

Politics as Self-Redefinition

The foregoing sections would seem to suggest that changes in Indian political culture have been initiated in roughly four interrelated but different dimensions or phases; in each of them certain key men and groups introduced changes in the mundane environment, as well as in metaphysics.

It was in the first phase, at the end of the eighteenth century, that the universalist, Western educated, pro-British, reformist literati and Brahminic symbol manipulators began their direct onslaught on Indian traditions. Their characteristic political style may be summed up as the attempt to incorporate extra-cultural elements on pragmatic or intellectual grounds, and then to justify this integration by appealing to traditional concepts of goodness. While the colonial system aided this "Indianization" process by favoring the elites who led the reform movements, support also came from the major institutionalized means of social mobility: Sanskritization. Identification with Brahminic norms came to imply, at least for the exposed sections of the society, identification with the Brahminic style in politics; as a result, diffusion of the imageries and symbols of this style became widespread within the modern sector.

This Brahminic mode held certain advantages until the middle of the nineteenth century. In an apolitical society, the reformist leadership enjoyed a comfortable autonomy from the masses who also, in their apathy, made few demands. Likewise, the leaders' maneuverability was enhanced by their own interpersonal contacts, and by the limited role of a few lower-level political "headmen" or "brokers." This first phase introduced several innovations in the culture of politics: the popularization of the concept of the state's relevance to daily life; the introduction of Hinduism and Indianness as important elements in elite identity, and initiation of a debate on the relationship between the two; the use of the state as a reform mechanism in Indian society (thus changing the concept of state from being Hinduism's antagonist or the dispassionate outsider and arbiter on religious issues);[33] and the acceptance of Brahminic intellectuals as a major political force.

When Rammohun Roy (1772-1833) began speaking about Hindus and Indians and Upanishads and Vedas, he was introducing a new concept of traditions, not based on *lokachara* or folkways, but on textual Brahminism. Social scientists, who offset Brahminism as a tradition remnant against "modern" politics, seem to forget that the Brahminic values within politics are themselves a recent innovation, deliberately introduced by the early modernists.[34] On the whole, these new Brahminic norms provided, for the first time, a basis for a collective political identity, open to foreign political ideas and less constrained by the primordial allegiances and fragmentations of the myriad folk cultures of India. Predominantly integrationist and liberal, these Brahminic values were also informed by a universalism and a positivism that had meaning for the major political actors, including the colonial rulers.

Politics as Self-Affirmation

During the second half of the nineteenth century and the first two decades of the twentieth, changes split Indian political culture. In emphasizing a different style of adaptation to modern inputs, the Brahminic counterelites, who had begun to organize themselves in the first phase of politicization, gradually came to dominate the political scene in this second phase.

The causes for this were various. First, the internalization of Brahminic norms had caused the loss of self-esteem, in being a Hindu or an Indian, for a sizeable section of the new, growing, urban middle classes;[35] it was a matter of truly coming to believe that they, as individuals and as Indians, were backward—economically, politically, and, worst of all, morally. The growing sense of British racial supremacy fed this feeling of moral anxiety. This racial tension was primarily a result of the increasing displacement of Indian feudal elements by the British middle class operating within the ruling circles in India. Justifying their chauvinism by referring to the new utilitarian ideas of progress and liberalism, these British groups sought in the concept of the white man's burden a counter to their still gnawing feelings of inferior status.

The most important factor, I suspect, in the transformation of Indian political culture was the discovery of Hinduism as an organized religion, toward the beginning of the nineteenth century. Hinduism crystallized with the establishment, by Rammohun Roy, of Atmya Sabha in 1815 and Brahmo Sabha in 1828; with the publication, by Roy, of the first modern translations of the Vedas and the principal Upanishads into Bengali and English, between 1815 and 1830; and with the founding, again by Roy, of a Brahmo church in 1830.[36] For the first time, Hindu religious organizations began to function, at least theoretically, within the entire Hindu community, including its social, economic, and political spheres, its different castes, sects and orders, and its numerous regional variants. As soon as Roy established the Brahmo Sabha, others started forming counter-organizations, which clearly split the political culture into two idioms: modernist and revivalist. In the beginning, the aggressively modernist idiom was dominant, but as time passed, and as new groups began to enter politics, the revivalist movement began gaining adherents at the expense of the modernist. Not only did this trend help certain individuals cope with their moral anxiety and inferiority feelings, but it also impelled others to enter the modern sector without feeling overawed and without being tempted to disown their traditional selves.

Although Brahmo Samaj and his successors, the more nativist Arya Samaj and Ramkrishna Mission, denied caste, their style was Brahminic and their leaders blue-blooded. The new idiom, growing out of the fragmentation within the same elite groups, used for awhile their technique of changing the culture of politics through a reinterpretation of sacred texts and of the Indian past. But the psychological needs were now different. The nativists tried to demonstrate, to themselves as much as to others, that many "Western" features of the modern world were not actually Western, but were also contained in Indian traditions, often in a "purer" form. Thus, they were not legitimizing the extraneous, but supporting the indigenous. These men were drawn from the urban elite sectors, from among those who had been exposed to earlier modernizing economic and social forces, and, frequently, from the English educated gentry. Their savage attack on the Western educated, urban, high caste gentry should not blind us to their origins. Bankim Chandra Chatterji, India's politically most influential novelist, one of the first to introduce the nativist idiom into nineteenth century India's political consciousness, and author of the anthem "Bandè Mātaram"—the war cry of both aggressive nationalism and fervent restorationism—writing of the Westernized urban gentlemen, the *babus:*

The *babus* will be indefatigible in talk, experts in a particular foreign language, and hostile to their mother tongue. . . . Some highly intelligent *babus* will be born who will be unable to converse in their mother tongue. [Their] . . . emaciated bony legs will be skilled in escape, their weak hands will be capable of holding pens and receiving salaries, their soft skins will be able to withstand imported boots. . . . Like Vishnu they will have ten incarnations, namely clerk, teacher, Brahmo, accountant, doctor, lawyer, magistrate, landlord, editor and unemployed. . . . They will be Christians to missionaries, Brahmos to the Brahmo leaders, Hindus to their fathers, and atheists to the begging Brahmins. *Babus* will consume water at home, alcohol at friends', abuses at the prostitute's and humiliation at the employer's.[37]

Who would suspect from this savage attack that Bankim Chandra was a district magistrate in the *raj,* and an English educated, pro-British member of the Calcutta gentry?

This element of self-criticism reveals that these men were more than revivalists; they were trying to lay the foundation of an Indian identity that would not humiliate the country's majority of Hindu inhabitants. On the one hand, they were deciding which elements of Westernization could be included within India's image of itself without destroying the basic self-regard around which the traditional identity was integrated; on the other hand, in rejecting the earlier adaptive mode of identifying with the aggressive, victorious British, they were seeking modern referents within the traditional culture itself.[38] Perforce these men had to assume a Brahminic tone, which, to psychologize M. N. Srinivas, was the traditional means of handling feelings of inferiority at the group level and of expressing one's search for parity, without breaking away from one's own historical roots.[39]

Politics as Autonomy Seeking

The first two phases of India's politicization were dominated by elitist politics. Changes in economic and political institutions and in public consciousness only seemed to confirm the historical role of the Brahminic elites as inventors of laws, interpreters of traditions, and "sanctifiers" of new means of livelihood. But this political style became scholastic and rigidly formal—a depot of Hindu chauvinism on the one hand, and of doctrinnaire modernism on the other. Those articulating the idiom had developed a vested interest in colonial politics, which certainly colored their perception of the political needs of the community. The modernists paid their homage by identification and imitation; the nativists, by compulsive and counterphobic rejection.

It was Gandhi in the 1920's who began to organize the fragments of a new style into the dominant language of Indian politics. This new idiom, while continuing to borrow from the Sanskritic world view, emphasized a more pragmatic, businesslike approach to politics which had been latent in the folk cultures of the Indian peasant. Like these self-confident, partially "closed" peasant cultures, this attitude toward political change was much less self-conscious and much more self-assured and autonomous. Gandhi, for instance, always claimed to be a *sanatani* or traditionalist; he never made a secret of his contempt for those who, like Rammohun Roy, had tried to reform Hinduism, because he felt that they were wrongly trying to redefine the Indian way of life.[40] The perversion of the original Indian way of life, Gandhi believed, accounted for the miseries of India. When Gandhi initiated new concepts of time, pacifism, or consensualism— and demanded ruthless conformity to them—he was convinced that he was not importing Western ideas of improving traditional values: he was merely using the only true Indian concepts. Gandhi also brought to the center of the political culture certain traditional character traits that had come to be associated with femininity and weakness. Elements which were considered by the earlier modernizers weaknesses of the society seemed now the strengths of an older, more compassionate order.[41]

The greatness of Gandhi lay not so much in his pacifism and nationalism, nor even in his mobilizational or organizational skills, but in his ability to bring to the center of political activity the hardy, non-ideological, albeit dull and low-key men for whom reformers and revolutionaries had long fought, but rarely "represented." Even before the new radicalism made it fashionable, the sleepy, conformist peasants were, for him, the revolutionary stuff out of which a new society had to be built. This approach had its roots—strange though it may seem to associate this with

Gandhi—in the native shrewdness, this-worldly individualism, and efficacy of peasant communities that had for centuries toiled against nature and fought a ruthless battle for survival.

This Gandhian phase established, for the first time in Indian history, the primacy of politics in the life of the Indian. Its ending marked the termination of the period of grace, which the earlier leadership had been given, for introducing political changes without disturbing the Indian masses, for working out the implications of the new political institutions with which the society was experimenting, and for making decisions about which the majority was not concerned. By the end of this period, India had also acquired a large body of discontinuous political traditions: a fact which may be said to mark the beginnings of post-traditionality in a society.

It is from these elements of Gandhism, rather than from Gandhi's saintliness, that one must trace many of the features of contemporary politics in India. Nevertheless, the latter also had a role to play. If Gandhi's pragmatism and organizational skills finished the liberals, as well as the nativists, his saintliness attracted former dissenters to the national consensus, negated the older concept of politics as amoral, and underwrote a concept of humane politics which may mean little to social scientists, but which makes a real contribution to the quality of life in a society.[42]

Politics as Banality

The politics of autonomy seeking may have established the primacy of politics, but its growth as a vocation is primarily a post-Gandhian phenomenon. This is natural; because colonial rule involved either sycophancy and collaboration, or defiance and high drama, it was only after independence that the real task of state formation could begin.

Freedom from colonial rule, however, does not automatically repair the damage to the self-identity of a culture. By reinforcing those traditional elements which suit it best, colonialism activates certain features of the modal personality system which later become dysfunctional, but nonetheless survive as important traditions in a society. Neither Gandhian nationalism nor post-independence politics has been able to wipe out these elements from Indian politics. India's past—two hundred years of colonial rule—remains a part of its living history. And the meaning which the society gave to subjection, in terms of indigenous theories of living, has ensured certain continuities. These continuities have arisen from efforts, during the first three phases, to either ascribe meaning to, or integrate, or institutionalize alien, external challenges, while at the same time rendering the society capable of dealing with its own problems in its own way.

The post-colonial political culture is more clearly oriented to economic rationality and political expediency; it assumes a broad congruence between an individual's self-interest and the society's good. Three processes have acquired primacy in this phase. First, the political culture of the districts is reaching out to the national center as mass politics consolidates its dominance.[43] This ruralization of politics, perhaps, merely indicates the assumption of power by men who run an established, stable political order in an inconspicuous, unselfconscious way. In a certain respect, its ascendence only reveals that the system is working, that it has grown roots, that somewhere the normative requirements of the order have overlapped with the pragmatic self-interests of the men constituting it.

Second, the establishment of a more clearly identifiable political center is expressed by the erosion of peripheral autonomy and by the tighter fit between the subsystems of the society. Today, compartmentalization is a less efficient coping mechanism and politics is spilling over its boundaries. It is also paying for its primacy by carrying an enormous "expectation load." Because politics has usurped some of the control functions of other subsystems, because it has a synthesizing and priority-setting role in the society, and because it has begun to "introject" demands and tensions generated within other subsystems, problems which would once have been considered under the jurisdiction of others—educationists or technocrats, for example—have become issues in which politicians may justifiably intervene and by which parties may justifiably be judged. Apparently the system has yet to "learn" to regulate, according to its long-term needs, which controversies should enter and which should be excluded from the political arena.

Third, with the reemergence of a dominant party and a paramount leader, the task of middle and lower level leadership has been changing from aggregation of interests to accountability to the center of the power structure. This is an aspect of the crisis of penetration which has yet to be fully worked out. Although this accountability has enormously increased the center's power, the center has also become more vulnerable, for it can no longer plead sabotage of policies at lower levels or produce scapegoats to explain failures. In this sense, lower level politics in India is gradually being taken over by two types of professional bureaucrats: the selected technocrats or implementers, and the elected policy supervisors.

To many of these professionals, the concerns of the earlier phases of Indian politics are distant history; the struggle for autonomy and the defensive self-affirmation of certain sectors of the Indian literati has, for them, only an increasingly esoteric ring. As the society moves toward greater freedom from its past, Indian politics seems to have gained the "inner" sense of autonomy for which intellectuals and other sectors of the society are still fighting. However, to the carriers of the liberal intellectual tradition, as well as to the inheritors of the Gandhian saintly style, this politics certainly seems a betrayal of the earlier modernizers and the surest sign of political retrogression and barbarization.

The Order of Change

Even though the four "phases" in the evolving relationship between politics and culture have not engendered exclusive styles for handling political problems, they do survive as four identifiable emphases in the culture of Indian politics. Those very forces which once determined the sequence of the phases also seem to regulate the present interplay and the relative significance of each style.

Take, for instance, the manner in which the leadership in the first phase tried to ascribe meaning, in terms of native symbols, to the disruptive inputs of a newly established colonial system. Colonial policies were not a matter of choice for them; what the leaders could deal with were the psychological reactions to these inputs, the fears and anxieties associated with cultural shock and structural change. These men handled the fears and anxieties by becoming uncompromisingly self-critical and catholic in their cultural inclusiveness.

Take also, for instance, the fact that efforts by this reformist leadership to alter Indian cultural identity provoked important sectors of the same elite to organize in protest, to redefine the nature of the challenge, and to devise adaptive strategies in terms more congruent with the self-respect of the community. Likewise in contemporary India, the politics of self-redefinition survives in certain forms of universalist liberalism and universalist radicalism, particularly among certain sectors of the babu intellectuals. Even in its defeat, this style contributes to national life by its greater ability to borrow from outside, to build intellectual and cultural bases to what is learned from other cultures, and to cushion the intellectual—especially the scientific and technological—spheres from pressures to become local and provincial. Similarly, the politics of self-affirmation checks any tendency by the political elites to stray too far from their task of searching for a political identity free of external referents, and warns against any flagrant impediment to the historical societies' freedom to pursue their own independent processes of change. Roughly in the same way that the phase of self-affirmation corrected the excesses of the politics of self-redefinition, the present interaction of styles has become a cultural radar for the corrective adaptations of the society.

However, the earlier modes of political participation must now operate within a system dominated by another, less "heroic" style; in this respect, they have become recessive, confined to small sections of the population. One may even speculate that, today, these earlier styles have come to reflect those levels of the nation's modal personality that are less frequently triggered by the society's adaptive needs. In other words, the cultural radar of the polity finds its extension within the personality of the modal Indian. The possibility of self-correction might suggest on the one hand, that the days of dramatic crises and drastic shifts in the political culture—

which once lead to vociferous, strident debates on the role and nature of political traditions—are nearing their end, and on the other hand, that India has moved into a phase where it should be possible to take for granted the cultural parameters of the polity.

There is always a temptation to write a postscript: here is mine. If the foregoing analysis suggests that the evolution of Indian political culture has, today, been completed, it is obviously the result of my attempts to retrospectively identify trends and impose a schema. Certainly the present culture of Indian politics cannot preempt other fundamental alterations. However, as the norms of a political order become more permanent and a part of everyday life, it also becomes increasingly difficult to change a nation's political culture. Stability has a cost. This hardening of the arteries is a necessary feature of the continuous tradition-building and institutionalization perpetuated by each state system, but nothing will eliminate the possibility that a society may begin to perceive as a threat what it once did not even define as a challenge; that societal concerns and goals, which once seemed only marginally important, may acquire a new centrality; and that what a society once took for granted may again become open to controversy. In this sense, the death warrant of every political culture is written on its birth certificate. That unmaking of a political culture, in response to changes in a society's unique definition of the human predicament and human destiny, is, of course, another story.

REFERENCES

1. Historical societies are not necessarily societies with a sense of linear history. Indian society, for instance, seems almost ahistorical to many because of its concept of cyclical time. There is a brief discussion of this in my "The Culture of Indian Politics: A Stock Taking," *Journal of Asian Studies,* 30 (1970), 57-80.

2. A recent review attempts to identify such civilizations. Roger W. Wescott, "The Enumeration of Civilizations," *History and Theory,* 9 (1970), 59-85.

3. Examples of empirical works based on these two complementary "emphases" within a unified conceptual orientation to political culture are L. W. Pye, *Personality, Politics, and Nation Building* (New Haven: Yale University Press, 1962); and G. A. Almond and S. Verba, *Civic Culture* (Princeton: Princeton University Press, 1963).

4. This position is compatible with the new neo-Freudian concept of culture as a collective defense. See a review of the latter position in B. J. Bergen and S. D. Rosenberg, "The New Neo-Freudians, Psychoanalytic Dimensions of Social Change," *Psychiatry,* 34 (1971), 19-39. Another similar conceptualization of culture at the level of small groups is in W. R. Bion, *Experience in Groups* (London: Tavistock, 1961). The present conceptualization, however, imputes greater maneuverability, self-

correction, and information-seeking to the society. Such processes can be seen as analogous to what at the individual level is "insight."

5. There is an enormous literature on the role of themes, traditions, and world views in politics. Nonetheless, these theme-by-theme analyses have given confusing and incomplete results. To begin with, any theme associated with politically developed statehood was considered "modern" and was sought in less fortunate nation-states with the zeal of a trained sleuth. Now the emphasis has shifted to the particular "mixes" of tradition and modernity which characterize politics at different developmental stages. Probably it is time to give more attention to the societal modes or methods of coping with traditions or themes, with reference to issues such as the extent of sanctity attaching to norms, the totalism of the traditional system, the importance and sanctity given to artificial or recreated history in addition to actual history, the society's ability to add new traditions to its original mass of traditions and its ability to particularize or traditionalize new elements, the ease with which in a society dysfunctional elements can be detraditionalized, the extent to which the society can draw upon different subtraditions within it or play one subculture against another, the tolerance of contradictory or unrelated norms coexisting in the polity, and the tolerance of normative ambiguity and chaos. Emphasis on these processes may make societies seem more like self-correcting systems and less like reactive, programmed organisms.

6. Elsewhere ("Culture of Indian Politics"), I have attempted to show how even such enduring themes as pacifism, consensualism, and cyclical time have carried different meanings at different periods of history, with each meaning greatly influenced by the political challenges facing the society at a given point.

7. The best illustration of this is certainly the epic Mahabharata. See M. N. Dutt, *A Prose English Translation of the Mahabharata* (Calcutta: Das, 1905); also R. Shamasastry, trans., *Kautilya's Arthasastra* (Mysore: Wesleyan Mission, 1923).

8. Rajni Kothari, *Politics in India* (Boston: Little-Brown, 1970), chap. 7.

9. On the concept of *dharma,* see P. V. Kane, *History of Dharmashastra,* vol. III (Poona: Bhandarkar Oriental Research Institute, 1946).

10. See a brief discussion of compartmentalization in M. Singer, "The Modernization of Religious Beliefs," in M. Weiner, ed., *Modernization* (New York: Basic Books, 1966), pp. 55-67.

11. The private symbolic associations of power at different levels of personality, expressed particularly as the fear of loss of potency and virility, are described in G. M. Carstairs, *The Twice Born* (Bloomington: Indiana University Press, 1957); and P. Spratt, *Hindu Culture and Personality* (Bombay: Manaktalas, 1966).

12. A. L. Basham, "Some Fundamental Political Ideas of Ancient India," *Studies in Indian History and Culture* (Calcutta: Sambodhi, 1964), pp. 57-71.

13. Hinduism, when it comes to social ethics, is individualistic with a vengeance. Religious values, as opposed to sacred rituals, are a matter of lonely pursuit. It lacks in this respect the collectivist orientation of Christianity and Islam.

14. It has been said that Indian cultural products are remarkably free from any expression of the oedipal hostility toward paternal authority. See Dhirendra Narayan, *Hindu Character* (Bombay: Bombay University Press, 1957). I leave it to the psychologically-minded reader to decide if this orientation could have been gen-

eralized to the political authorities—if they were also seen, at some level, as distant powers with whom one did not compete or quarrel, but tried to establish a *modus vivendi*.

15. See an interesting discussion of this in the context of Gandhi in Lloyd and Susanne Rudolph, *The Modernity of Traditions* (Chicago: University of Chicago Press, 1967), part 2.

16. In *Politics in India*, Kothari considers this tolerance of hyprocrisy to provide an important clue to the contemporary culture of Indian politics. This can also be explained in terms of the cultural tendency to pitch ideals too high for realization by the lesser mortals. See the Rudolphs, *The Modernity of Traditions*, part 2; K. P. Gupta, "A Theoretical Approach to Hinduism and Modernization of India," and "A Rejoinder," *Indian Journal of Sociology*, 2 (1971), 59-91, 213-216.

17. The most interesting attempt to work out the implications of consensualism in institutional terms is J. P. Narayan, *Swaraj for the People* (Varanasi: A.B.S.S., 1961); see also R. Kothari, "India: Oppositions in a Consensual Polity," in R. A. Dahl, ed., *Regimes and Oppositions* (New Haven: Yale University Press, forthcoming).

18. The metaphysical position from which this drew strength was *advaita* or monism. See a more detailed discussion of the political implications of this theme in my "Culture of Indian Politics."

19. This has been one of the main obstacles to the integration of the Islamic tradition in the mainstream of Indian politics. Islam is a politically conscious religion. It cannot give in on politics. Also, unlike Hinduism, it has a universalist core which competes with the secular universalism that political development assumes. Non-proselytizing Hinduism is truly particularist.

20. On the traditional concept of activism as *inter alia*, a characteristic of the feminine component of the godhead and of one's feminine self, see a brief discussion in my "Conformity and Defiance in Science: The Identity of Jagadis Chandra Bose," *Science Studies*, 2 (1972), 31-85.

Also suggestive is the ease with which "progressive" legislation is passed in India (the constitutional provisions for the untouchables, the Hindu code bill, radical economic measures, etc.) and the difficulty with which they are implemented, a difficulty which over the decades has generated a virtual "implementation crisis" in the society.

21. This apparently is comparable with some aspects of the Chinese political culture as analyzed by L. W. Pye, *The Spirit of Chinese Politics* (Cambridge: M.I.T. Press, 1968); and R. J. Lifton, *Revolutionary Immortality* (London: Weidenfeld and Nicholson, 1969).

22. On the role of intellectuals in the Indian polity, see E. Shils, "Influence and Withdrawal: The Intellectual in Indian Political Development," in D. Marwick, ed., *Political Decision-Makers* (Glencoe: Free Press, 1961), pp. 25-29. See also S. Tangri, "Intellectuals and Society in the Nineteenth Century," *Comparative Studies in Society and History*, 3 (1961), 368-394.

23. Whatever its end result, it was perhaps necessary for a few men to break away more or less entirely from the existing modes of living and thinking to look more dispassionately at their own society. And, these men *did* provide an intellectual basis for the integration of new cultural elements, for defining the challenge facing the society in intelligible terms, and for the alteration and reinterpretation of the

indigenous culture. Most important of all, their very activism was a living protest against the shared identity of the literati, who conceived of intellectual activity as an instrument of self-knowledge and personal salvation only.

24. A case study of the way in which the Gandhian style of political mobilization not only undercut the earlier liberal universalism, but also ultimately forced it to reveal its clay feet is J. Broomfield, *Elite Conflict in a Plural Society* (Bombay: Oxford University Press, 1968).

25. An indirect discussion, in the context of Gujarat, of the new role which Gandhi offered the intellectuals is in A. Bhatt, "Caste and Political Mobilization in a Gujarat District," in R. Kothari, ed., *Caste in Indian Politics* (New Delhi: Orient Longmans, 1970).

26. The antagonism towards the intellectuals has a history. The hostility of the intellectuals to the Gandhian movement was pronounced. They had taken their defeat in participatory politics in bad grace. Not only were they mostly outside the mainstream of political movements, but they also frequently led movements based on exogenous models of social engineering. These memories have persisted.

27. The political isolation of intellectuals is not, however, an indicator of low social status. If anything, with the spread of Brahminic norms, the intellectual has perhaps improved his social standing.

28. See a discussion of this in E. R. Leach, "What Should We Mean by Caste," in E. R. Leach, ed., *Aspects of Caste in South India, Ceylon and North-West Pakistan* (Cambridge: Cambridge University Press, 1960); Andre Beteille, "The Politics of Non-Antagonistic Strata," *Contributions to Indian Sociology*, New Series, no. 3, 1969; Kothari, *Caste in Indian Politics*. A systematic review of the caste-politics relationship is D. L. Sheth, "Caste and Politics," in R. Kothari, ed., *Survey of Political Science in India* (New Delhi: I.C.S.S.R., forthcoming). One result of this new relationship between politics and social hierarchy has been the rise of certain traditional groupings in social status. The anti-elitist bias brought into politics by these groups has been discussed in a later section.

29. To continue with the example of caste, there were caste systems of celestial bodies, gods, soils, temples, and gems, in addition to that of men. N. K. Bose, *Culture and Society in India* (Bombay: Asia Publishing House, 1967), p. 237.

30. This distrust and cynicism had support in some aspects of the modal personality system. See Carstairs, *The Twice Born*, particularly pp. 40-45.

31. Example of such attempts are Ramohun Roy (1772-1883), *English Works and Bengali Works* (Calcutta: Sadharon Brahmo Samaj, 1947): Ishwar Chandra Vidyasagar (1820-1891), *Rachanabali* (Calcutta: Mandal Book, 1966); Bankim Chandra Chatterji (1838-1894), *Rachanabali* (Calcutta: Sahitya Samsad, 1958); Swami Vivekananda (1863-1902), *Complete Works* (Calcutta: Advaita Ashram, 1964); and an account of such an attempt by Dayananda Saraswati (1824-1883), in Lajpat Rai, *Arya Samaj* (Calcutta: Orient Longmans, 1967).

32. The most succinct description of this process is of course in M. N. Srinivas, *Social Change in Modern India* (Berkeley: University of California Press, 1966).

33. The British, who were then yet to recover from the shock of discovering themselves the rulers of a continental land mass, tended to leave the social and religious systems untouched, to alter only the economic system, to recognize the Indian elites

as legitimate participants in the polity and—to the limited extent a ruling group can think so—as their equals. In fact, in the case of each reform, the British consolidated through legal measures, often after decades, the gains of the reformers only after their movements had acquired substantial momentum. This ambivalence ensured some support to the reformers, while containing the anxiety of the traditionalists.

At first it may seem paradoxical that it was the so-called core of the Hindu society, religion, which faced the first attack of men who themselves were supposedly the core carriers of Hindu traditions. Perhaps it was the sheer salience of religion in the society; perhaps it was the unorganized nature of Hinduism which made it look vulnerable and amendable to reform; perhaps it was merely the old hat of institutional rigidity and ideological pliability of Brahminism.

34. These were not always functional. The folkways were, after all, in some respects more responsive to changes in environment; the texts, from which these values mostly came, were less so. The Rudolphs, in *The Modernity of Traditions*, part 3, for instance, describe how the wholesale acceptance of such Brahminic norms did freeze the legal system around a stagnant concept of indigenous law.

35. For a study of an individual caught in the hinges of this process, see my "Defiance and Conformity in Science."

36. The growth of newspapers, in which again Roy and the Christian missionaries played important roles, also made religious issues live for a large number of elites. Brajendra Nath Banerji, *Sangbād Petrè Sekāler Katha*, vols. I and II (Calcutta: Bangya Sahitya Parishad, 1949); and Binoy Ghose, *Samayik Patrè Bānglār Samāj Chitra*, vols. I-IV (Calcutta: Bengal Publishers, 1962-1966). Unfortunately both the works are in Bengali.

37. Bankim Chandra Chatterji, "Babu" (1873), *Rachanabali*, vol. II, pp. 10-12. I have taken slight liberties with the translation, to eliminate the more abstruse allusions and the involved nineteenth-century Bengali sentences.

38. A fascinating attempt at self-esteem building on these lines was by Swami Vivekananda; see his *Prāchya o Prāschatya* (1900-1902) (Almora: Advaita Ashram, no date). The complex meaning of Hinduization of politics which began in this phase has been analyzed by Gupta, "A Theoretical Approach to Hinduism and Modernization of India" and "A Rejoinder."

39. M. N. Srinivas, *Social Change in Modern India;* also *Caste in Modern India and Other Essays* (Bombay: Asia Publishing House, 1962).

40. Stephen Hay, "Introduction," in Rammohun Roy, *Dialogue Between a Theist and an Idolator* (Calcutta: Firma K. L. Mukhopadhya, 1963).

41. The Rudolphs discuss this in *The Modernity of Traditions*, part 2.

42. I have not dealt with Gandhi's saintly politics in detail because a number of excellent analyses have become available in recent years. The most ambitious of these, of course, is Erik H. Erikson, *Gandhi's Truth* (New York: W. W. Norton, 1969). On the remnants of the saintly style in contemporary India see G. Ostergaard and M. Currell, *The Gentle Anarchists* (Oxford: Clarendon, 1971).

43. See a detailed analysis of this in M. Wiener, "India: Two Political Cultures," in L. W. Pye and S. Verba, eds., *Political Culture and Political Development* (Princeton: Princeton University Press, 1965), pp. 199-244.

NUR YALMAN

Some Observations on Secularism in Islam: The Cultural Revolution in Turkey

Extreme forms of repudiation of the past . . . are the analogues of the complete destruction of the past—which in its cult form is expressed by destroying property . . . such as occurs in 'cargo cults' and in small apocalyptic cults in our own society. Only by the destruction of every vestige of the past can the new order be ushered in . . . this will turn out to be one of the universal characteristics of human psychology.

—Margaret Mead, *New Lives for Old*

Violence in the colonies does not only have for its aim the keeping of these enslaved men at arm's length, it seeks to dehumanize them. Everything will be done to wipe out their traditions, to substitute our language for theirs and to destroy their culture without giving them ours.

—Jean Paul Sartre, Preface to Franz Fanon, *The Wretched of the Earth*

Will we recover? Yes, for violence, like Achilles' lance, can heal the wounds that it has inflicted.

—Jean Paul Sartre, *Ibid.*

Tradition and Revolution

THE SOCIAL sciences depend upon "ideal types." This concept, which lies at the center of Max Weber's sociology, and was not unknown to Plato, provides simplified models of social reality for the theorist which sometimes permit a clearer view of facts under consideration. Traditional and modern, among others, are two of the most frequently used "ideal types."

Weber writes more specifically of "traditional authority" that "legitimacy is claimed first and believed in on the basis of the sanctity of the order and the attendant forms of control as they have been handed down from the past, 'have always existed.'"[1] The past, especially *continuity* with the past, is a critical part of the "traditional" model. Continuity in certain key institutions and certain vital principles is what anthropologists usually write of as "structure." Absolute changelessness, impossible in any case, is not a necessary condition of a "traditional" model, but, at the same time, a model based on continuity with the past cannot accommodate fundamental

139

changes in the fabric of social life and upheavals in the key institutions and fundamental principles of organization. Such fundamental changes may be termed revolutions, and anthropologists in the Durkheimian tradition have been singularly shy of approaching the roots of these troublesome problems.

Weber did not specifically use the traditional-modern dichotomy implied by Eisenstadt in his essay in this volume. He had a more complex model with a range from "traditional" to "various forms of 'rational' (rather than 'modern') authority." Without going into the important problems of *Wertrational* and *Zweckrational*,[2] it may be observed that most writers have found the traditional-modern dichotomy a useful starting point. There is frequently little agreement on just what "modern" means, so that H. A. R. Gibb for instance, writes bluntly: "The plain truth of the matter is that 'modernization' means 'Westernization.' "[3]

In the hands of Eisenstadt, the ideal type "modern" seems to imply a successful society, rationally organized in the direction of sustained economic growth, and politically stable as well. There is little doubt that such a conception of "modern" is ethnocentric in that it represents a certain "materialist" stream in Western thought. Weber would probably have said that it left values (*Wertrational*) too much out of the picture and was not sufficiently attuned to the problems of the creation of a "good" or "just" society. He had recognized that behavior could be "rationally" directed towards the enhancement of certain primary values which could themselves be religious, or ethical, or even political without necessarily being directed towards "economic growth."

However, the world is getting smaller, and in the 1970's it seems clear that nations themselves are increasingly judging each other by the criteria of "economic growth." In this sense there are numerous societies which have cut their moorings with their traditional pasts and yet have been unable to start their economic engines. The concept of "post-traditional" draws attention to these drifting vessels. It also draws attention to the problem of a possible relationship (or the lack of it) between moorings and engines.

I am concerned in this paper with the cutting of the moorings in certain Islamic countries. It was indeed thought in the nineteenth and early twentieth century in these Islamic lands that there was some basic relationship between the "conservatism" and "fatalism" of Islam and the economic stagnation in Islamic lands. It was thought that Islam was a fundamental obstacle to "progress" and that the first task was to break the hold of Islam on the masses so that "progress" would almost automatically follow.

It is noteworthy that the issue was seen by "modern" intellectuals, particularly in Turkey, in these Comteian terms. As a matter of fact, one of the major political parties had adopted the Comteian title of "Union and

Progress" after the 1908 upheavals in the Ottoman Empire. The gradualist solution of Japan or India in which elements of tradition were interwoven into elements of political, social, and economic reforms was in Turkey, at a certain point, rejected. It had been tried for nearly 100 years in the Ottoman Empire (throughout the nineteenth century) but had been found wanting. In the 1920's and 1930's what would now be called a "cultural revolution" of unprecedented proportions was unleashed. This suggests only that there are no final arrivals in history, and that just as it is possible for India in the future to reject the gradualist solution in favor of more radical departures, it is also possible for Turkey to return to an attempt to reestablish contact with the broken ends of her own traditions. The task is to make the social roots of these extraordinary moves more intelligible in as systematic a manner as possible.

These various attempts at self-directed culture change are of great interest. The gradualist solutions are, perhaps, not so difficult to comprehend, but the radical attempts at social surgery, the intensity of ideological commitment to what must appear to be distant Utopian goals, the resulting cleavages in social life, the damage to hallowed institutions, the hatred and bitterness engendered even within families, and the specter of civil war waxing and waning, do merit the term "cultural revolution." In a perceptive paper on Turkey, Charles Gallagher writes:

> The third type is the revolution which, although it may to some extent encompass features of the two preceding ones [i.e., "palace" and "colonial" revolutions], gushes forth with such energy from well springs of deep restlessness and discontent that it involves a retouching of cultural identity and a serious attempt to enter and participate in another civilization. . . . Historical changes engineer changes which may seem only technical at first, but which by the energy they unleash lead to a vast rearrangement of the most fundamental social values and reveal a will for a new social personality. Examples are few but pertinent, Japan, Turkey and possibly Communist China.[4]

These "cultural revolutions" present a fundamental challenge to contemporary, especially "structuralist," anthropology. What is the nature of this challenge?

"Structural Anthropology" and Revolution

Looking back to the period of the 1950's in anthropology, it is striking to see how much has changed. American anthropology was always a luxuriant growth, difficult to channel into neatly marked streams, but British anthropology was beginning to be formalized into fairly rigid categories. First there was the distinction between culture and social structure; then there was the classification of social structures, often in effect, based on the kinship model—patrilineal, matrilineal, bilateral, and so forth. Culture was treated as a residual category, and being messy, difficult to grasp, including, in the words of Radcliffe-Brown, "books, works of art, knowledge, skill, ideas, beliefs, tastes, sentiments," it was left to Americans. (Hence "cultural anthropology" and "social anthropology.") There were many, of course, who suspected that to say that the Nayar of South India (Hindu) have the same matrilineal structure as the Minankabau of Sumatra (Muslim), or the matrilineal Bemba of Africa was not really significant; nor did the observation that the Nambudiri Brahmin of South India trace descent through the male line help the anthropologist to understand much (or indeed anything) about the Kurds of the Middle East who also had patrilineal ideas. The "structural tool" was too blunt an instrument. In all of these cases, what was most interesting were all those features of these societies which made them most different.

Actually, the limits of "social structure" as a tool of analysis were most clear in connection with the confusing, unclear kinship systems of Southeast Asia. These limits were also evident in that the whole spectrum of faith, belief, ideology, and mythology became difficult to manage.

It is at this point that Claude Lévi-Strauss opened Pandora's box. It was a good moment. The party was getting dull. In the pell-mell rush to catch some of the exotic shapes that have emerged, anthropology has been left in sixes and sevens.

What did Levi-Strauss say that was so peculiar? Anyone who reads the "Introduction" of *The Elementary Structures of Kinship* cannot but be impressed by the incisiveness of the logic which propelled the man. He says that kinship behavior in some of its most exotic manifestations depends upon systems of "rules"—but how do these rules arise? Where do they come from? I cannot go into the detailed answer, but it is in this roundabout manner that Lévi-Strauss succeeded in altering the deeply ingrained "behaviorist" bias in anthropology, and found his way back to a systematic study of "culture."[5]

I recall his lectures on the "Structural Study of Myth" at Cambridge in 1954. These are now widely regarded as classics. At that time, there was almost complete incomprehension, and total rejection of what was regarded as a preposterous French attempt to be more subtle by half than anyone else.

Why was the attempt so preposterous? This was so because Lévi-Strauss seemed to claim that "structure" did not exist at the level of action and behavior, but at the level of "thought." He seemed to argue that he could find "structures" in the mental processes of primitive peoples without being concerned with their "sociological" realities. He seemed to argue that the realm of mythology was worthy of investigation and attention *per se*, even if it did not relate too closely or immediately to social organization.

At a later date he was to speak more directly of this distinction between mental life and social organization.[6] He then used Marxist terminology: superstructures and infrastructures. In Marxist terms, it is the infrastructure which has primacy and which, in a complex manner, "determines" the superstructure. Thus, religious belief and thought are merely a reflection of the structure of power and domination in society. Lévi-Strauss, however, has called himself a "transcendental" Marxist: a phrase which should be repeated with some caution in the land of Thoreau and Emerson. The intention at least is to suggest, first, that the Marxist distinction is useful, and second, that it is not simply a matter of one level "determining" the other, but of a complex feedback between infrastructure and superstructure. While Lévi-Strauss has expressed himself in this vein in some private letters, in his publications he appears to be less and less interested in infrastructures and more and more drawn towards the analysis of superstructures.[7] Both *La Pensée Sauvage* and his tomes on the mythology of South America are mainly concerned with the "structure of customary thought." The question he has posed is: what are the internal and categorical constraints which channel the mythology of these peoples into predictable combinations and permutations of recognizable forms? This categorical scheme is like a kitchen utensil which cuts potatoes and carrots into certain set shapes.

Note, however, that even though Lévi-Strauss is writing suggestively of thought, of ideas, of ideas governing action like formulas governing mechanical tools, he does not say much about social or cultural change. I find most of Lévi-Strauss' writing on change to be various ways of evading certain key issues. The now notorious distinction between hot and cold societies is hardly a serious contribution to science, even though it shows Lévi-Strauss' predilection for culinary metaphors. Other suggestions to be found in various parts of his writings hint at tensions between certain categories of kinsmen which are glossed over, or "mediated" by mythology. This is again suggestive of Marxist thoughts—"religion is the opium of the people"—but the examples are not particularly illuminating.

In a footnote of criticism on G. Balandier he has expressed himself more fully on the problem of change and has revealed himself as a dyed-in-the-wool cultural conservative:

Au début d'une récente étude, G. Balandier annonce avec fracas qu'il est grand temps, pour la science sociale, de "saisir la société dans sa vie même et dans son devenir." Après quoi il décrit, de façon d'ailleurs très pertinente, des institutions dont le but est, selon ses propres termes, de "regrouper" des lignages menacés par la dispersion; de "corriger" leur émiettement; de "rappeler" leur solidarité, "d'établir" une communication avec les ancêtres, "d'empêcher que les membres disjoints du clan ne deviennent étrangers les uns aux autres," de fournir "un instrument de protection contre les conflits," de "contrôler" et de "maîtriser" les antagonismes et les renversements, au moyen d'un rituel "minutieusement réglé" qui est "un facteur de renforcement des structures sociales et politiques." On sera facilement d'accord avec lui, tout en doutant qu'il le soit luimême avec ses prémisses, pour reconnaître que des institutions, dont il avait commencé par contester qu'elles fussent fondées sur des "rapports logiques" et des "structures fixées" (p. 23) démontrent en fait la "prévalence de la logique sociale traditionnelle" (p. 33) et que "le système classique révèle ainsi durant une longue période, une surprenante capacité 'assimilatrice'" (p. 34). Dans tout cela, il n'y a de "surprenant" que la surprise de l'auteur.[8]

This may be called the gyroscopic theory of culture. We are asked to recognize a built-in tendency, almost an aesthetic sense of balance, which keeps ordering and reordering society, bringing the ship back on course after a buffeting by the forces of nature or history.

It seems to me that the question of social and cultural change, and especially radical ideological change, is still a major challenge now that Lévi-Strauss has cleared away some of the debris. Lévi-Strauss' contribution is essentially a contribution to "continuity." It is, therefore, all the more important to understand the nature and forms of ideological discontinuity in society. Hence this paper on secularism in Islam, and hence the interest in the momentous changes taking place in the community of Islam around the world.

The subject of social and ideological change is a preeminently anthropological subject. It is also one in which anthropologists have revealed themselves to be ostriches with their heads in the sands. It is difficult to read many monographs on the Middle East without being struck by the isolation of the anthropologists from the main currents of the time. The same is true of our work on Ceylon: there is not a hint of the tornado of Ché Guevara'ism that hit the island in April, 1971 in any of the dozens of monographs and Ph.D. theses written on this island in recent years.[9] Neither Malinowsky, nor Kroeber, nor Evans-Pritchard and Fortes, nor indeed the Wilsons, whose theoretical book *The Analysis of Social Change* was at one point much celebrated, had prepared us for the tidal wave of politics, anomie, revolution, and civil war which hit Asia and Africa so soon after the ebb of Imperial power.

The Decline of Islam

I turn now to discuss some of these momentous issues in the context of Islam.

M. Mahdi, in his remarkable study of Ibn Khaldun, observes that the picture of Islam in the fourteenth century is one of general decline and disintegration:

A few areas, notably South West Persia, Egypt and Muslim Spain were able to preserve some vestiges of what was once a dynamic expansive civilization. Western North Africa, where Ibn Khaldun grew up, was the worst part of the Islamic world. It presented a spectacle of chaos and desolation.[10]

With this background, it is not surprising that Ibn Khaldun should have been interested in the social reasons for the rise and fall of cultures. As is well known, his ideas on the role of "prophets" heralds Weber's ideas of "charismatic" leaders.

Mahdi writes of the fourteenth century. By the nineteenth century, the Turkish poet Ziya Paşa was to draw a similar picture of the House of Islam in some famous passages. There are many Muslims now who would say that conditions are only marginally better (perhaps worse) in the Islamic world since the nineteenth century. And as far as chaos is concerned, it reigns supreme at the level of ideology. On the one hand, we have Muslim leaders in secular Turkey claiming that *riba*, the taking of fixed interest on loan capital, is against the Qur'an and a sin just like adultery and prostitution; on the other hand, we have religious men in Pakistan saying that to see a true Islamic state in operation, there is no point in searching around in ancient texts—all one has to do is to see China, not the China of Taiwan, but that of Chairman Mao Tse Tung. For, it is said, Islam in the last resort is the vehicle for the creation of a community of equals. There are other elements in this puzzle, too, such as Prof. Erbakan, the leader of a right-wing party in Turkey, who wants to replace the works of Émile Durkheim in the Turkish public schooling system with those of the famous mystic Al-Ghazzali (who died in 1111).[11] On the total confusion, all would agree. Aziz Ahmad writes of Pakistan, for instance: "The situation is confused because the Western intelligentsia is as ignorant of Islamic religion and history as the ulema and the conservatives are of the pressures, stresses and challenges of the modern . . . civilization."[12]

What remains remarkable is the continuing attachment of the masses to the symbols and rituals of Islam. At times this attachment takes the form of a yearning for the Sharia, the legal code according to the Qur'an. At other times, the yearning for Islam produces movements around charismatic leaders, Seykhs, who can create in a *tariqat* (brotherhood) a sense of belonging, an Islamic community, a sense of legitimacy of the spiritual order which may appear to be lacking in the outside world. These *tariqat* are very much part of the social scene, even in a supposedly alien and godless republic like Turkey. They represent small-scale attempts to reproduce a particular understanding of the Islamic community in microcosm. I will not deal with the brotherhoods here, but they appear to be active aboveground or underground from Bosnia to Indonesia.

The attachment to the Sharia as a symbol is often cited as an example of the force of conservatism in Islam. Here the problem is more difficult. Some European jurists see it as follows:

Traditional Islamic ideology requires the total submission of man, in every aspect of his life on earth, to the divine will of Allah. Every Muslim, therefore, in theory is bound by the comprehensive system of duties, covering all human acts and relationships which represents the dictates of the divine will and which is termed the Sharia. As a code of behaviour the Shariat has a much wider scope and purpose than a simple legal system in the Western sense of the term. Not only does it regulate in meticulous detail the ritual practices of the faith such as prayer, fasting, alms and pilgrimage, but many of its precepts are also directed solely at the individual's conscience. . . . We are dealing with . . . a composite scheme of religious duties and morality, all of which is "law" in the Islamic sense and the ultimate purpose of which is to secure divine favour both in this world and in the hereafter.[13]

With thirteen centuries of accretions, elaborations, and adaptations from the Mongol Yasa Codes, with accommodations to local custom, such as the matrilineal codes of the Muslim Tamils in Ceylon and the Miangka-bau of Sumatra, the actual application of these "traditional models" represents many complexities for the community.

Note also that there is no place for secularism in this traditional conception. The dictionary definition of "secularist" is: "One who . . . rejects every form of religious faith or worship, and undertakes to live accordingly; also one who believes that education and other civil matters should be without a religious element." "Secularity" is defined as the character of being non-religious or divorced from religion. "Laic" is defined as "pertaining to a layman or the laity; lay, secular." "Laicize" means "to secularize; to put under the direction of or open to, laymen."[14] As Mahdi writes:

In Islam it is doctrinally essential that religion should not merely have an external concern with worldly affairs . . . or clearly distinguish between affairs of the Spirit and the affairs of the World. None of these would suffice. Religion itself must be politicized. This is the historical basis which led Muslim philosophers and Ibn Khaldun to reflect upon Islam and the Islamic community as a political regime.[15]

But there have been severe setbacks precisely in the day-to-day application of Islamic law. In much of the Middle East, the immediate background of the modern legal systems goes back to the nineteenth century Tanzimat reforms in the Ottoman Empire. These reforms started with the constitutional reforms of 1839, and developed further with a new commercial code in 1850, a penal code in 1858, a code of commercial procedure in 1861, and a code of maritime commerce in 1863 mostly based on French models. These codes involved a new system of courts, and by the end of the nineteenth century the Sharia courts had become essentially restricted to matters concerned with family law. A similar development appears to have taken place in Egypt. Under the Khedive Ismail, mixed courts were set up in 1875 and "native" courts in 1883. These applied civil and penal codes of French inspiration.

In India the situation was both simpler and more complex. After 1765, as the British progressively enlarged their jurisdiction, the Sharia law which they took over from the Moguls was gradually restricted in its application. By the middle of the nineteenth century, as Christians ruling over Muslims, they had also restricted the applications of the Sharia to family law.

This gradual restriction in the scope of Sharia law in the direction of family law is significant. It suggests, first, that governments have found it increasingly difficult to handle the problems in accordance with the strict interpretation of "traditional" law and have had to find ways and means to new legislation; and second, that, notwithstanding the great changes which have come about in the public affairs of Muslim states, the field of the family has remained relatively traditional and therefore still within the possible jurisdiction of the Sharia. It is not my intention here to follow the changes in the sphere of the family law even though these too are extensive; the new code in Tunisia may be said to have opened the famous door of the Ijdihat (independent interpretation) once again, after the Turks had, so to speak, exploded a bomb in front of this mythical door with their new European-inspired legislation during the Turkish Revolution in the 1920's.

It is in the field of constitutional law that the major problems have arisen. Where is the fountain of legitimacy in a Muslim state? The Qur'an? Or the people? Who is the sovereign? The people, or God? And who is to interpret this sovereign? Legislative assemblies somehow elected? Or the Ulema who have traditionally interpreted the body of Islamic teachings?

An "Ideological" State

This question is of more than mere academic interest. It has kept more than 100 million people in constant agitation in Pakistan ever since the separation from India. The tragic story of Bengla Desh is only a new twist in the desperate struggle of Islam in politics. The dimensions of the problem go far beyond the limits of Pakistan. It comes up insistently in Turkey, together with paranoic fears of what would happen if the Islamists, so-called, were to grab power. There are, perhaps, four political parties in the Islamic corner of the political spectrum who claim that they would like to create an Islamic state in Turkey. With all their sincerity, it is perhaps good that they do not know much about the ideological impasses of Pakistan.

An important Pakistani scholar[16] has written that Pakistan is an "ideological state." This means that Pakistan is to be governed by the goals and values laid down by Islam. "This . . . implies that Pakistan has these principles, policies, and program goals fully worked out on Islamic grounds which (will be implemented and embodied in a Constitution) just as various Communist parties, for example, have their goals and policies worked out in Communist terms—since Communist ideology too is total and not partial—so have the Pakistani Muslims worked out Islam."[17]

Rahman suggests that, in actual fact, Islamic imperatives are far from well-known and already agreed upon, and that it is not merely a matter of these imperatives being implemented, but also a question of discovery and agreement—which is another matter altogether. He continues: "When . . . we turn to the two Constitutions actually enacted [and abrogated] we are surprised to find that none of the things mentioned [above—viz. that Islam is well known and the imperatives worked out—none of this] is true; on the contrary, it is startling to find a) that Islam appears in these constitutions an item among a host of other matters . . . and b) that where Islam does appear it appears essentially *as a limitation,* as a "bounding" or limiting concept rather than as a positive or creative factor whence positive results are derived as values, goals or programs for human progress and enrichment." There are even stronger indictments bringing these endeavors of Pakistan into the target area of the Turkish "secularists," as we shall see.

Rahman writes: "The statements about the Islamicization of Law, particularly in the 1956 Constitution (clause 198.3), also strongly suggest that 'Islamicization' means bringing the existing law into conformity with *something that existed in the past.* In view of the fact that Islam is not yet 'there' in Pakistan, some . . . have suggested that Pakistan be designated only as a 'Muslim [not Islamic] Republic,' for the time being just as Communist states call themselves 'Socialist [not Communist] states.' The fundamental difference between the two . . . is that whereas Communism is *future-oriented,* Islam [as envisioned in Pakistan] is essentially *past-oriented.*"[18]

These are very serious observations regarding the nature of "Models." They must be seen in the context of the creation of Pakistan out of heterogeneous Muslim groups in the Indian subcontinent. Their common identity was forged both in the struggle against the Hindus and against the British, the very powers which demolished the Mogul Empire; these facts of history form important strands in the identity of Muslims in India.

The very identity of the new state was thus fed by deeply conservative groups who had preserved Islam in the days of its subjugation. The anti-British Ulema who maintained their conservative stand in the Deoband seminary, as one organized group, were both in close touch with the Muslim masses and mindful that the traditions had to be safe-guarded and maintained uncontaminated by Europeans. Together with this severely conservative reaction of certain groups, this instinctive withdrawal and turning inwards like a threatened procupine—an attitude repeated in the deep conservatism of many Islamic communities in their relation with Europeans from Kazan in Russia to Morocco in Africa—there was in Pakistan the political problem of how to bring together diverse Muslim groups who represented many facets of the thousands of caste and language categories of India. In this respect, the political expediency of the strong protestations of Islam is transparent. It was only Islam which held together Punjabi, Sindi, Baluchi, Pathan, Bengali, Bihari, and many others, not to mention the castes. It remained the only principle whereby West Pakistan maintained its military hold on East Bengal. It is said by certain intellectuals of Pakistan that Turkey and Egypt, with their firmly based national identities, can well afford to become "secular," but that "secularism" in Pakistan— interpreted as the abandonment of the attempt to set up an Islamic state based on an Islamic constitution—would mean the dissolution of the entity called Pakistan. The idea of a nation here is still in the process of being hammered out.

We may observe in this highly instructive case an attempt to return to the sacred mainspring of the culture in order to imbibe its strength and to reestablish a nation on the basis of an ancient and hallowed model. It is a typical case of emergence from the colonial twilight. The issue is the reestablishment of an identity—a Muslim identity. It will be readily observed that in such precarious conditions there can be no thought of a rechanneling of the cultural mainstreams of Islam. No attempt can be made to effect fundamental alterations in the sense of identity of the culture. Radical departures may, of course, still be in store for the future.[19]

An Anti-Scientific Ideology

If the colonial experience strengthened the desire to hold fast to symbols and principles of distinctive identity, how have the forgotten Muslims of the Soviet Union fared? Has Communism proved to be the solvent to melt the sense of distinctive identity? How has a universalist religion like Islam fared in its immersion into the universalist sea of Communism? We cannot go into more than a hint of the extraordinary issues here. Alexandre Bennigsen and Lemercier-Qulquejay end their brilliant study with, "there can be no doubt that the long period of isolation experienced by Soviet Islam from 1920 to 1960 is nearing its end. Is it probable that the years ahead will put the Muslims of the Soviet Union in the forefront of events? Formerly a mere cog in the internal development of the USSR, they are now in a fair way to becoming one of the major subjects of world policy."[20]

It is now estimated that there are about 40 million Muslims, 75 per cent Turkic speakers, in the Soviet Union. Islam has been under constant attack since the establishment of Russian rule over the Muslims. The Czarist period is characterized by missionary attacks on Islam which, with the Communist revolution, give way with certain noteworthy periods of respite to Communist attacks. " . . . All Soviet theoreticians insist that the campaign against the Muslim religion must continue," since "the attitude of the [Clergy] is one thing, and the essence of religion, which has been and always will be anti-scientific and profoundly inimical to Marxist-Leninist ideology, is another."

"Islam for the Marxist is 'the opium of the people,' a reactionary and anti-scientific ideology giving a fanciful and fallacious notion of society." At times these theoreticians wax almost poetic: Islam is a "primitive and fantastic religion," "a chaotic mixture of Christian, Jewish and pagan doctrines" founded "by a member of the feudal trading classes of Mecca with the object of providing a religious pretext for the plundering expeditions organized by the Arab aristocracy." In its social and cultural aspect Islam is "one of the most reactionary religions in the world"; "it has impeded all reform and has retarded the evolution of Turkestan" by preaching "the unconditional submission of the believer to fate and to his oppressors."[21] The Qur'an is a code of "injustice and inequality," and the Sharia is "a collection of laws among the most unjust which the world has ever seen."

This obviously rich vein of polemic has also been used by Chinese communists in Tibet by arguing that the Buddha, too, was a mere thief and a plunderer, lower even than a reactionary chauvinist nationalist.[22]

What is fascinating in the Communist attack is that it is meticulously organized for culture change. The party, the regional branches of the Marx-Engels, Lenin Institute, and the Ministries of Culture are involved. There is also now "The Association for the Spread of Political and Scientific Knowledge" which has taken over the tasks of the pre-war "Union of Godless Zealots." Bennigsen and Lemercier-Quelquejay provide marvelous figures: the Kazakh branch, with 15 regional and 209 urban sections, had under its control 815 propaganda bureaus. It organized in the space of three years, 30,528 public lectures of which 23,000 were devoted to anti-religious subjects. In Uzbekistan, the Association held more than 10,000 anti-religious lectures in 1951. In Turkmenistan, in 1963, the same Association held 5,000 anti-Islamic lectures. On top of this, it is coyly added, "anti-religious propagandists try to reach believers in their homes, where they oblige them to engage in private conversations." These efforts are apparently considered insufficient by the Soviet authorities. There appears to be much complaint that religious superstitions and even *tarikat* are of increasing importance.

The surface manifestations of Islam are subdued. In 1913 it was estimated that Russian Islam was served by 26,279 mosques, excluding Bukhara and Khiva. By 1942 these were reduced to 1,312 according to official bulletins. By 1964 it was reported that the number in Central Asia and Kazakhstan had fallen to about 250. The numbers for the clergy are 45,339 without Bukhara and Khiva before the Revolution in 1917. Bertold Spuler calculates their number for 1955 to be 8,052, which recent writers think has been further reduced.

Even so, G. E. Wheeler writes that, with all the disappearance of the outward manifestations, "it may be doubted . . . whether Islam is any less ingrained in the hearts and minds of the Muslims of Central Asia than it is elsewhere, for example, in Turkey and Persia."[23] Russian ethnographers at least do not fail to detect the tell-tale signs: 100 per cent observance of the rites of circumcision, for instance, or the absence of a single case of intermarriage between Russians and Muslims in the city of Ashkabad in the last 50 years, and other similar hints.

Models of the Past and Future

Here again we have an extraordinary example of induced culture change. We have the cadres and the doctrines of the new order which are forced, regimented, and rammed down the throats of the ignorant proletariat by their enlightened leaders, yet there are at least questions and doubts as to the direction of where this particularly interesting example of culture change is in fact heading.

The fervent ideals of Pakistan on the one hand, and scientific strivings of Marxist-Leninist cadres (Godless Zealots or not) on the other, set the wings of the stage in which contemporary Islam exists. Culture change does not come alone; it comes in the context of politics. Power relations are of the essence. It comes with organized groups, cadres, systems of education, internal dissension, and, probably, with the unpredictable appearance of creative and gifted men who can wrap the mantle of charisma, already prepared and ready to be offered by an expectant community, around themselves. In more mundane language, this is the "personality cult"; Ibn Khaldun spoke of them as "prophets." Arthur Koestler, Aldous Huxley, George Orwell (*1984* is almost upon us) had, of course, fully warned us of this form of "culture change," the kind that involves organized attempts at "double-talk" and "double-think," but it is obvious that as anthropologists we had not taken them sufficiently seriously.

The fact remains that the two major models of culture, one oriented to the past, and the other oriented to the future, exert subtle influences on the body politic: the "past" and Islam are inevitably conservative and the "future" and Communism open a path to self-righteous radicalism.

Disillusion with the Past

The situation in Turkey has elements of both the Soviet picture and that of Pakistan, yet it is unlike either in one crucial respect. In the above cases, we have the fact of colonial domination (for that is certainly what the Soviet case is, though the conspiracy of silence regarding Central Asia is almost eerie) and its attendant repercussions: the conservative reaction, the symptoms of withdrawal, the anxious protection of cultural identity, the surrounding of the community with a wall of aggression. The colonial aspect is weak in Turkey. To be sure, the Ottoman Empire was dismembered at the end of World War I, but the immediate experience of direct foreign domination was a brief one, restricted to the so-called Armistice at the end of World War I. This lack of domination, which, however, went hand in hand with an inability to dominate the European powers, had had a devastating and debilitating effect on Ottoman institutions.

In the frenetic self-examination to find and arrest the reasons for the continuing weakness of the Ottoman Empire, generations of intellectuals subjected their own institutions to the most devastating self-criticism. Reforms were undertaken by the Ottoman administration—often in the teeth of popular discontent—to alter the institutions of the Empire and bring them into line with European models. The reforms generated reactions, uprisings, downfalls of Sultans, or Grand Viziers, and much rolling of heads. Much of the Ottoman history of the nineteenth century is recounted in Turkish historiography as a progressive, contrapuntal development towards modern, I should say "Western," institutions. Moreover, the contrapuntal movement is seen to be generated by champions of reform and reaction who are placed on an equal horizontal footing. Prof. Tunaya's writing, for instance, is characteristic.[24] He discusses intellectual men on both sides of the Reformist-Reactionist divide. (The same division is also spoken of as the Secularist [Modernist] as opposed to the Islamicist groups.) In my opinion, the presentation of this issue as a simple *Kulturkampf* obscures the vital sociological dimension of these movements. In this model of reform and reaction there is also a vertical, hierarchical, social class dimension. The Ottoman reformists were almost invariably members of the elite, often in the Civil Service, generally well educated, and in some respect at least, men who had experienced some form of the domination of the Europeans over the Empire. The reaction, on the other hand, had deeper roots. It was said to draw support from the general, relatively ignorant, rather conservative masses. In this sense, then, the reforms undertaken by the members of the elite ruling institutions were rather like a sonar, a depth sounder, on a boat: they would send shock waves down into the masses, and would listen to the echo. Depending on the kind of shock the masses received, the echo would also be appropriately stunning.

At some point these Ottoman intellectual reformers got the idea that if they did not have to contend with these reactions, especially the reactions based on religious grounds, on some infringement of the Sharia rules, they would be more effective. It is at this time that they discovered the "scientific" attitude toward religion. Some simply state this bluntly: "Quand les peuples ont attent un certain degré de culture se débarassent naturellement de la religion"—a chance remark by an Ottoman in a preface to a book entitled *L'Effort Ottoman* (Paris, 1907). We need hardly go back to Proudhon and Comte for the paternity of these ideas.[25] Scientific non-religion fitted the intentions of these reformers. Some were obviously so dissatisfied with Ottoman institutions that they were ready to throw them over for something new. These reformist ideas could not be stated very openly in the Ottoman parliament. Riza Nur, in his recently discovered—and already banned—memoirs, describes how certain hints in Parliament by the philosopher Riza Tevfik, that the Ottomans had a history before they became Muslims, and that the Turks were probably Maenickean and Buddhist at some time in their history, are shouted down as he is made to beat a hasty retreat with his life in some danger.[26] However, Riza Nur, member of the Ottoman Parliament, later member of the Nationalist Parliament in Ankara, Delegate of Mustafa Kemal to Moscow and the second ranking delegate at the peace negotiations at Lausanne with Inonu, is himself a man of particular interest. His memoirs are now regarded by Conservatives as the ideological answer to the sweeping secularist reforms of Mustafa Kemal; he is seen as the spokesman of the conservative Turanists and Islamicists in Turkey, and yet he tells us in these embarrasingly candid memoirs that he is a man without religion. It is a noteworthy situation indeed when the defense of religion falls upon men who are themselves godless.[27]

This is not the place to go into the detailed examination of the Secularist reforms that were undertaken in Turkey by the new republic. They are familiar and have received exhaustive attention.[28] They sweep away the *ancien régime*. The Ottoman Sultanate is of course abolished. The "culture" associated with the old regime is brought under a devastating attack. The symbolism that is selected is important. The headgear, the red Morrocan fez, which was a distinctive mark of the nineteenth century Ottomans is abolished. Hats with brims are instituted in place of the fez: the brim would not permit the forehead to touch the ground if any believer could keep his trilby on while praying in the mosques. The veiling of women is forbidden by decree. All religious orders, schools, and *tariqat* are disbanded and abolished as mere receptacles of superstition and inequity. Later, the offices of the Caliph and Seyh-ul Islam, the highest religious offices, are dispensed with. Religious endowments are taken over by the State. Instead of these positions a General Directorate of Religious Affairs is established under the Prime Ministry with firm control over all *sunni* religious activities. Even more indicative of the Reformers' far-reaching cultural intentions, is the abolition of the Ottoman Arabic script and the adoption of the Latin alphabet. The Islamic calendar is abolished. The call to prayer is changed from its Arabic form to a Turkish form. And without fussing with the intricate problems of the Sharia, the Italian penal code, the Swiss civil code, and the German commercial codes are adopted.

It is all indeed a remarkable affair. Those who are more fortunate and look upon a continuity of tradition and an orderly—or even disorderly—development of institutions can hardly appreciate the degree of hostility shown towards the ideas and forms of the traditional past. The experience is not a conversion, perhaps (for there was no turning to Christianity), but an anti-conversion, a turning away from the Islamic tradition, without having anything very clear—at first—to turn towards. The point was made by Gökalp that a conversion to Western civilization was needed and this, to be precise, meant Rationality and Secularism. I will return to this, but will note in passing, how different this is, for instance, from the stance of the Sinhalese in Ceylon, who, upon receiving their independence from Britain, have been trying valiantly to reestablish the Buddhist religion, turning away from the Latin script and the use of English to rediscover the glories of the ancient Sinhalese script and literature. They have now instituted the ancient Buddhist calendar with its Moon days (instead of Sundays) and its weeks of uncertain duration. The thoroughness of the Turkish house-cleaning is not even matched by the Russian or Chinese Revolutions. They have their similarities, but at least neither of them tampered with the scripts of these peoples and, therefore, have allowed the new generation some access to their traditional history. In Turkey, the new Latin script has made it very difficult for the new generations to go back even to the newspapers of 1920, let alone to the nineteenth century.[29]

Taken as a whole, the intention of the Turkish Reforms is clearly to deal a mortal blow to an entire culture and to set up a new culture, with new men. Hence all the talk of the creation of a new Kemalist youth uncontaminated by the hopes and aspirations of a past that was regarded as backward, corrupt, rotten, weak, and shameful. And since Islam was at the heart of the *ancien régime*, it is Islam that receives the heaviest blow. There is a special chamber of the Topkapi Palace which houses the sacred memorabilia of the Prophet himself, which the Ottoman Sultans had brought to Istanbul from the holy cities of the Hijaz. In this holy place relays of "readers" had recited the words of the Qur'an for four hundred years without a break until the abolition of the Caliphate in 1922. They were apparently hustled out unceremoniously one morning on orders from Ankara. There was, it seems clear, a firm effort made to stop the main current of Islam from flowing into the minds of the new generations. To some extent this has been successful, but with unexpected results.

Illusions for the Future

I call the sum of these efforts, with the obvious analogy, the Cultural Revolution, since it seems to me there is a similarity of intention with China. In both cases we have countries with vivid ideas of grandeur who have been disappointed by their own past performances. In both cases the need is felt by those in power to go beyond mere corrections and adjustments in the culture which maintains their institutions. The intention is to raze the old decrepit house and to reharness popular energies for the creation of something new. Some optimistic and satisfying Utopian vision of the future is needed. This vision is the creation of a new culture, a new state, and a new future.

There are not many of these cases. Those that are available are highly instructive from the point of view of Western social science. The change in ideology, the new thoughts in the minds of new men, play a central part in the total change that is brought about. The reasons why such ideas arise, the nature of the soil which proves fertile to these seeds, repays analysis. Hence my excuse for returning to these issues.

What we have here is first a sense of disillusion, a feeling that old forms will not do, that the old faith is not enough, that new forms are needed. This sense of negation seems to go hand in hand with internal dissension, division, and a breakdown of social order. I suspect that this degree of disenchantment arises from a certain dissonance between what is expected in the world and what actually exists. In many countries the loss of power, of empire, of dominance, and of grandeur gave rise to deeply disappointed and gloomy appraisals of self-worth. In a minor way, France in 1958 went through such an experience.[30]

In Turkey, the total dislocation of World War I, the loss of province after province, and foreign occupation prepared the ground by fragmenting and shattering old social frameworks and especially the political institutions. New hope could only be injected into this context by the promise of grandeur and the restoration of pride in the future. The "model" of the future could not be Islamic. Nationalists had just been fighting the so-called Army of the Caliphate. It had to be "modern," Western, Nationalist.

It seems to me that it is in such times of great confusion, the dark and dangerous times of interregnum, that new models for society, new forms for ideals, and ideas for a new life are hammered out and propagated. It is also then that the internal social cleavages and dissensions become critical, because it is these internal frontiers which then become the frontiers of new ideas.

We do not know exactly around what ideological poles the resistance to Mao Tse-tung's Cultural Revolution in China is likely to develop. We know that the old bureaucracy has been identified as the recalcitrant villain. Chou En-Lai indicates that "the revolution" has not attained its goals (the transformation of China) and that it must be "carried on continuously."[31]

In Turkey, for special reasons, whenever Mustafa Kemal made efforts to establish a "loyal" opposition, it was the problem of Islam which kept returning to haunt the reformers. As the recollection of the Ottoman experience faded, the return of Islamic forms to the political arena in some form became a yearning difficult to resist. Unlike Russia, and unlike China or Mexico, Turkey held free elections in 1950. These elections, contested by men who formed a splinter group from within the ruling single party, resulted in the loss of power of the Reformist (CHP) party after a rule of almost 30 years. With all the great fears that a super-conservative Islamic party would reimpose the Sharia—however interpreted—in fact some kind of *modus vivendi* was reached which allowed free party politics to proceed in Turkey for awhile in a fashion entirely unexpected. After the extraordinary reforms, an extraordinary reaction could have been expected. That is indeed what the leadership of the Soviet Union and even of China, perhaps, would have to fear if ever there is a transition to open politics in these states.

The politics of Turkey gave the impression to the unsatisfied reformists on the left, who felt that "liberty" had been restored far too early, that the great reformist task had been left incomplete just as in China. It was felt that a new wave of reform must be instituted since the condition of the Turkish Republic was far from satisfactory. At the same time, with the restoration of liberty the Islamicists, so long under pressure, began to show their hand, at first rather tentatively, then more strongly, and lately (1971) forcefully enough to engender certain fears that an Indonesian style of uprising was being planned by the Islamic conservatives. In Indonesia in a frightening uprising many Communists were killed in a very brief span of days, and, as is well known, the regime lurched away from Socialism.

These two extreme wings, the yearning for the political restoration of Islam as in Pakistan on the one hand, and the yearning for Marxist-Leninist scientific rationality on the other, characterize the parameters within which the Turkish Republic is placed at this time. It is as if the battles of nineteenth century Europe—socialism against the traditional order—are now being fought on the home ground of Islam in Turkey. Rumbles of such struggles are heard in other Islamic countries, too. Their outcome may be civil war in some cases, domination by one side or the other in others; it seems too much to expect scholars to provide the ideas for a reconciliation between these implacable wings.

The Seeds of Civil Strife

We do not know whether a reconciliation is even possible in the Turkish case. Many elements of moderation are present, it is true, but the attempt to keep the central arena open and to allow the two massive popular parties, at the present at least, to get on with the task of government has placed the two extreme wings under the shadows. The extreme wings, the secret Islamic organizations directly or indirectly supported by large masses and a well-organized Communist underground movement, have evidently developed activist cells especially among the 100,000 University students. The elaborate network of secret leftist organizations apparently links up with the outlawed TKP (Turkish Communist Party) and some have called themselves the TKO (Turkish Liberation Army). Again, there is certainly an international aspect to these organizations so that the money from oil in the Middle East, from various Communist and other parties, and from a host of other sources, it is said, flows quite freely. The talk makes it appear as if the "Union of Godless Zealots" in the Soviet Union is pitted against the Jamaat-i Islami in Pakistan, but major world alignments are also at stake.

Every now and then an incident takes place which, like a flare, suddenly illuminates the major preoccupations of a society and brings troublesome issues to the surface. An incident of this kind, full of emotional overtones, took place two years ago in Turkey. One of the senior judges of the Supreme Court died. It was said of him that he was a self-admitted agnostic, if not an atheist. Certainly he had always shown himself to be hostile to the popular party then in power (AP), the party which if not openly Islamicist—for that is difficult in Turkey—had at least given the appearance of being sympathetic to Islam and had often received, alone, about 50 per cent of the popular vote.[32] Upon the death of this man, Öktem, the political tension in the entire country began to rise. It was said that mosque officials would refuse to perform the Islamic prayers and simple rituals at his funeral ceremony because an atheist such as Öktem could not be given an Islamic funeral. The funeral, a state occasion on account of the seniority of the judge, had brought together members of the top echelon of the political institutions of the Republic. Apparently, there was indeed some refusal to perform the traditional prayers, then much excitement, and when the aged leader of the Secularist and Kemalist opposition party (the CHP), Inonu, appeared on the scene to pay his respects he was caught in immense crowds. Thereupon, significantly enough, an officer, indeed a general, drew his revolver, pushed the crowd aside, and it is said "saved" Inonu from the crowd. The next day, Inonu announced that "Backwardism had risen from the grave (Irtica hortluyor), that the cultural reforms were in danger." The tension continued and in an amazing development the entire senior judiciary of the republic demonstrated in the streets in a silent march against the "Backwardism" that had risen from the grave. All these activities were, of course, directed squarely against the popular (AP) party in power and its leadership. They did, in fact, culminate on March 12, 1971 in a declaration by the commanders of the military establishment that the AP Prime Minister Demirel must resign. This he did and thereby averted, no doubt, the kind of *coup d'état* that had taken place against Prime Minister Menderes, leader of the same populist groups in May, 1960.

The forces that were aligned in the 1960 *coup* and the 1971 *annunciomento* are not quite the same. There has been a massive growth of left-wing organizations in the ten years between 1960 and 1971, but the Öktem incident does express with particular clarity the surface organizations which are ranged in flanks, though one can only guess at the secret organizations behind them, in the shadows. On the surface, at least, there is the Senior Civil Service and the administrative elite which we may re-identify as the ruling institution of Ottoman days ranged against the ordinary and nameless masses, probably sympathizers of the right-wing parties, and especially the mass party in power at the time (AP).

Metin Toker, the son-in-law of Inonu, brings this out with special clarity in his recent writing. He quotes the left ideologues as follows:

That Kemalism is not the ideology of the Petit Bourgeois but of the real Bourgeois is now better understood. In fact Kemalism is the name taken over by Turkish Nationalism, and it has got this name from its founder. . . . Nationalism is an ideology appropriate to the Capitalist period. . . . And Kemalism was the name of the ideology of the nation, of nationalism, current after the 1920's. The period of the War of Independence must be separated from the period of the Kemalist reforms at a later date. The reforms carried out at that date were certain actions carried out for the benefit of a bourgeois order. To bring the nation up to the level of the civilization of the day was the expression of the desire to reproduce a typical Western bourgeois nation. This is why the working class cannot make a common cause with Kemalist ideology. It cannot make a common cause with those who strangled, jailed, dominated the left.[33]

Toker then hopefully adds:

Those Kemalist civilian and military intellectual "enlightened ones," who shouted "the second war of liberation" in the streets, who distributed pamphlets without being aware of these realities and the sharp thinking on the Leftist Front are now probably a little ashamed of themselves.

Perhaps. I have said that the Kemalist reforms are felt to be an incomplete piece of work by the intellectuals of the Turkish left. Many now write that those reforms did not go much further than aping the West:

I do not believe that most Turkish intellectuals with all their good will will be helpful to socialism. For 200 years the Turkish intellectual has Aped the West; imitated the West. An Ape is not creative. It may look human but it is not creative. Since Turkish bourgeois intellectuals have aped the West for 200 years, they have not made any contribution to Humanity for 200 years. . . . Now after 200 years, when we say let us turn to our Identity, let us set up our own socialism, real socialism, then they turn against us, and start looking for models. . . . They look for the model of the Soviet Union, or the model of China. The entire struggle of Lenin has been to create his own model.[34]

Here, then, the story comes full circle, for Mehmet Akif, the Islamicist, had also written of the earliest reforms:

People of a nation whose religion is imitation, whose world is imitation, whose customs are imitation, whose dress is imitation, whose greetings and language is imitation, in short, whose everything is imitation are clearly themselves mere imitation human beings, and can on no account make up a social group and hence can not survive.[35]

Recent days have seen a rapproachement between the Moderates at the Center with the Activist radicals in the wings, but the seeds of civil war are well sown. Communism and Islam with their armed and well-heeled fanatic adherents are now pitted against each other, and the avoidance of civil war depends upon the ability to compromise of the political leaders at the Center. I say nothing about the Army here though I have written about this elsewhere, for the Army, too, neutral until recently, is being increasingly drawn into the irresistible polarization.

Is this going to be the fate of Islam elsewhere? One hopes not. At the same time, one cannot overlook Bernard Lewis' sobering assessment:

from time to time in recent years Middle Eastern thinkers have put the question: what is the result of all the Westernization? It is a question which we of the West may well ask ourselves too. It is our complacent habit in the Western world—the more so the further west one goes—to make ourselves the model of virtue and progress. To be like us is to be good; to be unlike us is to be bad. To become more like us is to improve; to become less like us is to deteriorate. It is not necessarily so. When civilizations clash, there is one that prevails, and one that is shattered. Idealists and ideologues may talk glibly of a "marriage of the best elements" from both sides, but the usual result of such an encounter is a cohabitation of the worst.[36]

Conclusion

I want to conclude with three theoretical observations: on the nature of cultural revolution and secularism, on the interaction of models as a theory of social change, and on charisma and culture change as a cyclical long-term process.

Gallagher, in his paper on Turkey quoted above,[37] distinguishes between three types of revolutions in the contemporary scene: palace revolutions, colonial revolutions, and cultural revolutions. The first he regards a mere change of personnel without altering the institutions. The second, colonial revolution, is described as the Nationalist reaction to the outside power which brings about an apologetic clinging to the past glories of the indigenous traditions. In India, for instance, there is the resurgence of Indian traditions, Indian dress, and Indian ritual developed in conscious and studied contrast to Western models. This process of self-discovery can be seen in the autobiographies of men such as Gandhi or Nehru. In Ceylon, there is a fascinating rediscovery and resurgence of Buddhism by Dharmapala, among others, with assistance of Col. H. S. Olcott and Madame Blavatsky, superbly described by H. Bechert.[38]

We have been concerned with the third type, the "cultural" revolution in which social institutions are pulled out from their very roots, and new values, new ideas, new blueprints are inculcated in new men. Gallagher speaks of this as an attempt made to enter and participate in another civilization, ideas which are echoed in the very words of the public prosecutor of Izmir, Turkey, who spoke recently at one of the common trials of a religious fundamentalist group. After accusing them of various cultural-political crimes, of trying to undermine the "secular" order of the republic, he said: "This case which in a sense involves the history of the Turkish Nation, its regime, its very existence and its future, is of extreme importance. At the same time this is a trial for progress [literally, 'age'] and civilization." He goes on to claim that these people—who include lawyers and other professional men in their ranks—are ignorant persons who "do not understand the value of Reason and Science."[39]

Certainly the literature on the attitude of Chinese intellectuals to their own traditions and religious forms seems remarkably familiar. C. K. Yang reports the same despair about tradition in the 1920's in China and the same view that "religion is a relic of man's primitive ignorance."[40] They, too, appear to formulate the contest between "objective science," a stage before one reaches scientific-historical-materialism, and "blind tradition." The writing of the Chinese on their Cultural Revolution, from the need for reform in the Opera and the Arts to the Red Guards, seems completely familiar from the perspective of Turkey. Here is a common experience.[41]

Maurice Freedman, in his Presidential Address to the Royal Anthropological Institute in London, observes: "What was intended was a further

stage in the total transformation of social and cultural life . . . by a campaign directed against the remnants of 'bourgeois' and 'feudal' mentality
and behaviour—the Four Olds . . . old ideas, old culture, old customs, and
old habits."[42] It is these that had to go.

Freedman appears surprised and even annoyed in this lecture that
these transformations should bring about such a religious fervor, such blind
fury, and unleash such aggressive energies against the remaining bastions
of resistance detected by fanatic hordes to be the prime targets. But, then,
we are always in danger of overlooking the intensity of the affect that has
been routinized and runs under the surface, as it were, of our most ordinary, even unconscious social arrangements. The intensity of this affect
comes through to consciousness only when our pet customs and habits and
ideas and institutions are seriously challenged. How natural it is for blind
fury to sweep the land while these institutions of a despised order which
have already been desecrated are being demolished. It is true that the
protagonists and the antagonists of different ideologies for the future of
the nation then begin to behave as if possessed by demons. But then again,
without this kind of almost religious and unquestioning commitment to
such ideals, how could they be realized? New forms can only be imprinted
on a community after desperate struggles. It calls for commitment and
sacrifice which, depending upon the centrality of the institution, may
require bloodshed. New men who are already converted to the new order
have to be put in charge. Others who cannot mend their ways or see the
light have to be eliminated. The demons cannot rest until the new order
is felt to be safe from attack—which, of course, it may never be. And the
greater and more total the transformation, the greater the passions and
the more bitter the sacrifices. Such passions subside only when the new
molds into which social action is directed and the new personality which
has been created are seen to be satisfactory in day-to-day operations. Then
with time and the healing of wounds one may get back to ordinary living.
It is clearly not an experience willingly to be wished upon one's friends.
The attempt to inculcate the personal qualities of such blind obedience to
duty and such commitment to utopian ideals, to allow men to suppress
questioning doubts, to stifle the temptations towards individual rationality,
and to accept the commands of the "Party" is indeed a striking theme of
early Communist writers. Sartre writes of this in his famous play, Les
Mains Sales, and Arthur Koestler has vividly described the internal debate
of the convert.

The struggle to transform a society, to effect a cultural revolution must
at the same time be a significant political act. Such acts demand those special qualities of leadership, of vision, of direction and charisma, of rationality
perhaps, but also those tenacious aspects of fanaticism and self-confidence
which run below the surface and without which men such as Mustafa
Kemal and Mao Tse-tung would not have accomplished much. Once power

is firmly established, however, the reins are in hand and the passions rechanneled into more mundane problems; then with patience and with care new institutions may be constructed, new habits and ideals may be carefully cultivated. Lévi-Strauss is right in calling affectivity the "darkest side of man." These questions concerning the release, the direction, the control, and the channeling of affectivity in terms of old and new cultural forms in whole societies is an area which would repay careful anthropological observation.

The Chinese Revolution is indeed remarkable. No country had disintegrated so tragically as a result of the combination of the colonial touch of death and internal dissension. The period of the fall of the Manchu dynasty, the 1920's, 1930's, and 1940's, is one of almost unrelieved horror and confusion for China. There were experiments with alternative models from the West, with Christianity and capitalism, but in a strictly understandable sense, the ideology that took root was one which was neutral in religious coloring and which presented itself (despite itself, for the Russians assisted Chiang Kai Chek) as an ideology of the oppressed against the "long noses."[43] Then Mao created his cadres for the propagation of Mao'ism just as Mustafa Kemal had created his cadres for the propagation of Kemalism. Mao's cadres, though more internationally-minded than Kemalists who are more strictly Nationalist, and in a sense old-fashioned by contrast, attacked the traditional bastions just as assiduously as did the Kemalists. Reading the passages of the material from the Great Cultural Revolution, one gets a strong flavor of the Turkish utopian zeal. The sudden imperious demands by the colorful Japanese novelist Yukio Mishima and his stunning act of traditional serial hara-kiri suggest a similar struggle going on beneath the surface between two civilizations, even in a Japan suffused with economic success—but this case is not, strictly speaking, comparable with the problems of China and Turkey. In any case, Mishima looks to the past of Japan.

The differences between the revolutions of China and Turkey should also be noted. The Chinese case, fought bitterly for almost thirty years among a host of warlords, invading armies, and warring factions in the twilight of World War II, involved an extensive social revolution as well. As is well known, entire classes were eliminated. An extraordinary and thorough land reform is said to have completely transformed the social structure of the rural countryside. There is little doubt that in Turkey there was no social revolution in this sense. The attempts at land reform were not very extensive. The effort made to eliminate certain commercial groups towards the end of World War II now remains merely a bad memory. In this sense, the social classes in the republic have simply evolved from former groups in the Empire. The Ruling Institutions are still ruling. Some left-wing intellectuals would say that the so-called "bureaucratic intelligentsia" is under attack from the mass parties of the AP (formerly

DP—Democratic Party) type, but, as was observed above, the army-civil service-universities coalition still manages to have the upper hand, even in the teeth of free elections, as the events of March 12, 1971 demonstrate.

Mao Tse-tung's attack on the entrenched bureaucratic hierarchies of China—and the mentality which produces such structures—during the Cultural Revolution is perhaps more comparable. The extreme left wing of Turkish intellectuals may have been on this Mao'ist path in the 1960's. Certainly the target of their attack was the class system of the Republic. They were in revolt against the entire social fabric of Turkey with its complacent peasantry, well-to-do local gentry, and relatively comfortable town-dwellers, and the revolt was launched by young men often closely related to the embattled bureaucratic elite and its entourage. Some of the most fervent fire-breathers turned out to be sons of generals and admirals. They had taken up arms against the mass parties and popularly elected Parliament under the banner of social justice. This attack, which culminated in the anarchic activities of the so-called Turkish Liberation Army, was naturally undertaken in the name of the masses and appeared to include a veiled attack on the bureaucratic apparatus as well. It is interesting that if, indeed, the attack had been successful—by which we mean the highly unlikely picture of Turkey behind the Iron Curtain in the Balkans—it would have brought about the dictatorship of a single party similar to those in Eastern Europe and would have enhanced the power and position of a new set of elite, bureaucratic *apparatniks*, themselves fairly closely related to the old set of bureaucrats.

It is not for nothing that that shrewd observer of the Middle East, Khedouri, remarks that there are only two classes in the Middle East, the ruler and the ruled. It has been so for a long time. The really revolutionary nature of the Turkish democracy and its free elections was that the ruled were about to become the rulers, as indeed the ex-General Secretary of the CHP (the party of the Ataturk revolution), Ecevit, and the leader of the right-wing AP, Demirel, both recognize with great clarity. They have never tired of saying it.

It is apparent that in both China and Turkey the clash between Western and Asian civilization first seems to produce a suspension of belief altogether and a lack of commitment, at least in the minds of the intellectuals. This seems to be the basic reason for secularism, which is a curious ideology and, in its political form at least, the result of an erosion of one culture by another. The weaker is pitted against the prestige and power, the science and materialism associated with the West.

The lack of commitment between ideologies, the uneasy coexistence, does not seem to last. Sooner or later it seems to turn into a commitment to available alternatives: either Nationalism, a return to a nostalgic past, or a plunge into an uncertain future. It is this last plunge which generates the greatest interest in Marxism-Leninism, since unlike Western humanism, it is both universalistic, apparently modern in its rejection of the old social arrangements, and a tightly and coherently argued doctrine of social revolution and promise. To frustrated persons struggling with a weakening religious commitment, with infuriatingly ineffective social and political institutions, with the continuing Imperialist gestures of the West it provides a source of ideological coherence, a mantle of scientific doctrine, and a hope of becoming a modern man. The appeal, as many observers have noted before but none as eloquently as Koestler in his *Memoirs,* seems to have an effect similar to conversion. And a conversion it is.

All conversions, one supposes, need an intervening period, a dark interregnum of uncertainty, confusion, anomie, perhaps of pain and humiliation. Times like this make all new departures suddenly seem possible. In more personal terms it is like the breakdown of a marriage, divorce, and, for the optimists, remarriage. There are such dark interludes in the lives of persons, and this seems to be true of peoples as well, even though the cases are rare. In cultural terms we would say that these are cases when the old model is discredited by a sufficiently large and important section of the population for an alternative new model to be reformulated, to take root and be developed.

The second point of theory comes from Edmund Leach. It relates to the analysis of these cases of social change between two poles.

In this book my descriptions of gumsa gumlao and Shan patterns of organization are largely *as if* descriptions—they relate to *ideal models* rather than real societies, and what I have been trying to do is to present a convincing model of what happens when such *as if* systems interact. A sociological description of process in social change, if it is to have any generality at all, must relate to a model of this type rather than to any one particular instance. It is not possible I maintain, to describe such a process of change directly from the observation of first hand ethnographic data. What one must do is first analyze out the ethnographic facts by reference to abstract whole systems conceived as existing in *unstable* equilibrium, and then postulate that the confusion arises from the interpenetration of these unstable ideal system.[44]

I hope I have shown that this is useful. It is a much neglected matter, and Leach was the first to point out the fertility of this approach in brilliant detail.

The third theoretical point concerns charisma and change. A good deal of my analysis depends upon a neo-Weberian view of statis and dynamics of cultural models. There are undoubtedly cases of statis in the anthropological repertory. There are many descriptions of societies working in a satisfactory fashion with a particularly well-articulated cultural model. There is indeed a beautiful anthropological myth that somewhere a society exists which is pristine and entirely integrated. Frederik Barth gave a lecture recently on a society totally isolated and only recently contacted in New Guinea.[45] It certainly gave the impression of a wholesome integrity in which nature, experience, social, cultural, and religious life appeared like a well-oiled mechanism. The total number of persons were 183 souls. The forms were well-established. The symbols of the system penetrated through the whole culture.

I have been thinking of the opposite case, when the symbolism has broken down and much desperate confusion marks the scene.

The cases which demand our attention are those messy ones with a degeneration and disintegration of old forms and a regeneration and reintegration of new forms. The midpoint, that dismal but fertile interregnum of anomie, the dissolution of Proudhon, is critical. Weber never really analyzed this, and Durkheim did not say much about it either. But Weber has drawn the outlines in the process of the regeneration of forms. He has written of charisma (at least in its personified form), of routinization and the final establishment of traditional—legal—rational authority. He has not seen this in cyclical terms and has not analyzed that critical process of the loss of charisma in outdated institutions, in those too inflexible, unworkable systems. These are conditions in which the superstructure is out of phase with the infrastructure and collapses under its own weight. It is only after a period of disintegration and dissolution that the search for new charisma begins and the opportunities for the new charismatic leaders arise.[46]

These observations on Cultural Revolutions are intended to draw attention to the gargantuan dimensions of the task of transforming "traditional" societies. Evolution may simply not provide a sufficiently speedy timetable. Revolution must inevitably destroy. The more central and effective it is, the greater the destruction. The period of rebuilding that may follow—for the likelihood of the disintegration of the body politic is not negligible—must deal first of all with the problem of order in its most general sense. This involves beside political, social, and economic order the establishment of goals, the sense of purpose, and direction. This used to be called "destiny," a word which is used with noteworthy insistence by the myth-makers of the non-Western world.

The problems of economic growth, the rise in the marginal productivity of labor, are of course interwoven into this story. One may recall the bizarre experiment with backyard smelting furnaces in the Communes during the Great Leap Forward in China. But these economic problems, though a vital part of the design of the future, pale in significance when seen in the immediate perspective of near revolutionary politics. Even when there are parliaments and free elections, as in Turkey, the memory of the social and cultural cataclysm may be too near for the leaders to be able to devote their full energies to the growth of the economy. In the din of post-revolutionary politics the economic effort becomes displaced and fragmented. It is surely instructive that the most successful effort at economic growth of a non-European country has taken place in Japan, a society whose central institutions and historic national traditions were successfully preserved against the tide of millenarian cultural revolutions. That luxury was not available for Turkey and China. There appear to be very few countries in Asia where conditions of stability, respect for traditional political institutions, effective economic organization, and pragmatic leadership are combined for a repetition of the Japanese "Great Leap Forward."

REFERENCES

1. Max Weber, *The Theory of Social and Economic Organization* (New York: Free Press, 1964).

2. Oversimplifying, these mean, respectively, rational behavior directed towards "ultimate values" (patriotism, religion, etc,) and rational behavior directed towards "immediate ends."

3. H. A. R. Gibb, "The Reaction in the Middle East Against Western Culture," delivered in 1971 in Paris, *Studies on the Civilization of Islam,* eds. S. J. Shaw and W. R. Polk.

4. Charles F. Gallagher, "Contemporary Islam: The Straits of Secularism," American Universities Field Staff Reports, *Southwest Asia Series,* 15, No. 3 (1966).

5. See Overture, *The Raw and the Cooked* (New York, 1970), pp. 9-10 for Levi-Strauss' own explanation of his progress from Kinship to Mythology; on the behavorist bias, see Edwin Ardener, "The New Anthropology and its Critics," *Man,* 6, No. 3 (September 1971).

6. Claude Levi-Strauss, *La Pensée Sauvage* (Paris, 1962).

7. *Ibid.,* p. 174; "l'ethnologie est d'abord une psychologie."

8. *Ibid.,* p. 311.

9. The work of H. Bechert in particular must be singled out as a striking exception. See his *Buddhismus, Staat und Gesellschaft in den Ländern des Theravada Buddhismus,* vol. 1 (Frankfort, 1966); vol. 2 (Wiesbaden, 1967).

10. M. Mahdi, *Ibn Khaldun's Philosophy of History* (Chicago: University of Chicago Press, 1964).

11. Erbakan's party was outlawed and Erbakan tried in secularist courts for his non-secularist ideas in 1971.

12. Aziz Ahmad, *An Intellectual History of Islam in India* (Edinburgh: University Press, 1969), p. 15.

13. J. N. D. Anderson and N. J. Coulson, "Islamic Law in Contemporary Cultural Change," *Saeculum XVIII,* 1-2 (1967), p. 14.

14. Webster, *New International Dictionary of the English Language,* 2nd edition (Springfield, Mass.: G. & C. Merriam Company, 1959).

15. Mahdi, *Ibn Khaldun's Philosophy of History,* p. 247.

16. Fazlur Rahman, "Islam and the Constitutional Problem of Pakistan," *Studia Islamica,* 32 (1970).

17. *Ibid.*, p. 276.

18. *Ibid.*

19. On the intellectual history of modernism in Pakistan, see Aziz Ahmad's brilliant study, *Islamic Modernism in India and Pakistan, 1857-1964* (Oxford: University Press, 1967).

20. Alexandre Bennigsen and Chantal Lemercier-Quelquejay, *Islam in the Soviet Union* (London: Pall Mall Press, 1967).

21. *Ibid.*, pp. 175-176.

22. Bechert, *Buddhismus; Staat und Gesellschaft in den Ländern des Theravada Buddhismus.*

23. G. E. Wheeler, "Soviet Central Asia," in "Islam in Politics: Symposium," *The Muslim World*, Hartford Seminary Foundation, 56, No. 4 (1966), p. 239.

24. T. Z. Tunaya, *Turkiyede Islamcilik Cereyani* (Istanbul: Baha Matbaasi, 1962).

25. Proudhon writes in 1860, "All the traditions have been used up, all the beliefs are abolished; in turn, the new programme has not been created, or at least it has not entered the consciousness of the masses; hence what I call dissolution. This is the most atrocious moment in the life of societies. Everything unites to desolate men of good will: the prostitution of consciences, the triumph of mediocrities, the confusion of right and wrong, the contortions of principles, the lowness of the passions, the looseness of customs, the oppression of truth, the reward of bad faith. . . . I have few illusions and I do not expect to see reborn in our country, tomorrow, like a flash of lightning, liberty, the respect of law, public honesty, freedom of opinion, good will in the papers, morality in government, reason among the bourgeois and common sense among the plebians.

"The killings are coming and the prostration which will follow this blood bath will be horrible. We do not detect the work of the new age; we fight in darkness; we must make arrangements to support this life without too much sadness in doing our duty. Let us help one another; let us invite ourselves into the shadow, and whenever the occasion arises, let us be just. . . ." *De la création de l'ordre dans l'humanité, Oeuvres complètes* (Paris, 1927), p. 205f., and p. 187f.

26. Riza Nur, *Hayatim ve hatiratim*, 4 vols. (Istanbul: Altindag Yayinevi, 1967).

27. The authentic element of chance in the reforms comes through with some clarity in these memoirs. As Istanbul was under occupation, and as the Nationalists began to consolidate their position in Ankara, Riza Nur thinks of the future of the State. He feels that the Sultanate, already 600 years old, should continue to provide the legitimacy of the movement. So he writes a letter to one of the Royal Princes in Istanbul, inviting him to escape from the capital under foreign occupation and join the Nationalists, so that, when they win, they should have with them a legitimate link at least with the Imperial House of Osman. This letter is passed on to the occupying powers, and the royal family evidently remains adamantly disposed against the Nationalists. Riza Nur claims that it is this very incident which confirms him in his suspicions that the blood of this Hanedan (lineage) has been much too watered down with all their non-Turkish marriages. (Riza is an unrepentant racist who believes in the genetic and historic destiny of Turanian genes.) Therefore, he goes back to the National Assembly and immediately draws up a bill abolishing the ancient Sultanate in Istanbul by the will of the Nationalist Legislature in Ankara. He claims that Mustafa Kemal had no idea of doing this, but only

chanced upon Riza as he was collecting signatures for his bill in the corridors of the Assembly. This incident, which is of some general interest, should be checked in the Archives. If true, it would throw some more light on the enigmatic and dominating personality of Ataturk.

28. For a superb study, see Bernard Lewis, *The Emergence of Modern Turkey* (London: Oxford University Press, 1961 and 1965).

29. There are some suggestions that the script in Turkey was changed to fit in with the Soviet moves of changing the scripts of the Central Asian and Caucasian Turkish Republics. The Soviet, as is well known, changed the Muslim scripts of the USSR first into Latin, and after Turkey followed suit, into Cyrillic. The matter has not received much attention.

30. Some aspects of the prelude to the Spanish Civil War seem very suggestive. Hugh Thomas writes superbly of this period in Spain, *The Spanish Civil War* (New York: Harper and Row, 1961); see also G. Brenan, *The Spanish Labyrinth* (Cambridge, Eng.: The University Press, 1943).

31. "During his youth, he went on, he only imagined that the revolution would attain victory. At that time he thought that revolution was quite simple; it was only after suffering several setbacks that he learned how to make revolution from the teachings of the Communist party Chairman Mao Tse-tung.
"After the triumph of the revolution, according to Marxist-Leninist principles and Chairman Mao's thoughts, he said, *the revolution must be carried on continuously to win complete victory over the reactionaries.*" Chou En-lai, *The New York Times,* May 21, 1971, p. 10.

32. The reformist party (CHP) usually gets a popular vote of between 29-42 per cent.

33. Metin Toker, *Milliyet*, 14.v.71.

34. Yasar Kemal, *Milliyet*, 19.iv.71.

35. Mehmet Akif, quote by Tunaya, *Turkiyede Islamcilik Cereyani.*

36. Bernard Lewis, *The Middle East and the West* (Bloomington: Indiana University Press, 1964).

37. Gallagher, "Contemporary Islam: The Straits of Secularism."

38. Bechert, *Buddhismus, Staat und Gesellschaft in den Ländern des Theravada Buddhismus.*

39. Reported in *Cumhuriyet*, September 3, 1971, with the banner headline "This is a trial for progress and civilization."

40. C. K. Young, *Religion in Chinese Society* (Berkeley: University of California Press, 1967), p. 365.

41. *The Great Cultural Revolution in China*, ed. Asia Research Centre (Tokyo, 1968).

42. Maurice Freedman, "Why China?" *Proceedings of the Royal Anthropological Institute for 1969* (London).

43. For an excellent account by an anthropologist, see C. P. Fitzgerald, *The Birth of Communist China* (Pelican Books, 1964); see also S. Schram, *Mao Tse tung* (New York: Simon & Schuster, 1966), and Schram, *The Political Thought of Mao Tse tung* (Pelican Books, 1969). For more detailed accounts, see *Party Leadership and*

Revolutionary Power in China, ed. J. W. Lewis (Cambridge, Eng.: The University Press, 1970); see also F. Schurmann, *Ideology and Organization in Communist China* (Berkeley: University of California Press, 1966).

44. E. Leach, *Political Systems of Highland Burma: a Study of Kachin Social Structure* (Boston: Beacon Press, 1970), p. 285.

45. Lecture at the University of Chicago.

46. Some of these problems concerning "charismatic-revolutionary" leadership, in contrast to "bureaucratic-pragmatic" (Anglo-Saxon), and "ideological" (Soviet third generation) leadership are examined with remarkable clarity in an important article by Henry A. Kissinger, "Domestic Structure and Foreign Policy," *Dædalus*, 95, No. 2 (Spring 1966). His types may be identified as second generation concepts from Weber: thus, charismatic (Maoist), traditional (Soviet), and rational (Anglo-Saxon) authority. His analysis of the relationship between these types of leaders and the relation between the U.S., the U.S.S.R., and China is quite penetrating.

ŞERIF MARDIN

Center-Periphery Relations: A Key to Turkish Politics?

"SOCIETY HAS a center." Yet just as certain societies have stronger centers than others, the materials of which centers are forged vary greatly between societies.[1] The Middle East has had a long history of attempts to construct the institutional framework of such centers, even though efforts to marshall these "free floating"[2] resources were, more often than not, ephemeral. Here, the Ottoman Empire emerges as an outstanding exception. There was, in the Ottoman Empire, a lasting center supported by a sophisticated network of institutions.

The methods the Ottomans used were ingenious and varied. By co-opting in the ruling elite individuals largely recruited at an early age from religious minorities, by socializing them into the official class, by tightly controlling, though not necessarily centralizing, the system of taxation and land administration, and by dominating the religious establishment, the center acquired strong leverage in the spheres of justice and education, and in the dissemination of the symbols of legitimacy.[3] These imperial achievements emerge even more clearly in relation to the situation in neighboring Iran. Iranian rulers were often merely "grand manipulators," gingerly juggling the many social forces over which they were unable to establish control. But Ottoman success in these matters cannot fully be evaluated by a simple contrast with the institutions of its neighbors.[4] To establish a fuller perspective another comparison is in order, one that places the Ottoman Empire side by side with the emerging, Western centralized state, and its successor, the modern nation-state.

Both "Leviathan," the form of government which emerged in the West in the middle of the seventeenth century, and the later nation-state had a role to play in the development of Ottoman institutions. At first they were seen as rivals who were beginning to excel in precisely those areas where the Ottomans had traditionally prided themselves for achievement. Eventually, however, during the process of modernization, the Ottomans looked to these new forms of the state as models for reform in their own government.

Leviathan and the nation-state are also important for Turkish history

169

because they present structural contrasts to Ottoman institutions. The forces that shaped the state in the West seem to vary significantly from those that shaped the Ottoman state before modernization set in. Because of its feudal antecedents, the process of centralization that created the modern state included a series of confrontations leading to compromises with what may be called the forces of the periphery: the feudal nobility, the cities, the burghers, and later, industrial labor. The consequence of these compromises was that Leviathan and the nation-state were relatively well articulated structures. Each time a compromise—or even a one-sided victory—was obtained, some integration of the peripheral force into the center was achieved. Thus the feudal estates, or the "privilégiés," or the workers became integrated into the polity while, at the same time, obtaining some recognition of their autonomous status. These successive confrontations and co-optations had important consequences. The confrontations had been varied: conflicts between state and church, between nation builders and localists, between owners and non-owners of the means of production. These cross-cutting cleavages introduced a variety of political identifications which provided for much of the flexibility of modern Western European politics.[5] Also, the center existed within a system of linkages with peripheral elements: medieval estates found a place in parliaments; the lower classes were accorded the franchise.

In the Ottoman Empire before the nineteenth century these characteristics of multiple confrontation and integration seem to be missing. Rather, the *major* confrontation was unidimensional, always a clash between the center and the periphery. In addition, the autonomy of peripheral social forces was more than anything *de facto,* an important difference from the institutional recognition accorded, for example, to estates in Western Europe, which were "separate from the Lord or Prince"[6] even when they were "dependent corporations."[7] Until recently, the confrontation between center and periphery was the most important social cleavage underlying Turkish politics and one that seemed to have survived more than a century of modernization. This paper takes up the ways in which this cleavage was perpetuated during modernization.

The Traditional System

There were many reasons why the opposition of center and periphery became the outstanding issue of Ottoman political and economic life. One of these was the incompatibility of urban dwellers with the always large contingent of nomads in Anatolia, the core of the Empire. The state's difficulty in dealing with nomads on the periphery was endemic. But more than this, the clash between nomads and urban dwellers generated the Ottoman cultivated man's stereotype that civilization was a contest between urbanization and nomadism, and that all things nomadic were only deserving of contempt. A residue of this basic cleavage between nomad and sedentary population can still be seen today in Eastern Turkey where the statistical data, social structure, and basic issues of thirteen provinces with settled agriculture contrast so sharply with those found in the four provinces with a pastoral economy and residues of nomadism.[8]

Another component of the center-periphery cleavage was the suspicion of the center towards the remaining traces of a pre-Ottoman nobility and a number of powerful families in the provinces whose star had risen with that of the Ottomans. The provinces were also hotbeds of intractable religious heterodoxy. Turbulent sects, syncretic cults, self-appointed messiahs presented a long-lasting and well-remembered threat. When the Ottoman provinces occasionally became havens for pretenders to the throne, the periphery gained the added onus of having served as a launching pad for rebellions.

All of this occurred against a background of localism tolerated by the center, for Ottoman social engineering stopped before insurmountable organizational tasks. As the Empire expanded, the Ottomans dealt with the new social institutions they encountered by giving the seal of legitimacy to local usages and by enforcing a system of decentralized accommodation toward ethnic, religious, and regional particularisms. No attempt was made for a more complete integration when loose ties proved workable. One may count among these semi-autonomous groups the non-Moslem communities controlled by their own religious leaders. Thus, in the more general, ecological sense, the center and the periphery were two very loosely related worlds. This aspect of Ottoman society, together with social fragmentation, set one of the primary problems of the Ottoman establishment: the confrontation between the Sultan and his officials on the one hand, and the highly segmented structure of Ottoman Anatolia on the other. Anatolia is particularly important for modern studies since it is the territorial component of modern Turkey.

Those who opposed segmentation, the officials, were set apart from the periphery not only by being, so to speak, on the other side of the fence, but by virtue of certain distinctive status characteristics, as well as by certain symbolic differences. For a long time, one of the distinguishing marks for a number of high—and low—officials was that many were recruited from non-Moslem groups.[9] This practice was designed to establish an ideal pattern, that of the bureaucrat becoming the Sultan's slave (kul in Turkish). In this ideal scheme, the official figured as a person with no ascriptive ties and as totally devoted to implementing the goals of the dynasty. The establishment was, therefore, open to accusations of having excluded free-born Moslems from these posts; obviously, this impediment to access rankled. Friction also existed between the kul and the members of the religious establishment who, barring certain exceptions, were closer to the daily life of the lower classes. The religious institution was thus on the border line between the center and the periphery. During modernization, and because of the secularizing policies of the center, it was increasingly identified with the periphery.[10]

The bases of the distinction between the official elite and the periphery were to be found in economic variables as well. Officials were not subject to taxation; when the Empire was flourishing their income compared favorably with that of the richest merchants. This was partly attributable to the administrator's costs for employing certain personnel and other office expenses, but it was also an aspect of Ottoman legitimacy: the wielders of political power, not the merchants, were the first citizens of the realm. The tight control established by the state over the economy was a further example of the primacy of politics in the Ottoman Empire.[11] Officials wielded extensive power in their administrative capacity. Conversely, because of their *kul* status, they were subject to special, administrative law and lacked the "civil rights" of the Moslem population.[12] In a wider perspective, the entire life-style of the patrimonial official and free-born Moslem contrasted.

The confrontation between the center and the periphery was not, however, due to a hereditary transmission of official status. On the contrary, by and large, advancement was by merit; this was a feature of the way official careers were made when the Empire was most vigorous. Some families with a history of service to the state held privileged positions, but this second pool for the recruiting of officials provided its members only with indirect privileges of access to officialdom. It was only after the Empire reached its nadir that the practice of official patronage or the influence exerted by court circles seem to have become more important.

One aspect highlighting the difference between all types of officials and the masses, both rural and urban, was the operation of the bureaucratic core of the state. Its arrogation of the major control of the economy and society, its control of the commerce of foodstuffs, the limitations it placed on land ownership, and the strictness with which it tried to enforce social stratification through sumptuary regulations were all designed to maintain the state's authority over the nodal points of society and to build a corresponding image of paramountcy.[13] Property relations were included in this system. The Sultan had full property rights on arable land outside the cities. He could alienate land when he chose, but, in fact, relatively little land was given out in freehold. *Latifundia* existed, but most of them were usurped and could, when necessary, be confiscated by the state. Conversely, peasant land could only be expropriated by fraud, by circumventing the original understanding under which the land had been granted. The state was always alert to the suggestion that such fraud had been perpetrated, but action was restricted by three major considerations. In some regions land had been granted as freehold, while in others, perpetuation of property rights was based on the feudal system in operation at the time of the Ottoman conquest. Finally, in many regions the state did not have the power—or the will—to oppose the seizure of land by notables. A number of changes away from the original system of military "fiefs" worked in the long run to favor notables in this respect. When the state could re-assert itself, as it did during the nineteenth century, it tried to protect individual peasant holdings by adopting statutes to hamper the consolidation of land.[14]

The state's claim to political and economic control was bolstered by its title to cultural preeminence. Relative to the heterogeneity of the periphery, the ruling class was singularly compact; this was, above all, a cultural phenomenon. Two elements, one positive, one negative, may be isolated here. On the one hand, the entire mechanism of the state was permeated by the myth of the majesty of the Sultan; on the other hand, there were restrictions placed on the common mortal's access to the symbols of official culture. For much of the population, nomad or settled, rural or urban, this cultural separation was the most striking feature of its existence on the periphery. Rulers and officials were heavily influenced in the cities by the culture of earlier, successful, urban cultures such as the Iranian. Iranian bureaucratic culture in particular was diffused into Ottoman institutions. For example, the rulers adopted languages—Persian and Arabic —that were foreign to the lower classes and worked these into the official culture.[15] The periphery only benefited from one of the educational institutions that trained members of the establishment—the religious training institutions. Not surprisingly, the periphery developed its own extremely varied counter-culture, but it was well aware of its secondary cultural status, an awareness best illustrated by its clumsy imitation of the styles of elite culture. This was particularly true of the lower classes, both rural and urban, for in this matter the urban masses could also be counted as part of the periphery. Even at the height of the Ottoman power, when the image of the Sultan as a provident father had a tangible economic reality, the court, officials, and politics were grim things from which the populace kept apart. Today, *siyaset* means *politics* in Turkish, and *siyaseten katl* means *condemnation to death for reasons of state,* but in earlier official parlance *siyaset* (politics) was also a synonym for a death sentence imposed for reasons of state. This grim connotation is the one which *siyaset* still retained for peasants in a study carried out in 1968 and 1969.[16]

These aspects of the style of state domination and of official status and culture together made up a cluster, an institutional code. In this code the set of principles which kept officials alert to the erosion by the periphery of the achievements of the center occupied an important place. On the other hand, the forces of the periphery, such as locally powerful families, saw the central officials as persons with whom they had many points of contact, and also as rivals who tried to get the greatest possible share of the agricultural surplus and other values for the center—which meant less for themselves. Because of the fragmentation of the periphery, of the disparate elements that entered into it, it was to begin to develop its own code much later. In earlier times this code simply consisted of an awareness of the burdens imposed by the center.

The world-view of those opposing the state's incursions into the economic and social life of the periphery made up an attitude if not a code that spelled localism, particularism and heterodoxy. What have been called "primordial groups"[17] played an important role in the periphery, and identification with such a group was one of a variety of forms that this peripheral stance could take. In fact, however, the many different forms of the peripheral stance were similar only in sharing a negative view of officialdom. When local notables were used in an official capacity, and the state was often obliged to use them, this attitude softened, but the lack of any real legitimization of anyone outside officialdom kept alive the potential for tension.

During the heyday of the Empire, this potential for violent confrontation between the center and the periphery materialized only sporadically, both because of the normal fragmentation of social forces and because of the linkages with the periphery which counterbalanced this possibility. Among these one may count the regular system of recruitment of free-born Moslems into some parts of officialdom, the judicial system penetrating to the subprovincial level, the tradition of public works and charitable foundations, and the wide net of the religious institution—the real hinge between center and periphery.[18] The system of military "fiefs" was a particularly efficient integrative mechanism; the normal fief holder at the time of the rise of the Empire being a cultivator with close ties to the peasant.[19]

It was only with the decline of the Empire that Ottoman officials became plunderers of their own society, and that the relation between officials and the periphery—especially the peasant heavily burdened with taxes—increasingly showed the mark of "Oriental despotism," a type of exploitation basically different from the grimness of Sultanic rule in earlier times and comparable to the earlier system only in the way it perpetrated the cleavage between the governing elite and those excluded from it. Likewise, the local population increasingly relied on local notables who emerged at this juncture to articulate local interests. Despite the growth of their influence and authority, these notables still had no autonomous status comparable to that of the European feudal nobility. While their legitimacy was acquired in their role as agents for the center, increased autonomy could only be obtained by defiance of state power or by outright rebellion.[20] Thus, only those notables rich in land and powerful enough to stand up to the state could gain greater autonomy. There are some signs that where this occurred, the local notables were no less interested in squeezing the peasants than was the state, but at least they saw it was in their interest to provide those minimum services that kept the system going.

One urban form of a new type of estrangement of the Ottoman periphery from the center appeared in Istanbul in 1730 in the form of the so-called Patrona revolt. Through their guilds, the artisans of Istanbul had been asked to contribute heavily to a military campaign that fizzled out because of the timidity and incompetence of the Palace. By then the lower classes in Istanbul had for some time witnessed the Westernization of Ottoman statesmen and the Palace through various attempts to copy the pomp of Versailles and the libertinism of eighteenth century France. When called to arms to prevent the subversion of traditional ways, they responded.[21]

There had been many rebellions in Istanbul before, but this was the first to show a syndrome that was thereafter often repeated: an effort to Westernize military and administrative organization propounded by a section of the official elite, accompanied by some aping of Western manners, and used by another interest group to mobilize the masses against Westernization. Turkish modernists have concentrated exclusively upon the background of political intrigues by statesmen which, indeed, was an aspect of this and similar revolts. However, for a complete picture we should also dwell on the cultural alienation of the masses from the rulers, of the periphery from the center. During later phases of modernization, this alienation was to be compounded.

Ottoman Modernization During the Nineteenth Century

Three outstanding problems stood out as demanding solution in the Ottoman Empire during the nineteenth century. All were related to the Ottoman reformers' attempt to build a state modeled after the nation-state, and all brought into play the relations of the center with the periphery. The first was the integration of non-Moslem groups within the nation-state, and the second consisted of accomplishing the same for the Moslem elements of the periphery—to bring some order into the mosaic structure of the Empire. Finally, these "discrete elements" in the "national territory" had to be brought "into meaningful participation in the political system."[22] This last development was not initiated until the middle of the twentieth century; however, through the first tangible co-optation of notables into politics, a beginning of integration began to be seen after 1908.

The national integration of the non-Moslem components of the Ottoman Empire was more than anything achieved by default, by losses of territory during the nineteenth century and early twentieth century. With its policy of exchanges of population, the Turkish Republic made the situation even simpler. In the years following the exchange, the Republic might have continued to take a suspicious view of non-Moslem minorities, but only in rare cases did minority problems constitute the substance of an outstanding political issue.

Although it is usually overlooked, the national integration of Moslem components was just as much of a problem as that of the non-Moslem groups. The architects of the Turkish reform policy, the *Tanzimat* (1839-1876), had already set a foundation stone here through their fiscal and administrative reforms.[23] By the third quarter of the nineteenth century, the Ottoman state was an increasing presence in the daily life of the periphery. Sultan Abdulhamid II (1876-1909) tried to continue the integration of the periphery by compelling the remaining nomads to settle down. At the same time, the Sultan attempted to bring to the Moslem Ottoman periphery a sense of its unity with the center. As is well underlined by Sir William Ramsay, Abdulhamid's policy of Pan Islamism was not so much a dream of uniting all Moslems as an effort to establish some form of proto-nationalism, to unite his people around an Islamic-Imperial idea. As Ramsay notes:

Until very recent times, the motley population of Asia Minor appears to have been perfectly content with tribal and racial designations. The Turkmen or Avshahr was satisfied to be Turkmen or Avshahr, and did not think so far as I know, of a national or imperial unity to which he belonged; and therefore there was no general name by which the Unity of the Empire could be expressed.

Whether Abd ul-Hamid attached any importance to the adoption of one name or general designation for the Moslem subjects of the Empire, I am not aware. Perhaps it was outside the sphere of his interest . . . but at least it is inevitable that a process such as he was attempting to carry out should find a name to give expression to it, and the wide adoption of an imperial name in Anatolia is a marked feature of his reign, as I can assert from positive knowledge. The name was an old historic title, and the diffusion of it was a fact of Ottoman government long before Abd ul-Hamid, by his policy gave strength to a natural process in the Empire. . . . So far as I can learn there existed previously little, if any, tendency to real unification of feeling in the country, and therefore unification of name had little vitality. The tie to the Sultan sat very lightly on the many nomad and semi-nomad tribes in the country, while all Christians, Jews and certain heretic Moslems had no desire and were not accorded the right to call themselves by a name appropriate to imperial Turks. There did, however, exist a name which gradually established itself as an expression of unity in a Turkish-Moslem Empire. This name was the name Osmanli.[24]

But Abdulhamid's success at national unification should not be exaggerated. At the turn of the century, "Arab," "Laz," "Abaza," "Tcherkess," "Arnaut," "Kurd," and "Lezgi" were still words that referred to the social reality of the Empire.

The Young Turks (1908-1918) took over at a time when only this partial unification of the population of Asia Minor had been achieved. They tried to enforce a policy of cultural and educational unification throughout other areas of the Empire where much clearer ethnic cleavages existed and local groups were better organized. Their ineptitude and incipient nationalism combined to undermine what support they might have gathered for their regime. Lack of integration, demands for decentralized administration, as well as provincial opposition to what were considered the secular ideas of the Young Turks are a main theme of their years in power and appear within, as well as outside, Anatolia.[25]

Thus, Mustafa Kemal (Ataturk), who limited his objectives to redeeming Anatolia for Turkey, did not begin with a clean slate. In the earliest stages of organizing the movement for national independence, following the Ottoman withdrawal from World War I, his nationalist forces in Ankara were surrounded by insurgent groups supposedly working for the government of the Sultan opposed by Mustafa Kemal. While these groups proclaimed their aims to be the elimination of a rebel against the Sultan and to work for the greater glory of Islam, they also seem to have represented the forces of the periphery reacting against what they considered to be a continuation of Young Turk rule and a policy of centralization. Between 1920 and 1923, the fear that Anatolia would be split on primordial group lines ran as a strong undercurrent among the architects of Kemalism trying to establish their own center, and it remained as a fundamental— although often latent—issue of Kemalist Policy to the end of one party rule in 1950.

The problem of politically integrating this segmented structure only partly overlaps with the problem of national integration and may thus be taken up under a separate heading.

Social Cleavages in the Nineteenth Century

The end of the nineteenth century saw the beginning of the penetration of market values into certain more developed regions of Anatolia. Thus, the local notables' earlier basis of influence was gradually transformed, as notables of all types and origin took an increasing interest in economic pursuits. In this respect, the upper tier of the provincial periphery began to acquire a uniformity—if not a unity—which it never had had before. While one facet of this uniformity was the new focus of the notables' activities, another facet involved the new ubiquity of the opposing force: the greater penetration of the state into the periphery. These developments placed the parties to the center-periphery cleavage in a new confrontation that embodied elements of the earlier clash, but also partly transformed the nature of that conflict.

With regard to the notables, this transformation centered in the new area within which patronage began to operate. Patronage and client relations had long permeated Ottoman politics, but a structural transformation after the middle of the nineteenth century changed the total picture. For instance, the determination of the nineteenth century architects of reform

to make citizens out of the subjects of the Ottoman Empire, and to bring
the state into the periphery by imposing new obligations—taxes, military
service, various registration procedures—as well as by offering new benefits
—roads, the regulation of justice, land registration—placed the individuals
in the periphery in closer contact with the administrative and judicial
process. Before the gradual penetration into the periphery of a system of
centralist administration, inaugurated in 1864, notables still served as a
transmission belt of administration through locally elected councils working with provincial governors. This role, though modified with time, continued throughout the nineteenth century;[26] notables thus became more
clearly the hinge between the lower classes—the peasantry—and the
officials. Largely because of the hold that the state still maintained over
the economy, the new economic pursuits of the notables, where these
had become important, established a second link between notables and
officials. In addition, while the number of positions in the Ottoman administrative system had been considerably increased after 1876,[27] middle
and lower-rank officials were only paid in a desultory fashion. The
notables thus established a symbiotic relation with the officials, and bribing
acquired a new dimension. This was as much a necessity for the advancement of the notables' own interests as it was one for the rendering of
services to their clients. Among this new stratum of notables, one may
also place the provincial men of religion, a number of whom were property
owners and also belonged to the class of local "influentials." However, their
influence and leverage over the lower classes was also established through
involvement in religion and education. Faced with increasing secularization, these men became more clearly involved with the periphery.

With the success of the Young Turk Revolution of 1908, notables began
to appear in the ranks of Ottoman political parties and in parliament.
Where their influence can be traced, we see they stood for administrative
decentralization and for a continuation of local control over culture, which,
in fact, meant an attempt to keep the hold that men of religion had established over the system of values and symbols. This was especially true for
the poorer clerics, the men of religion who had no other basis of status
than their standing as men of religion.[28] But the view of Islam as the crucial touchstone of the Ottoman patrimony was shared by non-religious
notables. To this extent, an Islamic, unifying dimension had again been
added to the peripheral code; what had thus become a characteristic ideology of the periphery was not merely an idiosyncratic proposal of *Lum-
penulema*. One reason for this is clear: modern educational institutions had
perpetuated the pre-modern, cultural cleavage between the center and
the periphery. Modernization of Turkish educational institutions had begun with those of the officials. The provinces lay on the margin of the
world of elite education; the great majority of the provincials—even of influential provincials—were unable or unwilling to send their children to

modern schools. What data we have today suggest that only the brightest ones were packed off to the capital with hopes that they would be able to establish a channel of communication with official circles. In 1903 in the province of Konya—an area that had had some development—there were 1,963 students in the modern sector of secondary education, as opposed to 12,000 students in 451 *Medrese* (religious schools) providing the traditional equivalent.[29]

Entrance into the modern sector of education was much easier for children with fathers who were already part of the class of reformist officials, or even any part of the bureaucracy. In one of the key new educational complexes, the military schools, school socialization counted for more than family socialization, by its extension of education to middle school and by its recruitment of a large portion of students from less privileged families. In this military *milieu*, the critical view of the provinces as a backwater of civilization emerged sharply. The modernization of media and of cultural life in Turkey generally increased, rather than decreased, the gap between the "little" and the "great" culture. A clinging to Islam, to its cultural patrimony, was the province's response to the center's inability to integrate it into the new cultural framework. The provinces thus became centers of "reaction." Most significant, however, was the fact that the provincial world as a whole, including both upper and lower classes, was now increasingly united by an Islamic opposition to secularism. No doubt the decentralist notables found this development heartening. The lower classes in the Ottoman capital were also part of the periphery in this new sense of persons who had difficulties in joining the stream of modernization. In this newfound unity, the periphery was challenged by a new and intellectually more uncompromising type of bureaucrat.

Modernization as the Westernization of the Bureaucrat

Ottoman statesmen, although obliged to compromise with powerful notables, were never resigned to see them acquire real autonomy: this was the core of the code of the traditional bureaucrat. However, bureaucracy was also changing in Turkey during the nineteenth century. By the end of that century, the aspects of Ottoman bureaucracy that could be called "patrimonial" or "sultanic"[30] were giving way to a "rational" bureaucracy. The applicability of this Weberian formula is limited, however, in the sense that "bureaucratic" elements, such as hierarchical structure, were much more evident than "rational" claims, such as rewards based on performance.

One section of the Ottoman bureaucracy had been attuned to the requirements of modernization relatively early and had taken the leadership in reform during the nineteenth century. This reformist bureaucracy selected as the earliest nodal point of reform the modernization of the educational institutions preparing the military and the civilian bureaucracy. Taking over the French model of the "Grandes Ecoles," which was directed to aims very similar to those of Ottoman statesmen, the nineteenth century Ottoman reformers succeeded in producing a well-trained, knowledgeable bureaucratic elite guided by a view of the "interests of the state." In a way, the earlier elite was then perpetuated. It was now formed in molds that brought out a product in many ways comparable to the earlier official.

With the penetration of the state into the provinces, a new dimension was added to the traditional concern with shoring up the center. An attempt was made to establish a direct relation between the state and the citizen, which was partly the revival, in a new form, of an ideal of Ottoman statesmanship that there should be no intermediate allegiances between the Sultan and his subjects. During the later stages of reform, the creation of credit institutions and other facilities made a reality of the idea of the state as a provident father. When notables preempted these resources, they invited the antipathy of reforming statesmen.[31]

But to this opposition of reformist officials to notables we must add still another source of opposition which began to appear toward the end of the nineteenth century. The new conflict resulted from administrative modernization during the reign of Sultan Abdulhamid II. More precisely, it was a product of the Sultan's policy of half-way modernization, for while the Sultan worked hard to rationalize Ottoman bureaucracy, he also relied on individuals who countered his achievement-oriented directives. It is as yet unclear how successful in reaching access to higher positions were the graduates of the School of Political Science—an institution to the modernization of which the Sultan had given his full support.[32] Nevertheless, the younger bureaucrats and the military, who began to oppose the Sultan actively at the end of the nineteenth century, did believe that the highest administrative and governmental posts were staffed by persons characterized more by their loyalty to the Sultan than by their ability. As for the military, the Sultan's modernist reforms did not fit in well with his prohibition that large military units engage in maneuvers with live ammunition near the Capital. The attitude seeking to eliminate these contradictions and looking for a "closure" of the system might be called "national" bureaucratism, as opposed to the earlier, Ottoman ideology of "reason of state."

A further point at which the new, school-trained, national bureaucrats felt at odds with the Sultan was in their impatience to establish a modern state in Turkey. They allowed much less time for the elaboration of the nation-state as compared to the Sultan's more gradual—sometimes timid—approach. The national bureaucrat's impatience partly reflected the diffusion of nationalist ideologies into the Ottoman Empire. These ideas had affected part of the Ottoman intellectual establishment and created an intransigence not to be found among earlier reformers. No doubt the new view of science as the touchstone of truth, which had become influential in modernist circles of the capital after 1885, fitted in well with this attitude.[33] The old Ottoman motto of preservation of "religion and the state" thus emerged refurbished in the Young Turk slogan of "Union and Progress." After these new men took the Sultan out of the picture, following the Young Turk Revolution, the provincial notables seemed to them much more evil than they had been for the traditional bureaucrats, or even for early reformers. In the Young Turk parliament the notables' bills aiming at decentralization and less military control singled them out for suspicion at a time when separatist currents were beginning to be seen as a real threat.[34]

During the Turkish War of Independence (1920-1922), this center-periphery duality appears once again within the directing organ of the national resistance movement, the Grand National Assembly. Here the Kemalists were pitted against a diffuse group which was mainly the party of notables led by alienated members of the official class. This group has been known as the "Second Group." But in the Assembly they were augmented by a larger, more inchoate cluster of representatives with Islamist and decentralist tendencies whose membership cut across group lines.[35]

These men formulated a series of extremely interesting policies regarding representation, the military, religious instruction, and religious practice. They wanted to impose a five year residence requirement in an electoral district as a prerequisite to candidacy for election as a deputy; they attempted to control the military and began to attach the gendarmerie to the Ministry of the Interior, stating that the gendarmes were preying on the civilian population; they strongly supported education through religious schools; they passed a statute prohibiting the consumption of alcohol. Because we have no precise studies of the composition and uniformity of this group, we cannot say much about their cohesiveness, but the cluster certainly served as a rallying point against Kemalists.[36]

On the other hand, the more radical elements among the Kemalists protested that in the new law of municipalities "the people" were not represented on municipal councils. They also accused the notables of Bursa of having sold out to the Greek forces with whom the Kemalists were engaged in a life or death struggle. Both sides claimed to be working for "the people," but for the Second Group this expression had clear connotations of decentralization and economic and political liberalism, whereas for the Kemalist core it had undertones of plebiscitarian democracy and the state's duty to eliminate "intermediate" groups.[37]

The symbolic expression of the Kemalists' opposition to the Second Group and to provincials focused on religion. For the moment, however, Mustafa Kemal did not show his hand.

With the end of the War of Independence and the victory of the Kemalists, it became easier to assume a hold over politics. Sophisticated political tactics, as well as intimidation, were used with persuasion. The Republican People's Party, the Party of the Kemalists, successfully established discipline among its members. When an opposition party was formed whose activities coincided with a Kurdish revolt in 1925, a Law for the Maintenance of Order was passed giving the government wide powers for two years. Although there was no link between the Party and the revolt, the new opposition did represent decentralist aspirations. It was suppressed the same year because of what were said to be its links with "religious reaction," and indeed this, more than "Kurdishness," had been the central theme of the revolt.[38]

Although the primary aim in the suppression of this Party seems to have been the elimination of political rivals, the context in which it was made should be underlined. The nightmarish fissions seen before and during the War of Independence had traumatic effects; the Kurdish rebellion brought them to the surface. A second trauma, this time connecting political parties, the provinces, and religious reaction, occurred in 1930. At that time an experiment with multi-party politics which received strong support from the many groups opposing Kemalism, resulted in a minor "Patrona" type revolt in the town of Menemen.[39] The province, the primary locus of the periphery, was once more identified with treason against the secularist aims of the Republic. It is understandable, in this light, that beginning in the early 1930's, Mustafa Kemal should have devoted his energies to linguistic problems, cultural matters, and historical myths. It is no coincidence that he personally stepped into the picture at this time to forge a new national identity for the Turks.

In 1946 after Ataturk's death, when an important opposition political party was formed for the third time, the warning that went out from the Republican People's Party was characteristic: "Do not go into the provincial towns or villages to gather support: our national unity will be undermined,"[40] meaning "provincial primordial groups will be resurrected as political parties." Regardless of whether this argument was disingenuous, the fact is that between 1923 and 1946 the periphery—in the sense of the provinces—was suspect, and because it was considered an area of potential disaffection, the political center kept it under close observation.

Given all this tension, what is remarkable is that a sizeable portion of the provincial, notable class was successfully co-opted into the ranks of the Republican People's Party. This compromise did not differ radically from what prevailed at the time of the Young Turks, or even earlier. Dependent as it was on the notables, the center had few means of realizing the perennial Ottoman dream of working through ideally supine local intermediaries for the benefit of the peasantry. In fact, the Kemalist revolution could have been achieved in a number of ways: by an organizational revolution in which the notable was actively opposed, and/or by providing real services to the lower classes, and/or by an ideology focussing on the peripheral masses. In fact, the builders of the Turkish Republic placed the strengthening of the state first in their priorities, even though it meant the perpetuation of dependence on notables. This might have been a very wise decision, one that allowed Turkey to survive despite the economic and military weakness of the new Republic. Yet this option seems to have been derived not so much from what, in retrospect, seem rational considerations, but from the bureaucratic code: the center had to be strengthened—partly against the periphery—before everything else. It is this aspect of the bureaucratic code that was profoundly unrevolutionary, despite the populist themes which the Republic developed.

The Republican People's Party, the single party through which Republican policies were channeled, was unable to establish contact with the rural masses. The movement "toward the people," for which so much clamor had gone up in the first years of the Ankara government, was thin, and the possibilities opened up by the Republic for establishing new links between government and peasants were not fulfilled. In fact, the meager surplus of the agricultural sector financed much of the reconstruction of Turkey. The peasant still depended on the notables for credit, social assistance, and, in some regions of Turkey, protection. The symbol of the peasant as the "fundamental Turk" came up very early in the Kemalist movement, but Kemalist energies were devoted to the building of symbols of national identity, rather than to radically altering the place of the peasant in the system. This is fairly understandable in view of the limited resources of the Republic. But the problem, in fact, went deeper.

The members of the bureaucratic class under the Republic had little notion of identifying themselves with the peasantry. This is perhaps an unfair judgment, given the large literature on the village question that appeared in Turkey at the time and given the experiment of village institutes. I do not, however, recall any members of the ruling elite having constructed an operative theory of peasant mobilization, Russian or Chinese style. As for attempts by officials to identify themselves with the peasant, these are limited to a few radical teachers. Again, one has a feeling that the traditional Ottoman relation with the periphery is being perpetuated. Investments in education, which might be used as a shorthand notation to recapture the multiple layers of this attitude, show that what little capital there was came to be invested in institutions that would shape a generation of true Kemalists at the center.[41]

One consequence of apprehending the problem in these terms was the ideational cast of the Republican program: peasants were "backward" and would only be changed by transforming the laws of the land, such as the highly unrealistic village law—what Marxists would call the superstructure.

Integration from the top down by imposing regulations had been the general approach behind Ottoman social engineering. The characteristic features of Kemalism show that this view of society was still preeminent. In the Kemalist program, a theoretical commitment to the peasant repeated an old Ottoman theme, while peasant advancement was to be achieved by integration from the top down, an idea which also had an element of *déjà vu*. Altogether, the Kemalists had a fine understanding of *regulation,* but they missed the *revolutionary-mobilizational* aspect that, in certain contemporary schemes of modernization, mobilized masses for a restructuring of society. To the extent that regulation had always been a maxim of Ottoman rule, their ideas about modernization had an unmistakably traditional component. The only current within Kemalism which took note of the organizational-mobilizational side of modernization was the publication *Kadro* (1931-1934) which had a number of Marxist activists in its ranks. Just as the Kemalists missed the mobilizational aspects of modernization, they also did not see too well the nature of the *integrative* network of modern society, or were unable to legislate it into existence.

The thinness of Kemalist ideology has to be seen in this light. Ataturk was trying to do with ideology what he had not achieved through political mobilization or through a commitment to radical changes in social structure. This was a hard burden to shift onto ideology. The Turkish countryside, already suspect as separatist, was not brought closer to the center by these policies. While showing a remarkable ability for small but sustained growth, the periphery could see that it was paying for the prosperity of the cities, that it was being given speeches as consolation, but being denied the haven of its religious culture. Thus, it is not surprising that local notables kept their hold over the peasantry, and that the state was unable to drive a wedge into the unity of the periphery. The Democrat Party, founded by some erstwhile and prominent members of the Republican People's Party in 1946, was not so much a party of notables as it was a party that speculated with a political ideology which it thought would be strongly supported by the rural masses and by their patrons. This was the old Ottoman idea of the state being solicitous of the interests of its subjects: the protective state distributing justice on the one hand, and abundance on the other. But this time it was the periphery who had preempted this stance. To show that the issues that were so central to the opposition had their roots in the alienation from the center, we have only to look at the themes that won the Democrat Party 81 per cent of the seats in Parliament in the first multiparty elections. The new party promised it would bring services to the peasants, take his daily problems as a legitimate concern of politics, debureaucratize Turkey, and liberalize religious practices. Finally, private enterprise, equally hampered by bureaucratic controls and angered by its dependence on political influence, was also promised greater freedom.

Until 1946, the Republican People's Party had been at most a "means for political action." After this date, when parties emerged, it became "a medium for public participation in politics," but this transformation was not sufficient to entice the periphery to it.[42] On the contrary, the electoral platform of the opposition, especially as seen in Democrat Party political propaganda, in newspapers, and in the media, established the lines of a debate between "real populists" and "bureaucrats." This symbolic and cultural paraphernalia—the conspicuous patronizing of mosques and religious rituals by members of the Democrat Party and the reluctant follow-up by the Republican People's Party—laced with protests that secularism was being lost, identified the Democrat Party with the culture of the periphery. Ironically, its four official founders were just as much part of the bureaucratic "class" as other People's Party members.

The high resonance achieved by the Democrat Party's appeal to Islam as the culture of the periphery acquires greater significance in the light of a discovery by the Turkish sociologist Behice Boran in the 1940's. Boran found that as villages came into greater contact with towns, the villager began increasingly to see his village ways as inferior. The electoral campaigns of the Democrat Party intervened at just the right time to provide many transitional rural areas with the belief that they were not inferior. The Democrat Party relegitimized Islam and traditional rural values.[43]

The blows dealt to the power and the prestige of the bureaucracy between 1950-1957 endeared the Democrat Party to both the notables and the peasants. The alliance was now continued under new conditions; the laws of the Republic, the growth of the judicial apparatus, and the success of the Republic in building the infrastructure of reforms had gradually changed the master-servant relation between patron and client, except in the still undeveloped regions, such as Southeastern and Eastern Turkey. Economic power, rather than domination, increasingly set the relation between notables and villagers. Smaller men surrounding notables saw new opportunities for economic success. Deals, trade-offs, and bargains became much more pervasive than in the earlier situations, and client politics flourished on a new level. This was not the form of mobilization that the Republican People's Party would have approved, but it was undeniably a form of mobilization, a *form* that brought a greater portion of the masses into a meaningful relation with the center than had been possible under the Republican People's Party.

The Democrat rural following might not have realized that the very possibility of these bargains stemmed from the success of the Republican People's Party in building an economic infrastructure. The workers, who at the time usually voted for the Democrat Party, might not have thought that the Republican People's Party's earlier, progressive legislation had kept them from becoming a rootless proletariat, but then, gratefulness, as some members of the Republican People's Party have continued to believe, is not an element of politics. Moreover, in the early 1950's Turkey was still relatively land rich, and thus land redistribution was not a major issue. Altogether, the notable-peasant alliance, whose framework was a common understanding that collaboration would bring greater benefits to either side than would state control, worked rather well.

In these straits, instead of seeing its future tasks in terms of organization and mobilization, the Republican People's Party stood fast for the preservation of Kemalist ideals. And, thus, the bureaucrats selected it as the one party with which they could best cooperate. There were now good reasons to claim that the Republican People's Party represented the "bureaucratic" center, whereas the Democrat Party represented the "democratic" periphery.

The Revolution of May 27, 1960 once more underlined the cleavage between the center, now identified with the preservation of a static order, and the periphery, the real "party of movement." The old polarization of center against periphery acquired a new form: the preservers of the Procrustean, early Republican order against those who wanted change. The deposed president of the Republic, Celal Bayar, has recently commented that the difference between the Turkish Constitution of 1924 and the new constitution adopted after the revolution of 1960 amounted to the constitutional legitimization of the bureaucracy and the intellectuals as one source of sovereignty in addition to the "Turkish people," who had earlier figured as the only source of sovereignty in the Kemalist ideology.[44]

All of the protests mounted by the Republican People's Party that it was the real Party of change and the real supporter of democratic procedures were thus lost. Even the latest appeal of a faction of the Party to "populism"—an attempt to get down to the grass roots—dissipated, because the issue was not so much getting down to the grass roots as providing an alternative *means of fundamental change.* The grass roots had no confidence in the progressive, democratic, and populist policies outlined in the various electoral program of the Republican People's Party, because it placed no confidence in its methods of change.

It was easy for the periphery to identify the recent (1971) intervention of the military in Turkish politics with a desire for a return to the rigidity of the old order. Regardless of the intentions behind the move or the popular support for the reestablishment of law and order, the elements of the periphery still believe that their down-to-earth, direct, personal, observable method of mobilization and integration, with its short-run gratifications, is more tangible and presents fewer risks than the Turkish bureaucracy's system of mobilization by planned economy. Insofar as the center's attitude toward the periphery has been marked more by patronizing advice than by identification with the plight of the lower classes, they would seem to have a point. Planning seems to relegate all control over one's fate to the limbo of bureaucratic decision: once again, *regulation* raises its ugly head. Whether this is a correct assessment of the implications of planning is irrelevant; the polarity that the perception of regulation creates is that of officials versus all others.

Once my thesis is stated this simply, I should add that the picture is, in fact, more complex. Organized labor is not completely a part of the periphery. The cross-cutting cleavages of owners against non-owners of the means of production are an aspect of Turkish politics that could change the picture. A party representing the Shi'ite minority has emerged, and rumblings concerning Kurdish attempts at separate organization have been heard for some time. There is evidence both of new cleavages and of differentiation *within* the periphery. Certain members of the bureaucracy are now quite aware of the demands of a differentiated and integrated modern system, and some of them are defecting to parties representing the periphery. But these are future aspects of Turkish politics, and center-periphery polarity is still one of its extremely important structural components.

In retrospect, two facets of the peripheral code seem to have emerged with clearer outlines during modernization: the periphery as made up of primordial groups, and the periphery as the center of a counter-official culture. Both were *bêtes noires* of the Young Turks and of the Kemalists. But the policies of the modernizers, as well as fortuitous developments, worked to highlight the second facet of peripheral identity. Since this identity emerged in almost all of provincial Turkey, it was able to submerge —if not to overcome entirely—that aspect of the peripheral code that harked back to primordial allegiances. Later, this identity as counter-bureaucracy also provided a nationwide basis of allegiance for a party operating at the national level—the Democrat Party, and also for its successors. Thus, paradoxically, one aspect of the peripheral stance—of which the center was so suspicious—produced a national unity in the sense of provincial unification around common themes; it was used by the Democrat Party in its rise to power. The paradox is that this common code of the periphery which unexpectedly was productive of a unifying national skein, would probably not have emerged if the policies of the center toward the periphery had been more conciliatory.

REFERENCES

This article was written while the author was in residence at Princeton University as a Fellow in the Program of Near Eastern Studies. The author is grateful to the University and the department for the many facilities that were made available to this end.

1. My initial formulation is derived from Edward Shils, "Centre and Periphery," in *The Logic of Personal Knowledge: Essays Presented to Michael Polanyi on His Seventieth Birthday, 11 March 1961* (Glencoe: Free Press, 1961), pp. 117-130, here p. 117.

2. For "free floating" resources see S. N. Eisenstadt, *The Political System of Empires* (New York: Collier, Macmillan, 1969), *passim*.

3. For a general survey of these features see Halil Inalcïk, "The Rise of the Ottoman Empire," in P. R. Holt, Ann K. S. Lambton, Bernard Lewis, eds., *The Cambridge History of Islam*, Vol. I, *The Central Islamic Lands* (Cambridge: University Press, 1970), pp. 295-323, and compare with the earlier more assertive study of H. A. R. Gibb and Harold Bowen, *Islamic Society and the West*, Vol. I, part I (London: Oxford University Press, 1950-1967), pp. 39-199.

4. I owe this expression to Prof. Y. Abrahamian who uses it in a forthcoming article in the *International Journal of Middle East Studies*.

5. For relevant aspects of the development of the state in Western Europe see Reinhard Bendix, *Nation-Building and Citizenship; Studies in our Changing Social Order* (New York: Wiley, 1966), pp. 1-142; C. J. Friedrich, *The Age of the Baroque 1610-1660* (New York: Harper, 1952), p. 14ff.; R. R. Palmer, *The Age of Democratic Revolution*, Vol. I (Princeton: Princeton University Press, 1959); *passim,* and especially important here Seymour M. Lipset and Stein Rokkan, "Cleavage Structures, Party Systems and Voter Alignment: An Introduction," in Lipset and Rokkan, eds., *Party Systems and Voter Alignment: Cross-National Perspectives* (New York: Free Press, 1967), pp. 1-64.

6. Friedrich, *The Age of the Baroque,* p. 19.

7. *Ibid.,* p. 20.

8. The literature on this subject for the time of the formation of the Ottoman Empire is summarized in Speros Vryonis, *The Decline of Medieval Hellenism in Asia Minor and the Process of Islamization from the Eleventh through the Fifteenth Centuries* (Berkeley: University of California Press, 1971), pp. 258-285. J. Cuisenier, a French anthropologist, could still state in 1966: "There are truly two Turkeys, one of old urban tradition which is the Turkey of government, the other of rural tradition, a direct descendant of the Oghuz and Turkmen tribes to which belong 4/5th of today's Turks." *Etudes Rurales,* No. 22-26 (1966), pp. 219-242, here p. 224. For Eastern Turkey see Ismail Beşikci, *Dogu Anadolunun Düzeni* (Ankara: E. Yaÿnlari, 1969), p. 23.

9. See Gibb and Bowen, *Islamic Society and the West,* pp. 39-199 and compare with the more nuanced article "Devshirme" *E.I.,* 2, No. 2, pp. 210-213.

10. See Gibb and Bowen, *Islamic Society and the West,* Vol. I, part 2 (London: Oxford University Press, 1957-1969), *passim.*

11. See Halil Inalcïk, "The Ottoman Economic Mind and Aspects of the Ottoman Economy," in M. A. Cook, ed., *Studies in the Economic History of the Middle East from the Rise of Islam to the Present Day* (London: Oxford University Press, 1970), pp. 206-218.

12. See Ahmet Mumcu, *Osmanli Devletinde Siyaseten Katl* (Ankara: Ajans-Türk Matbaasi, 1963) Ankara Universitesi Hukuk Fakültesi Yayinlarindan no. 180, p. 71.

13. See Halil Inalcïk, "Osmali Padişahï," *Ankara Üniversitesi Siyasal Bilgiler Fakültesi Dergisi,* 13 (December 1958), pp. 68-79.

14. See Halil Inalcïk, "Land Problems in Turkish History," *The Muslim World,* 45 (1955), pp. 221-228. Land ownership was an important element in the boundary between center and periphery. Officials who acquired land surreptitiously—as well as the few who acquired legal title to it—usually shifted into a peripheral stance once they had gained control of these resources.

15. F. B. Kramers, "Ottoman Turks, History" *Encyclopedia of Islam,* first ed., Vol. IV, p. 959 ff. and M. C. Sahabeddin Tekindag, "Şemsuddin Mehmet Bey Devrinde Karamanlilar," *Instanbul Üniversitesi Edebiyat Fakültesi Tarih Dergisi,* 14 (March 1966), pp. 81-98.

16. For the traditional setting see "Askeri," *Encyclopedia of Islam* I, (2), p. 712. For the situation in 1968-69, see Ozer Ozankaya, *Köyde Toplumsal Yapi ve Siyasal Kültür* (Ankara: Sevinç Matbaasi, 1971).

17. For this concept, see Clifford Geertz, "The Integrative Revolution" in Geertz, ed., *Old Societies and New States* (Glencoe, Free Press, 1963), pp. 105-157.

18. See Gibb and Bowen, *Islamic Society and the West,* Vol. I, part 1, *passim.*

19. See *ibid.,* p. 247 and Ömer Lutfi Barkan, "Türk Toprak Hukuku Tarihinde Tanzimat ve 1274 (1858) tarihli Arazi Kanunamesi," in *Tanzimat: Yüzüncü Yildönümü Münasebetiyle* (Istanbul: Maarif Matbaasi, 1940), p. 325.

20. For the earlier importance of notables see Halil Inalcĭk, "The Nature of Traditional Society, Turkey," in Robert E. Ward and Dankwart Rustow, eds., *Political Modernization in Japan and Turkey* (Princeton: Princeton University Press, 1964), pp. 46-48. For later developments Stanford Shaw, *Between Old and New: The Ottoman Empire under Selim III 1789-1807* (Cambridge, Mass.: Harvard University Press, 1971), pp. 212-217.

21. See M. Munir Aktepe, *Patrona Isyanĭ: 1730* (Istanbul: Istanbul Üniversitesi Edebiyat Fakültesi Yayĭnlarĭ No. 808, 1958), *passim.*

22. See Joseph G. LaPalombara and Myron Weiner, "Conclusions: The Impact of Parties on Political Development," in LaPalombara and Weiner, eds., *Political Parties and Political Development* (Princeton: Princeton University Press, 1966), p. 413.

23. See Halil Inalcĭk, "Tanzimatĭn Uygulanmasĭ ve Sosyal Tepkileri," *Belleten,* 28 (1964), pp. 623-690.

24. W. M. Ramsay, "The Intermixture of Races in Asia Minor: Some of Its Causes and Effects," *Proceedings of the British Academy* (1915-1916), p. 409.

25. For provincial opposition to secularism at the time of the Young Turks, see the 96th and 97th sessions of the Ottoman Parliament, May 24-25, 1910, also 71st session, April 3, 1911.

26. For the Administrative Law of 1864, see Roderic H. Davison, *Reform in the Ottoman Empire 1856-1876* (Princeton: Princeton University Press, 1963), pp. 136-171.

27. Enver Ziya Karal, *Osmanlĭ Tarihi VIII: Birinci Meşrutiyet ve Istibdat Devirleri 1876-1907* (Ankara, 1962), (Türk tarih kurumu Yayĭnlarĭndan, 13 ser., No. 16, Dunya Tarihi 5), p. 329.

28. See Celal Bayar, *Ben de Yazdim: Milli Mäcadeleye Giriş* (Istanbul: Baha Matbaase, 1966), pp. 451, 475.

29. Server Iskit, *Türkiyede Neşriyat Hareketleri Tarihine bir Bakĭş* (Istanbul: Devlet Basĭmevi, 1939), p. 113.

30. I take this terminology from Max Weber, *Economy and Society,* Guenther Roth and Claus Wittich, eds., 3 vols. (New York: Bedminister Press, 1968), Vol. I, p. 229.

31. "Yeni Belgelerin Işığinda Kâmil Paşanın Siyasal durumu," *Belleten*, 35 (January 1971), pp. 60-117, here pp. 110-111.

32. Andreas Kazamias, *Education and the Quest for Modernity in Turkey* (London: Allen and Unwin, 1966), p. 90, note 12. I was alerted to this information by Joseph L. Szyliowicz, "Elite Recruitment in Turkey: The Role of the Mulkiye," *World Politics*, 23 (April 1971), 386, but cannot concur with his interpretation that 10 per cent of graduates in higher posts is "significant." This data is also at variance with that given by Leslie L. Roos, Jr., and Noralou P. Roos, *Managers of Moderniza-tion Organization and Elites in Turkey (1950-1969)* (Cambridge, Mass.: Harvard University Press, 1971), p. 20.

33. See M. Orhan Okay, *Beşir Fuad* (Istanbul: Hareket Yayinları 1969), *passim*.

34. See Celal Bayar, *Ben de Yazdim*, Vol. II, p. 449, note 1.

35. On the Second Group, see Tarik Z. Tunaya, *Turkiyede Siysî Partiler* (Istanbul, 1952), pp. 538-539 and Halide Edib [Adivar], *The Turkish Ordeal* (New York: Century Press, 1928), p. 183.

36. On the control of the gendarmerie by the civilians see *Turkiye Büyük Millet Meclisi Zabit Ceridesi* I, 29/6-7-1336. Latin script edition Vol. II, pp. 182-183.

37. On municipal boards not being representative of the people see *Türkiye Büyük Millet Meclisl Zabit Ceridesi*, I, 43/3-8-1336, Vol. III, p. 85; on notables evading military service, *ibid.*, Vol. II, p. 433; on notables as persons primarily interested in protecting their property, *Ibid.*, Vol. II, p. 260.

38. See Tunaya, *Turkiyede Siyasî Partiler*, p. 617 on article 14 of the party program. On the revolt see Bernard Lewis, *The Emergence of Modern Turkey*, 2nd ed. (London: Oxford University Press, 1968), p. 266.

39. See Lewis, *The Emergence*, p. 417.

40. F. Köprülü, "Partiler ve Millî Birlik," in *Demokrasi Yolunda* (The Hague: 1964), p. 304.

41. M. T. Özelli, "The Estimates of Private Internal Rates of Return on Educational In-vestment in the First Turkish Republic 1923-1960," *International Journal of Middle East Studies*, 1 (April 1970), pp. 156-176.

42. Osman Faruk Logoglu, "Ismet Inönü and the Political Modernization of Turkey 1945-1965," Unpublished Ph.D. Dissertation, Princeton University, 1970, p. 135.

43. Behice Boran, *Toplumsal Yapi Arastirmalari* (Ankara: Türk tarih Kurumu basimevi, 1945), pp. 218-219. Boran points out that this was a transitory situation but it nevertheless served the Democrat Party well.

44. Celal Bayar, "Başvekilim Adnan Menderes," *Hürriyet*, June 29, 1969.

ERNEST GELLNER

Post-Traditional Forms in Islam: The Turf and Trade, and Votes and Peanuts

ORIENTALISTS ARE at home with texts. Anthropologists are at home in villages. The natural consequence is that the former tend to see Islam from above, the latter from below. I remember an anthropologist specializing in a Muslim country telling me of his first encounter with an elderly and distinguished Islamicist. The old scholar observed that the Koran was interpreted differently in various parts of the Muslim world. The young anthropologist remarked that this was indeed obvious. "Obvious? Obvious?" expostulated the older man angrily, "It took *years* of careful research to establish it!"

The story has various morals, but one of them is that the diversity of Muslim civilization is now a well-established fact, amply documented by scholars and by field workers, and it no longer requires further documentation. In its day, it was no doubt a useful corrective to the simplistic view which took Islam at face value and assumed that, because Muslim life is the implementation of *one* Book and its prescriptions, therefore Muslim civilization is homogeneous. This view need no longer be fought. The time has come to re-assert the thesis of homogeneity, not so much as a thesis, but as a problem. For all the indisputable diversity, the remarkable thing is the extent to which Muslim societies resemble each other. Their traditional political systems, for instance, are much more of one kind than were those of pre-modern Christendom. At least in the bulk of Muslim societies, in the main Islamic block between Central Asia and the Atlantic shores of Africa, one has the feeling that the same and limited pack of cards has been dealt. The hands vary, but the pack is the same. This homogeneity, in as far as it obtains, is all the more puzzling in the theoretical absence of a Church, and hence of a central authority on Faith and Morals. There is no obvious agency which could have enforced this homogeneity.

It is worth trying, rashly but tentatively, to identify some of the main cards in this pack, as a preliminary to an examination of some curious examples of what happens when hands drawn from that pack are dealt in a modern context.

191

The elements which go into what one may call the Islamic social syndrome fall into two main groups: the ecological/technological, and the ideological. All this refers to the traditional context, defined loosely and summarily (and perhaps question-beggingly) as the conditions preceding the impact of the modern and Western world on Islam.

Ecology and technique: Muslim societies between the Hindu Kush and the Atlantic were characterized by the symbiosis of urban, literate, centrally governed, trade-oriented communities, with tribal ones. Tribes may be defined as rural communities which partly or totally escape control by central government, and within which the maintenance of order, such as it is, is left largely to the interplay of local groups, generally conceived in terms of kinship. What is so striking a characteristic of Muslim civilization is the numerical and political importance of tribes. Tribes were not unknown on the margins of Christendom or Hinduism—but they were far less important. This fact is mirrored to this day by the popular Western stereotype of the Muslim as a fanatical turbaned tribesman on a camel— what one may call the T. E. Lawrence, North West Frontier or Beau Geste image. This is of course in striking contrast to Islam as seen from inside, as an urban faith, practicable only with difficulty in an illiterate milieu of desert or mountain.

One may rephrase this characterization in terms of the technical and institutional equipment of Muslim societies. They assumed literacy, urban life, long-distance trade, and central authority. But they also assumed, or had to live with, the fact that the central power and the towns could not effectively control outlying tribes, though at the same time they constituted, economically and religiously, one community with them. All this assumes a level of population which has forced enough people to live in marginal mountain and desert regions, and to be sufficiently numerous out there to constitute a threat. The central power does not possess adequate technical and organizational resources for the effective subjugation of the tribes; at the same time, the general ecology of the tribes is such that they need urban markets and specialists, and remain in sustained contact with the towns. (In Platonic terms, the tribes resemble the inflated rather than the self-sufficient and simple city, and hence autarchy is not open to them. As Ibn Khaldun noted—and it sounds surprising to Western ears—economically, the tribes need the towns, rather than vice versa.) This economic need is reinforced by what may be termed moral ecology: the tribesmen identify with a religion which, through literacy, ultimately must have an urban base. These factors lead to that characteristically violent symbiosis of tribe and urban-based government.

What are the ideological cards which are dealt by Islam? The crucial ones are: a scriptural faith, a *completed* one (the final edition, so to speak) is available, and there is no room for further accretion or for new prophets; also, there is no warrant for clergy, and hence for religious differentiation;

and, third, there is no need to differentiate between Church and State, between what is God's and what is Caesar's, since it began as a religion of rapidly successful conquerors, who soon *were* the state. These are the basic data, as they emerged when Islam shook down, so to speak, to its settled form in the early centuries of its existence.

Islam is trans-ethnic and trans-social: it does not equate faith with the beliefs of any one community or society (even the total community of the faithful). But the trans-social truth which can sit in judgment of the social is a Book, plus the traditions—a recorded Revelation, rather than an institution. Thus by implication Islam is not clearly tied to any one political institution or authority. But at the same time, this implication fails to obtain reinforcement or support from any tradition of state/church opposition. The early community was both church and state, and thus this differentiation never fully developed, as it does in a faith which organizes itself long before it captures the state. The Shi'ites, who did need to organize before they captured the state, and organized in order to do so, did develop a theory, *taqiya*, not so much concerning what is God's and what is Caesar's, but concerning the permissibility of telling Caesar what he wished to hear, while keeping the truth to oneself.

The consequence of all this is that the trans-social standard which judges the social is a Book, and not a Church. This can then be socially incarnated either in the corporations of literate interpreters of the Book, or in such spiritual leadership which emerges as best it can, notwithstanding the lack of a clear charter for it.

This is the setting, these are the elements in the power game which limit the available political and doctrinal moves. Within the limits thus set, what were the options? The dominant notions available for political legitimation, in these circumstances, were:

Communal Consensus	The Book	Organization, Leadership, Ancestry

These are the three central ideas that were available, arranged along a spectrum, from a kind of Left to a kind of Right. The Book is, on the whole, shared ground: few extremists go so far as to actually suspend its authority in favor of either spiritual leadership (on the Right) or of Communal Consensus (on the Left). Though such extremist deviations do occur on the Left and on the Right (particularly on the Right), they remain relatively rare. An extremist Left deviation, in this sense, would allow the consensus of the community to override the Book; an extremist Right one (and this has been known to happen) would deify an individual and allow *him* to over-rule the Book. "Left" and "Right" are here in effect defined in terms of egalitarianism versus hierarchy and hereditary inequality. The tension between these two is endemic in Islam: the egalitarian element is inherent in the universalist, scriptural, no-clergy, proselytizing elements of the faith. The inegalitarian element is inherent in large and complex organization, and the articulation of inequality in terms of heredity follows from the fact that the societies incorporated in Islam were and remained kinship-oriented societies. Conventionally, two somewhat contradictory theories are given by historians of the *origin* of this conflict: one, that the impetus to inequality came from the early conquerors and their desire to maintain their privileges against the conquered and the later converts; the other, that the egalitarianism was rooted in Arab tribal traditions, while the inegalitarianism originated in the monarchic inheritance of the Persian converts.

Origins need not concern us in the present context. What does concern us is that the tension is inherent in the situation. In practice, extremism was rarer than either the moderate Left or Right positions—which are the fusion of a cult of the Book either with a cult of the Community, or of Leadership (and hence, of hierarchy and organization).

The interesting thing is that the tension and conflict can be played out in two different ways—which I shall call the Unbounded and the Bounded. Chronologically, the Unbounded comes first, the Bounded becomes more common later. The reason for this sequence seems straightforward. The Unbounded way of playing out the conflict is the consequence of the *early* situation when no bounds, no limits, had yet clearly emerged, and hence protagonists were easily pushed into relatively extreme positions. No markers were there to signpost danger and to encourage caution. The Bounded style, on the other hand, is a consequence of a certain maturity, of the emergence of well-known and recognized limits which protagonists respect and which they cannot and will not easily violate. At the start, they could hardly help violating them, for the boundaries were not laid down. Later, when the boundaries became well known and revered, the average participant in the religious-political game—and the vast majority of the participants are, naturally, rather ordinary and unexceptional people—will hardly dare brand himself as a heretic by transgressing them. A scriptural religion which believes its Revelation to be complete has a natural tendency towards delimiting the possible moves in the game.

In concrete historical terms—in the early years of Islam, the plugging of either the egalitarian or the inegalitarian card led to the crystallization of the Kharejite and the Shi'a sects or heresies respectively. Neither of these tendencies need in normal circumstances be extremist, nor push either communal consent or the cult of personality to its utmost limits (though in Shi'ism, the tendency towards deification of personality was present and on occasion emerges). In normal times, either principle can be fused with a recognition of the Book and the Traditions.

But it is characteristic of the early centuries that, for the lack of established and familiar bounds to the game, these two tendencies did end up as outright sects—heresies from the viewpoint of the main community and of each other. If we are right in the claim that the tension between the egalitarian and the organizational principles was inherent in the situation, what happened to it in later centuries?

Basically, people learned how to keep it within limits: clear bounds emerged, and being clear, were more easily enforceable. The tension which, at the beginning, emerges as that between the two *heresies*, one each at either end of the spectrum, the Kharejites and Shi'ites, appears at a later stage *within* the fold, between the ulama and the Sufi. Sociologically speaking, the Sufi is an addict of leadership, of the cult of personality, who does not allow it to run away with him, or whose leader knows how to remain within the bounds of orthodoxy. The member of the corporation of the ulama is a member of a tradition which has found a compromise between the sovereignty of the community and the sovereignty of the Book, by having within the community a non-sacramental guild of scribes-lawyers-theologians, guardians and interpreters of the social norm, who yet do not claim deep or hereditary differentiation of spiritual status.

All this, though no doubt contestable, is not original. But it was necessary to rehearse the manner in which the traditional, pre-modern situation generated a certain possible span of religious-political attitudes, of styles of social legitimation. There were, as stated, two spans—one broader, one narrower; both were generated by the same basic tension between an egalitarian faith and inegalitarian social requirement, but one span *dépassait les limites* and was articulated in terms of rival heresies, and the other managed to stay within bounds. As far as I can see, the main reason why the same tension sometimes did, and sometimes did not, break out of limits was simply the clear demarcation of those limits, and this in turn was a matter of age and maturity. Movements which in the early days of Islam would have made a bid for a total takeover of the whole community, and would in consequence have ended as outright heresies, in *later* centuries, when the Community as a whole seemed too stable and well-established to be available for take-over, generally contented themselves with more modest claims *within* the faith.

There are various common theories of the origins and roots of the Sufi movement within Islam: the influence of mystical traditions springing from Christianity; India; pre-Islamic Middle Eastern thought; local cults; a reaction to the aridity of scholastic Islam; a reaction to foreign encroachment. There are no doubt important elements of truth in these various theories. But the most important factor, at least sociologically, seems to be the inescapable requirement of religious *organization* and *leadership*. Formal Islam is capable of providing this only to a limited degree: it can do so when the State is strong, as in the Ottoman Empire, by linking religious organization with political authority; and it can, and does, provide the legal "schools," the corporations of scribes/teachers/jurists, who moreover can provide leadership of a limited kind only. Being numerous, they can ratify better than they can initiate, and being scholars, they can make their weight felt only in the kind of milieu in which they are respected and in which they flourish. But if we reconsider the ecological and military balance of Muslim societies, the manner of the symbiosis of tribe and city, we see that the Muslim world does not *everywhere* provide a milieu which favors the scholarly legal schools and makes their members adequate for the problems of leadership. Nor does it always favor a strong state. Sufism provides a theory, terminology, and technique of leadership, far more generally usable, in tribe, village or town, under government or in anarchy, but one which, unlike Shi'ism, does not normally transcend the limits of orthodoxy. Sufism is a kind of Reformation-in-reverse. It creates a quasi-church.

So much for traditional society. What is especially interesting are two well-documented specimens of adaptation of old Islamic movements to *modern* conditions. Each of our two specimens is drawn from the "Right" end of the spectrum, from organizationally complex and inegalitarian movements. One is Shi'a, one is Sufi: in other words, one is older and operates, conceptually, outside the bounds, and the other can claim to have remained within the orthodox, Sunni fold. Both are conspicuous success stories in the modern world, and in each case the success is highly paradoxical: for generally speaking, the conditions of the modern world favor literacy, sobriety, rationality, formal equality, all of which are found on the moderate "Left" of the Islamic religious spectrum. The modern world has not favored Sufism; and Shi'ism, though it holds its own relatively speaking, has all in all not been an active political force, and its characteristic, distinguishing features have not been conspicuously displayed. One suspects a tacit shift to the left within it.

Here we have two relatively extreme movements, neither of them particularly attuned to the allegedly rational, production-oriented, and egalitarian spirit of the modern world. Each of them, one should have said, was doomed to fare ill under the cold wind of either colonial commercialism or the subsequent cult of economic development. Neither had any good reason to welcome the modern world, and each of them had good cause to fear it. Any resemblance between these particular Shi'ites or Sufis, and the puritanical entrepreneurs of popular sociological theory, is not so much coincidental as downright unbelievable. Yet, strange to tell, each of these particular movements is not merely famous for the success of its adaptation to modernity, but owes this success, above all, to brilliant *economic* performance. This paradox deserves consideration.

Within the Shi'ite part of the Muslim spectrum—in other words, the segment of Islam turning towards a cult of personality rather than consensus mediated by scholars—there were further internal differentiations and dissensions. The *Ismailis* tended to extremism. Of the Shi'a as a whole, Bernard Lewis writes: "A recurring feature is the cult of holy men . . . who were believed to possess miraculous powers. . . . Among the beliefs attributed to them are those of reincarnation, the deification of the Imams . . . and libertinism—the abandonment of all law and restraint."[1] Expectation of miracles and a suspension of all Law—of such material successful orderly entrepreneurs are *not* made!

Within this general tradition, the Ismailis are not among the moderates: "The imam is central to the Ismaili system of doctrine and of organization, of loyalty and of action. . . . The imams . . . were divinely inspired and infallible—in a sense indeed themselves divine. . . . As such, [the imam] was the fountainhead of knowledge and authority—of the esoteric truths that were hidden . . . and of commands that required total and unquestioning obedience."[2]

These were large claims. Their implication for political theory are plain: "For men to think of electing an imam is . . . blasphemy. He was revealed by God . . . the imams are perfect sinless beings. The imam must be obeyed without question . . ."[3]

The implications for political practice are even plainer. If you believe that you, or your Leader, is "infallible . . . [and] the executor of the word of God," you possess a fine legitimation of revolution against current rulers who are not so remarkably qualified. Hence, from the viewpoint of those rulers, you are not merely a heretic, you are also a most disagreeable political danger. And as you constitute such a menace to others, your own chances of survival must be correspondingly small.

And so it was. Not surprisingly, many of the varous lineages of pretenders to the Imamate were violently eliminated and became extinct (quite unlike those very numerous lineages that also claim descent from the Prophet, but without extravagant political or theological pretensions, and which have multiplied exponentially in the Muslim world). The various sub-segments of the Shi'ites have diverse beliefs covering the disappearance of the Imam: some believe that the last Imam known on earth is still living incognito and will reappear, others believe that the Imam is incarnated in a different person in each generation, but remains concealed. But as luck would have it, *one* at least of these lineages survived, or is believed to have survived, and is represented not by someone hidden or transcendent, but by a living and identified person. At the same time, the theological claims made on his behalf remain undiminished.

The sect which, presumably by the hazard of history, has survived with a concrete, tangible Imam is the *Shia Imami Ismailia* which, thanks to the activities of recent Aga Khans, its leaders, is well known and incorporated into popular English (and perhaps now international) folklore. The modern history of the movement begins in 1840 when "the first Aga

Khan . . . fled from Persia after an unsuccessful rebellion against the throne."[4] Nothing unusual or interesting about this: this is the normal stuff of Muslim history. A leader endowed with a religious aura and some tribal support tries his hand at challenging the central power. Normally such efforts fail. If the leader is unfortunate, his severed head is displayed on the city gate by way of demonstration of the inefficacy of his charisma. If he is fortunate, he manages to escape. This one did: to British India. There he rendered some valuable service to the British Raj, and was awarded a pension and the title of Aga Khan. In due course, he settled among some of his followers located in Bombay.

But all was not well. Certainly not as well as one might expect, if one remembers the absolute and total claims made by members of the sect for their Imam. If he was truly infallible, sinless, and the executor of the word of God, in a sense indeed divine, the followers behaved in a manner which can only be characterized as impious. Divine or not, they disputed the payment of tithes, and forced the sinless one to take them, not to the Last Judgment, but to the High Court of Bombay. Moreover, these litigants against their own living Imam had some very interesting arguments on their side, in defence of their practice of using Sunni, non-Shi'a officials to officiate at their weddings and funerals: this practice had begun in the days of *taqiya,* the officially sanctioned Shi'a doublethink permissible in the face of a hostile unenlightened government, and they felt they could continue it now, though Caesar was no longer hostile, but neutral.

The dispute remained unsettled and went to the courts again in 1866. The opponents of the Aga Khan among his supposed followers put forward something that was, in substance, a non-Shi'a position, one which shifted sovereignty, and in particular the control of communal funds, to the community rather than the divine leader. Under the Pax Britannica, of course, religious sovereignty could no longer signify temporal power—but it could still signify financial power. The decision was now in the hands of a British judge.

His judgment was the crucial event in modern Ismaili history. From the viewpoint of Shi'a Ismaili theology, his judgment was impeccable, and resulted in the absolute transfer to the Imam of communal property, without responsibility of trusteeship. Given Ismaili theology, he could hardly do less. Whether Mr. Justice Arnould's sociology was as sound as his theology is a question we may leave aside.

With the wealth he now controlled, thanks to Shi'a theology and British law, the then Aga Khan had the means to live in a princely Indian style which gave him, and his successors, social access to the British rulers. The third Aga Khan went to Europe in 1897 and dined with Queen Victoria. He maintained his position as somehow a member of the British ruling class, of the international aristocracy of title and wealth, and as the divine reincarnation of his own sect. His story and that of his successor is familiar from the world's press. What is surprising is that its sociological morals have been so seldom spelled out, though they are not hard to discern.

Shi'a theology is of a kind familiar on the "right" wing of Islam, whether that right wing goes beyond the limits of orthodoxy, or stays within it (as with the Sufis). By stressing a person at the tacit expense of the Book and at the open expense of the Community, it verges on, or reaches, anthropolatry. But the significant thing is that under the "normal" conditions operating in the traditional Muslim world, the extreme claims of obedience are balanced by the social reality of power. The claims to absolute and total obedience (though not the approximations to divine status) are made even by minor little Sufi shaikhs. But the "normal" religious movement within Islam is constituted of dispersed pockets, tribal and urban, physically separated from each other and operating in a partly anarchic environment. The government may be hostile, and whether or not it is, travel is perilous and arduous. Under such circumstances, whatever the theology may say, the effective control by the leader of his followers and lodges is inevitably loose and precarious: effective control rests, if it rests with anyone, with the local representatives of the leader. The leader himself can only maintain his leadership, and hope to receive some tithes, if he skillfully manages and plays off the various local leaders—if, in effect, the prestige pay-off for *them,* of their connection with *him,* is greater than the loss they incur by submitting, more or less, to his authority. Of course, he may try to seize political power, so as to strengthen his position. For that particular end, he will value and cultivate his tribal supporters rather than his urban adherents. Urban adherents may come on pilgrimages and pay tithes, but to reach the throne one must be carried by a cohesive tribal group, as was stressed by Ibn Khaldun.

The weakness of the then Aga Khan vis-à-vis his urban followers was only too clearly demonstrated by their willingness to take him to court. So was the fact that their urban position evidently tempted them in the direction of theological moderation and of Sunni orthodoxy, with which they were blatantly flirting. All this is true to type, as was his attempted rebellion against the ruler of Persia.

But now a completely new set of circumstantial factors begins to operate: British India was an effectively centralized state, in which the verdicts of the courts were properly enforced. So when Mr. Justice Arnould found in favor of the Aga Khan, this was not an empty verdict, nor a mere preliminary to endless further litigation. On the contrary, it settled the matter. Moreover, under the Pax Britannica, the more taxable Ismaili traders of Bombay, with a greater tithe potential, so to speak, were *far* more valuable adherents than the tribesmen driving their flocks somewhere in the Persian mountains. With luck, the tribesmen might once have carried their Imam to the throne, but that throne was now out of reach, and from the viewpoint of long distance tithe collection, those tribesmen were probably, if not a dead loss, at least not a very impressive asset. The traders of Bombay were a different matter. No one could ever have ridden to a throne with their help, but when it came to tithes—a different matter altogether.

So far, however, only theology provided a sanction for the payment of those tithes. Mr. Justice Arnould's verdict added the existing communal wealth, and thus the means for adopting a style of life which gave the leader access to the topmost British rulers. And at this point, we witness a crystallization of a new social form.

After the court verdict, presumably the Ismaili traders of Bombay could do little to recover their existing communal property, now handed over without accountability to the Aga Khan. There was nothing to stop them from drifting away. But this they did not do, or at least a significant proportion of them did not. At some point, the reality of a new situation must have dawned on them, and converted them to a more pious and deferential attitude, however (if at all) they may have articulated it to themselves.

They were a trading community in a well-governed state, and their divine Imam had access not merely to God but also to the otherwise very distant and not fully intelligible British rulers. Every little holy man claimed privileged access to God, but Lord Dufferin, the British Viceroy, was socially more exclusive. Under an effectively centralized colonial regime, such as British India, where countless communities competed in a very complex society, real direct contact with the rulers was an incredibly valuable asset. So, evidently, the Ismailis of Bombay overcame their egalitarian, orthodox, Sunni leanings, and reverted to a theology whose exaggerations of human divinity had been elaborated in so different, and near-anarchic, a context (for the anarchy and indiscipline of which they had indeed been intended as a kind of over-compensation). But now, there was no chaos to compensate: British India was well governed. So the exaggerated claims, effectively enforced by the courts, gave the communal leaders the financial and social means for doing something quite different—namely meeting the rulers on the turf and the polo ground. And this was no matter of mere worldly frivolity. Who was better placed to protect and aid his community than one who had the ear of the rulers, one who had access to the centers of power and information?

This remarkable combination of an ideology, worked out in one set of circumstances (and seldom effective there, though it may have been the best thing available), with a completely different and unforeseen set of circumstances, is the real sociological clue to the familiar story. No doubt, the remarkable women—Persian, British, or jet-set—whom the successive Imams married and who busied themselves with the movement's affairs, were a great help. The success was not possible without some individual ability and energy. But the real clue remains elsewhere. The Ismailis could not have brought it off without the historical accident of possessing a living and manifest, rather than a hidden and transcendent Imam. The fact that they possessed, within their ranks, an urban trading population, as well as some tribal populations in the Iranian highlands, was not an accident. Most movements do have such a diversified following. But among the Ismailis, under the new order, the center of gravity of the sect moved to this part of the followership.

The "right wing" theology, in terms of the Islamic spectrum, continued to be invaluable. A "left" community which requires consensus, mediated by the guild of scholars, makes reform, and in particular drastic and rapid reform, extremely difficult or impossible. Some of the scholars will always see heretical innovation in any change, and if you try to push through some reform, the community will tear itself apart in inner conflict. But if the leader is authoritative and near-divine, if the person of the leader, rather than Book or consensus is the heart of the faith, reform becomes relatively easy, always assuming that the leader is inclined in that direction. The social contacts of the Aga Khans aided their perceptions of the direction of the winds of change. Who could challenge the leader's innovations? We have then the pre-conditions for a kind of purely spiritual Stalinism, or a spiritual Peter the Great, for dramatic development made possible by the concentration of leadership in one center. And, in this case, the Stalinism could indeed be spiritual, and employed means quite other than physical compulsion: a trading population, operating under a centralized colonial regime, had every motive for following a leader who could, through his political contacts, do so very much for them, and who was ideologically legitimated for doing this. They did not need to be compelled. If Paris is worth a Mass, then the trading opportunities of the British Empire were surely well worth the Shi'a principles of incarnation, succession, and divine leadership, all the more so if you are already nominally committed to them anyway. And so it was. The Ismailis prospered famously, displaying entrepreneurial virtues and ideology which is virtually an inverse Weberian paradigm.

With the end of colonialism, the situation changed again drastically. Minority trading communities, now even more dispersed and minoritarian through their very trading success, could no longer rely for protection on a leadership with contracts primarily with the erstwhile colonial rulers. On the contrary, as a minority, and a rich one, they found themselves the natural targets of economic and social nationalism. It is a curious feature of the 1972 Uganda crisis that the present Aga Khan, who combines divinity with an official position as U.N. Commissioner for Refugees, has not been openly *visibly* conspicuous as a protector of his followers. But it is an indication of the remarkable success of the movement in the preceding era, that it is by now so well established that it may salvage a good deal even from the present, far more unfavorable, circumstances.

The Murids of Senegal are the objects of a recent brilliant study.[5] Like the Ismailis, they too are famous for a specific *Wirtschaftswunder*. They are not as famous as the Ismailis, but nevertheless, fame of their economic exploits is part of Africanist folklore, and the religious-authoritarian manner in which they appear to achieve it arouses the indignation of the international Left. The power they appear to have to cause peasants to cultivate a new cash crop in arduous circumstances, opening up new lands in the process, for very meager material rewards, must also inspire much envy among economic developers. These Muslim holy men appear to have succeeded where the British Groundnut Scheme failed so notoriously. How do they do it? As in the case of the Ismailis, a simplistic answer is available and is indeed current: they persuade their followers that they will go to paradise if they work like blacks growing groundnuts in this world, and their credulous followers do as they are told, thus enabling their "feudal-religious" leaders to live in opulence. Were it so simple!

The followers of the Murid religious brotherhood are recruited mainly from one ethnic group, the Wolof. The Wolof had a strong state organization within what is now the republic of Senegal. Their society was sharply stratified, with a middle stratum of peasantry and a top stratum of royalty, court, and warrior class, and a low or perhaps ambiguous stratum of slaves or servants. This latter class is normally classed as a *low* in the literature, but it seems possible that, like military or administrative slave personnel in some Middle Eastern states, their position could vary considerably. Be that as it may, it was the top and the slave strata which were most affected by the French destruction of the state of Kayor in 1886.

Prior to the French conquest, the Wolof were already strongly but not completely Islamized. The diffusion of Islam in the societies of black Africa takes many forms: Islamic scribes may be imported as administrative technical aids to government: or they may exist to justify opposition to government. Islam may be carried by nomads, or by traders.[6] Amongst the Wolof, it would seem that Islam appealed to the classes resenting the oppression by the warrior aristocracy. Nevertheless, warm relations evidently existed between the ruler and Muslim religious leaders.

The man who was destined to found this brotherhood, Amadu Bamba, had but a handful of disciples at the time of the battle of Dekkilé in 1886, when the French finally destroyed the native state. After some peregrinations and two exiles, and a religious revelation around 1891, his movement, formally an offshoot and segment of the great Qadiriyya brotherhood, came to have 70,000 followers by 1912, the date at which it began to have good relations with the French authorities. It continued to grow and became one of the greatest economic, social and political forces in modern Senegal.

How was this achieved? Anyone can claim to have the key to salvation, and ambitious preachers and thaumaturges are not lacking in West Africa. What concatenations of circumstances, what special crystallization accounts for this most remarkable success?

Donal Cruise O'Brien's excellent study documents the answer admirably. The French thoroughly destroyed the old local state and the social hierarchy sustained by it. At the same time, their conquest increased the opportunity for marketing cash crops: they encouraged such cultivation, and of course colonial taxation in itself creates a need for a cash income. Inside the land of the Wolof, there was a socially displaced population, which had lost the roles it had enjoyed under the old order. Re-creating the old order was impossible: the chiefs tolerated or created by the French were small-fry, not comparable with the old rulers. As in the case of displaced populations in many parts of the world, religion offered the most plausible alternative form of organization. The most easily available model and leadership was that of a Sufi religious brotherhood.

Inside the Wolof area there was a dislocated population; but outside it there was uncultivated and under-used land, well suited for groundnut cultivation, and owned in an ambiguous way, as these things go, by Fulani pastoralists. An obvious solution would be for the uprooted Wolof to settle these new lands, prosper with the help of a new and desired cash crop, help the new rail lines to prosper, and bask in administrative approval for this economic enterprise. But it was not quite as easy as that. An individual Wolof settler-squatter on Fulani territory would soon find himself attacked and destroyed by the Fulani. Even if he could stand up to them, which was unlikely, he probably would not know how to produce groundnuts successfully. The erstwhile aristocrat or slave from a Wolof state did not necessarily possess either the required skill or the equipment. Before the human need and the physical opportunity could meet, some organization was required which would bring them together.

Here was the basic key to the Murid success. It possessed the framework of an easily understood—because familiar—type of organization, and a kind of organization which can easily be expanded when recruits are available. The loose hierarchy of shaikh and follower, with a ranking of leaders in a pyramidal federation, is familiar in Muslim lands and can easily be emulated. But, of course, this advantage was shared by other religious orders. A special, and as it happens, both an ideological and organizational twist was required, to adapt this religious brotherhood for the particular task for which it was destined.

One of the earlier important converts of the founder of the movement was Shaikh Ibra Fall, a Wolof aristocrat with a strong personality, no scholarly leanings whatever, and a curious, indeed idiosyncratic, penchant for physical work. He did not seem inclined to the scholarly and/or mystical initiation which is the stock in trade of Sufi religious leaders. It was he who started and organized the *working* novitiate, which turned out to be such a crucial innovation in the structure of this Order.

There is nothing inherently novel in the performance of a voluntary corvée by the devotees of a religious leader, either as a substitute or a supplement of voluntary tithes. To cultivate the living saint's field, or help build his house, are perfectly familiar notions in, for instance, North Africa. What was original was the systematic organization and expansion of this principle by a lieutenant of the leader, himself of prestigious lay origin, who somehow canalized the enthusiasm which his class had once felt for their status and for warfare, into a positive ethic of work. It is not true, apparently, that the Murids believe work to be a substitute for prayer: but they do lay unusual stress on work as the form taken of the submission which is required by the follower vis-à-vis the leader. This submission, theoretically total, is a common trait of these religious orders or brotherhoods. The follower, it is characteristically claimed, must be in the hands of his shaikh as is the corpse in the hands of the washers of the dead. Otherwise no mystical illumination will come. What was novel here was that the submitting "corpse" was required or encouraged not to scholarship and mystical exercise, but to the planting of groundnuts without much or any remuneration.

But this "ethic of work" did not achieve this remarkable human and social transformation unaided. More mundane motivation, more concrete circumstances were also operative. The population was uprooted. It knew that land was available, if only it could be seized, and that a profitable cash crop could be grown and marketed, if they learned how to grow it. The religious kibbutzim, so to speak, at which the novitiates worked so self-lessly, with apparently nothing but spiritual salvation in mind, were in effect agricultural training centers, and the adepts took no vows for life, but could look forward, after some years of service, to the reward of an individual holding. Furthermore, a family with one representative at the Murid agricultural labor settlement was thereby linked to a powerful movement and system of protection and patronage. In the meantime, the organized kibbutz, protected by a religious aura and a powerful, extensive, well-organized and well-connected religious Order, favored by the administration (which could look forward to economic development through its activities), had an incomparably better chance of seizing Fulani land— and making it prosper—than individual squatters could ever have had.

We have here something very similar to the Zionist movement, with a religious brotherhood performing the role of the Jewish Agency, and the Fulani in the role of the Arabs. Free-lance Jewish settlements in

Palestine, without organization, could hardly have withstood Arab opposition. Moreover, they could hardly have transformed a nation of non-farmers into farmers in difficult and initially most unrewarding circumstances. Zionism was fortunate in having, in Socialism, an ideology which already and independently pervaded the mental climate of 19th- and 20th-century Europe, and which, through its populist elements, prized collective work on the land without individual remuneration, and which thus ratified a human transformation which had to be accomplished anyway if Jewish resettlement of the land of Israel was to become a reality. (Without the presence of such an ideology, that resettlement might have resembled those European settler populations in Africa which were either driven out, as in Algeria, or forced into repellent extreme measures of a caste society, as in South Africa.) The Murids could not draw upon any such general socialism; they were fortunate in the accident of the enthusiastic enlistment of a secondary leader who was ill-suited for normal Sufi pursuits, but who had a splendid penchant in the right direction, and great organizational ability.

It is worth noting that in certain senses, Muridism is Zionism-in-reverse. The Wolof once had a state, and Muridism gave them a religious organization instead—where Eastern European Jewry had had a religious organization and exchanged it for a secular state. Jewry had been occupationally specialized and Zionism diversified it; the Wolof had possessed a state with a diversified stratification and the Murid movement (though it created a leadership of its own) turned this diversified population into a more homogenous set of groundnut-growers.

It is useless to try and explain the success of the order by simply invoking the authoritarian traditions of Sufism. For one thing, all the countless other orders share them. For another, the cult of submission is very deceptive. It is the equivalent, in Sufism, of the tendency to deify the leader found in Shi'a Islam. In neither case can it normally be taken at face value. It is precisely because organization is normally so very weak, that the doctrine of discipline is so very exaggerated. Ideological excess tries, vainly, to compensate for organizational weakness. The typical Sufi order is a loose and dispersed federation of holy centers, where the minor ones balance the losses inherent in submission against the advantages gained from the spill-over of prestige from some famous center. Sanctions of central authority are weak. The Murids, however, had unusual incentives and opportunities for making the submission more significant, and they had some special doctrinal and organizational features which could bring motivation and opportunity together.

Their opportunities did not end with the settlement of land and the extensive cultivation of groundnuts. Senegal was one of the first of the French overseas territories to become involved in French electoral politics. The Murids could and did peddle votes as well as peanuts. With the approach of Independence and the struggle for power of the early years of Independence, votes were particularly valuable. Thus the organization resembled not merely the Jewish Agency, but also the American Democratic Party. It is not only immigrants who need aid and protection, and repay it at the voting booths. Colonial dislocation had made the Wolof migrants in their own lands.

As in the case of the Ismailis, the favorable circumstances were not to last forever. New lands for groundnuts were not unlimited. Novices cease to be such, and in the end must be rewarded. Once power crystallizes in a new African state, elections cease to be serious and votes become less valuable. Recent reports suggest that groundnuts have lost much of their economic attraction. All the same, a powerful organization, once established, has its own momentum, and its fame and past achievements are in themselves valuable assets. It is too early yet to speak of the fate of the movement in post-colonial conditions. It is not without resources and may yet deploy them to good effect.

These are two striking cases of "post-traditional" social forms. Both are paradoxical, not to say piquant. In each case, a fortunate combination of circumstances has enabled a particular set of organizational and ideological elements, inherited from a tradition in which they were but slight variants of a standard pattern, to make a marked impact in novel circumstances. Shi'ism is an unpromising candidate for the Protestant Ethic, but the followers of the Aga Khan are famed as entrepreneurs, and it seems unlikely that without their Shi'a faith, they could have been as successful as in fact they have been. Sufism does not resemble socialism and looks like most unpromising ideological equipment for the formation of agricultural kibbutzim, but, in its Murid form, this is just what it has achieved. It too was essential for an unusual achievement. In either case, an explanation in terms of the faith alone and its preaching is woefully inadequate, but in either case, the faith played a crucial part.

REFERENCES

1. Bernard Lewis, *The Assassins* (London: Weidenfeld and Nicolson, 1967 and 1970), p. 24.

2. *Ibid.*, p. 27.

3. H. S. Morris, *The Indians in Uganda* (London: Weidenfeld and Nicolson, 1968), p. 67. My account of the Ismailis is heavily indebted to this admirable book.

4. *Ibid.*, p. 68.

5. Donal B. Cruise O'Brien, *The Mourides of Senegal* (Oxford: Clarendon Press, 1970).

6. I. M. Lewis, ed., *Islam in Tropical Africa* (Oxford: Oxford University Press, 1966).

ELBAKI HERMASSI

Political Traditions of the Maghrib

THE CONTEMPORARY Maghrib offers such a complex array of institutions, values, and attitudes that almost any theory can find sufficient illustration to lend credance to its validity. Depending upon one's theoretical perspective, the Maghrib may be described as either traditional or modern. The gap between theories generated and shaped by European, colonial experiences and the spectrum of local realities is usually bridged by the deliberate selection of case studies. With rare exceptions, anthropologists are drawn to Morocco, where they perceive a nearly unbroken continuity of the traditional order. Political scientists seem more at home in Tunisia, where the existence of modern political institutions affords them the opportunity to substantiate theories of political development. Algeria, on the other hand, provides ammunition for many diverse interpretations. The massive involvement of the peasantry in the war of liberation justifies those who see in Algeria elements of revolutionary change, while those who prefer to look at inter-elite conflict have read into this involvement the manifestation of ancient tribal rivalries.[1] Despite the close scrutiny and the detailed analyses, these theorists have not been able to explain the range of variation between these societies or to compare the general features of nation building in the Maghrib with other regions of the world. They tend, for the most part, to lack a historical perspective from which to analyze both the continuities and the discontinuities in the symbolic and structural dimensions of these societies.

By inquiring into past and present political orders, this paper attempts to clarify some of these issues. It is argued that the political order has been historically problematic. Throughout the history of the Maghrib, the center-forming collectivities have generally lacked an integrative framework and a basis for legitimation. The state usually drew legitimacy from Islam, a value system which cut across state boundaries and seriously undermined any one state's claim to ultimate loyalty. The state also failed to control from the center the marginal communities. Thus, the major legacy of the pre-colonial Maghrib has been one of collectivities normatively unified and politically divided.

The establishment of the nation-state represents, however, a fundamentally changed situation. I hypothesize that the challenges for contemporary national elites have ceased to be those of national integration. Marginal groups have been generally—sometimes violently—incorporated into the central national framework; and a community of political destinies irreversibly links all Moroccans, Algerians, and Tunisians to the ultimate fates of their nations. The conditions under which national unification was achieved highlight institutional integration as the major challenge for nation building.

The nation-state came to be accepted prior to the development of institutional facilities that would include rural and urban populations. This is related to the ways in which a legacy of external unification and the grafting of a modern colonial economy eroded the foundations of the traditional society without bringing sufficient structural and occupational differentiation to the society at large. In contrast to Europe, where the nation-state was accompanied by a commercial, industrial, and political revolution which profoundly altered the social structures and created a residue of secondary organizations, much of the Maghrib has yet to develop an institutional infrastructure that might channel the different sectors' aspirations and activities and involve the periphery in the policy choices of the center. As a result, regimes tend increasingly to be evaluated on the strength of their performance in building institutions and offering social and economic opportunities, rather than on the mere upholding of "Tradition."

An analysis of the history of national state formation—or the ways in which a nation's particular structure has evolved—can provide us with an understanding of the coherence and transformative capabilities of the existing political orders. It can delineate the vast range of variations for dealing with the institutional dilemmas by which the states are pressed.

The adoption of Islam in the eighth and ninth centuries represented a great cultural revolution. The scattered Berber communities, which had lived until then only in the shadows of Punic, Roman, Vandal, and Byzantine history in North Africa, were compelled to move to the center and build their own civilization. But while Islam formed them as historical empires, the classic polarization between the political, economic, and cultural life of the centers and the tribal hinterlands was too deeply enmeshed in the ecological structure to be easily erased. Until quite recently, the relationship between political centers and their peripheries, which anthropologists describe as segmentary and marginal,[2] oscillated between violent confrontation and uneasy accommodation.

During the formative period, political crystallizations were largely legitimized by Islamic ideals. These crystallizations typically emerged as unitarian and puritan movements whose predominant objectives were the social integration and the spiritual homogenization of tribal structures within an all-embracing political and religious community. These were, in other words, self-conscious reenactments of pristine Islam. The most significant efforts to forge an empire orginated in Ifriqiya (present-day Tunisia) with the Fatimids and Zirids in the ninth and tenth centuries, and in the western Maghrib (present-day Morocco) with the Almoravids and the Almohads in the eleventh and twelfth centuries.

These unitarian movements allowed the Berber population, which might otherwise have graced our memories only as a folk culture, to construct a civilization of its own, creating the Maghrib as a distinct cultural area, shaped by Islam and Arab culture but different from Arab, Persian, and Turkish civilizations. With a forged identity and a set of political traditions, the Berbers were to achieve, in only a few decades, relative political autonomy. Henceforth, only within the territory of the Maghrib would political and religious tensions be worked out. However, since belligerent tribes and utopian sects competed to impose a new vision upon the area of the Maghrib as a whole, the new states were completely at the mercy of the same peripheries from which they had been created. Every medieval state was structurally condemned to an insurmountable political instability.

The dynamics of such a political system are lucidly analyzed by the participant-observer, Ibn Khaldun. He argues that under normal conditions regimes are protected from disintegration at the center by the tribal proclivity for fragmentation. He uses the concept of "Asabiya" to denote both the propensity of peripheral segments to neutralize each other in local feuds, and their capacity to intermittently overcome internal segmentation through corporate cohesion. He further identifies religious prophecy and reformist leadership as being highly instrumental in stimulating the tribal corporate action that was most corrosive of the existing dynasties.

The reason why Islam legitimized political revolutions must be sought in the inherent tensions of early Islam as well as in its lack of orthodoxy. Medieval dynasties were required to be both just, in order to fulfill religious aspirations, and powerful, in order to control the periphery and defend the empire against external encroachments. These requirements were often contradictory. For example, the reenactment of pristine Islam required that taxes be imposed only on the conquered, sparing the believers. Controlling the periphery, however, demanded the presence of an independent and permanent army. Sooner or later the rulers were led to impose non-canonical taxes: an innovation (bid'a) which was immediately exploited by competing religious sects. In the absence of mechanisms for accommodation, ideological conflicts tended to be intense and total. Given this background, we can appreciate the scenario which was enacted every three or four generations, with marginal units, toughened by the harsh environment and enflamed with religious fervor, overthrowing the weak and immoral dynasties. Once it became an empire, the movement confronted the same old problems of community and polity; and it, too, eventually succumbed to the easy urban life, losing its spartan virtues and, in its turn, was replaced.

This, in essence, is Ibn Khaldun's theory of the tribal circulation of elites.[3] The vulnerability of the political order led him to define the problem as one of tragic antithesis between social cohesion and civilization. Only the tribesmen were able to construct the kingdoms upon which the cities depended but were unable to build for themselves; yet only within the city did civilization flourish. This dilemma remained insoluble.

The collapse of the prophetic unitarian movements in the fourteenth century brought in its wake a second period characterized by two major trends. One was a spiritual fragmentation known as the "Maraboutic Crisis"— essentially, a drift of the local communities away from involvement with the centers and the appearance in their midst of local holy men. This crisis most deeply affected Morocco, shaping its political future up to this day. Clifford Geertz writes:

Morocco splintered, in this period, into a collection of larger and smaller polities centered around holy men of one sort or another . . . a proliferation of zealous, insular, intensely competitive hagiocracies, sometimes called maraboutic states, though most of them were more like utopian communities, aggressive utopian communities, than proper states.[4]

The rise of the Alawite monarchy in the seventeenth century introduced the cult of personality into the matrix of central rulership, endowing the Moroccan state with the traditional style it has since maintained.

The second trend consisted of the central power's relative stabilization and the end of the tribal circulation of elites. This trend became even more pronounced after the establishment of the Turkish administration in Algiers and Tunisia in the sixteenth century. In these places, the state proceeded to consolidate itself without any concern for either transcendental legitimation or the expression of the community's aspirations. The state managed to achieve differentiation through the foundation of makhzens (Establishments) that were free of the problematic tribal support and based on an independent army. The ubiquitous result was the emergence of military monarchies capable of thwarting tribal takeovers, though still unable to incorporate the periphery. Indicative of this stabilization, the ensuing dynasties each lasted more than three centuries, some enduring until the contemporary era.

This whole evolution of political structures was regarded by local historians as a period of decadence. The feeling among the literate and urban strata was one of nostalgia for the former era that, despite its violent symbiosis, had brought together the scattered pieces of the society. What followed was a widening gap between the center and the periphery, each living its own life until the first stirrings of nationalism.

The major preoccupation of the consolidated patrimonial system was to secure resources in order to meet the needs of the administration and army and to support the ruling class in the life-style to which it was accustomed.

Thus, the cost of stabilization, in the context of marginal dissidence and subsistence economy, was to reinforce the conception of society as merely a domain for resource extraction. In the continuing differentiation between the inner and outer Maghrib, regimes were usually able to control and tax the towns, villages, and coastal plains where they appointed governors, rendered justice, and owned rural domains. They could rely on the support of the newly formed religious orthodoxy which above all stressed obedience to authority. With the exhaustion of Islam's revolutionary potential, however, and with the withdrawal of the rural community from central concerns, there were limits to effective taxation. Tribal communities, in particular, managed to elude taxation, organizing their resistance in such a way that they remained bound to the rest of the community. They were led in this resistance by holy men and religious brotherhoods that continued to settle disputes and to interpret Islamic Law in what was variously named *bled-es-siba* (land of insolence), *bled-el-Khela* (land of abandonment), and *bled-el-baroud* (land of gunpowder).

In order to provide for its maintenance, the state came to rely upon Mediterranean trade to supplement its insufficient internal resources. Although this benefited the existing makhzens, Mediterranean trade encouraged trade monopolies, permitting European powers and their merchants to become too involved in the politics of the Maghrib. Moreover, the resources created by this trade permitted the existence of any regime, whether or not it had local support. At any rate, the maladjustment of state to society precluded a genuine unification, or any economic breakthrough.

A political order whose existence depended less on its institutional and symbolic expression of the social order than on its propensity for manipulation and expediency could endure only to the extent that it recognized and negotiated with local constellations of power.[5] The lack of meaningful communication between the state and the peripheral populations created the very conditions suitable for the emergence of local leadership. Local leaders were able to capitalize on the centrifugal tendency of tribal communities who fled from the crushing burden of taxation. Under the increasing pressure for centralization in the nineteenth century, intermediary leadership was able to use the state to buttress its position in local dealings, while at the same time using the tribal communities to defend its prerogatives against official encroachments. To the state, the intermediaries presented themselves as the integrators of anarchical subjects, and to the tribes as the last rampart guarding against a fatal submission.

The most significant variation in styles of governance as well as in degrees of political unification depended primarily on the type of relationship between the state and the diverse forms of intermediary leadership. In Algeria, the political vocation of empire-building was comparatively weak. There were scarcely any central traditions available to the Turks, who, as a result, used Algiers more as a Mediterranean base for piracy than as the capital for unifying and building a country. Thus, beyond the radius of a few miles from Algiers, Titri, Wahran, and Constantine, most of the population depended on local military and saintly leaderships. This tradition of dual government tempted the European powers to substitute one foreign minority for another.

The drive for unification from the hinterland was accelerated when the precarious equilibrium between Turks and Algerians was upset in 1830 by the French conquest. The local leadership, not the Turks, defended the Algerian soil. "Abd-el-Kader," writes Tocqueville,

is in the process of building among the Algerians . . . a form of power more centralized, more agile, more strong, more experienced, and more ordered than any of its predecessors for centuries. . . . It is, thus, necessary to try to prevent him from accomplishing this frightful work.[6]

With the termination of this sole effort for unification, future Algerian political elites would find it difficult to utilize any past residue of organization to provide a sense of national identity.

In Morocco, as previously mentioned, the institution of the Sultan as both ruler and holy man did not fulfill the requirements for political integration. First, there was a disassociation between power and sanctity. Whereas the Arabized urban population was attached to the Sultan as a political ruler, the Berber tribes of the Rif and Atlas held to his sacred person but opposed his political establishment. Second, the makhzen, almost forming a society of its own, was in constant competition with parallel forms of power: religious orders, intermediary leaderships, armies, and foreign nations. In a society that remained fundamentally plural, the monarchy employed its sanctity to aid in arbitrating between micro-polities, in the same manner that local saints had settled tribal disputes. It is important to note from the outset that the monarchy acquired the capacity to govern, beyond the classic role of mediation and compromise, only with the inheritance of a French colonial administration.

The population was cohesive and urbanized in Tunisia. There were neither linguistic, nor ethnic divisions, and the country was able to claim a long history as an autonomous political unit. In achieving its autonomy from the Ottoman Empire, the Husaynid Dynasty managed to attain a modus vivendi, if not a relative symbiosis, with local elites and old families who were entrusted with the daily administration of the country. The Husaynids even attempted to introduce limited measures of "modernization," such as the proclamation of a Constitution in 1861, the encouragement of economic activity among the peasantry, a fiscal exemption for twenty years, and land redistribution. They also created special schools, a central bank, and a military academy. However, these reforms suffered the same fate as those introduced by the young Turks in the Ottoman Empire and by M'hammet Ali in Egypt. While they created the first Tunisian generation of reformers, they also exposed the inadequacies of the governmental machinery and the indifference of the masses to world trends.

As the states in the Maghrib became more stable, tribes never appeared again as the bearers of new dynasties. The Abd-el-Kader and Abd-el-Krim movements against the French pursued political directions different from the traditional ones of religious revivalism.[7] Islamic ideals no longer regulated the society, and the government was accepted only insofar as it provided public order and did not frustrate customary practices. In no way did the government decompose the fundamental mixture of pride and suspicion which marked the political culture. One observer asked local leaders why they bothered to put up a fight against governmental troops when the taxes were so minimal. They answered:

It is true that the sum is not much, and that the Kahiya [governor's representative] is a decent man who does not demand too much from us. Still, if we pay without causing any difficulties one year, he may well be tempted to increase the levy the following year. In any case, it would be shameful for mountaineers to pay at the first demand.[8]

For institutional as well as technological reasons, the political system clearly failed to provide an integrative framework. The only symbols of unity were to be found in the attachment to the homeland (patriotism), which increased with foreign contact, and religion, which continued to provide the verbal environment for identity despite the altered situation.

With the exception of Tunisia, which will be treated separately, the superimposition of the colonial system brought the periphery under full control. Rural resistance to French occupation lasted nearly a quarter of a century in Morocco and Algeria. It was followed by the final submission of the marginal areas and the transformation of frontier zones into fixed boundaries. By breaking down the old barriers between groups, the colonial system undeniably established frameworks for national consciousness and national integration.

However, from the viewpoint of the societies in the Maghrib, these frameworks were not created by integration into modern economic networks, by the introduction of new political institutions, or even by the formation of new and distinctively national, cultural orders. Rather, the paramount reality of colonialism was one of administrative and military control. Sustained by these coercive instruments, the colonial state juxtaposed the European population to the native population within a quasi-caste system which institutionalized differences in power, economic position, and cultural identity.

Essentially, the new colonial system proceeded through the existing framework of the pre-colonial order, exacerbating its inner tensions. Economically, for example, the area was divided into the "Maghrib utile"—the mild and irrigated coastal plains—and the "Maghrib inutile"—the steppes and the Atlas Mountains. The natives were driven from their fertile lands into the rugged parts of the country, while the Europeans were supplied with the land, machinery, and markets necessary to undertake the commercialization of North African agriculture. In this process of superstratification, local landowners and merchants, from Tunisia and Morocco especially, were allowed to take advantage of the newly-created economic opportunities, but the rest of society was abandoned to the principles of Ricardian political economy.

Politically, beyond the generalization of taxation, a total form of administration, and a downgrading of status, nothing sustained the new order save coercion. "We did not," writes Tocqueville, "bring in Africa our liberal institutions. We rather dispossessed it of the only ones which resembled them."[9] From the start, the colonial system reflected its built-in inconsistencies: on the one hand, it provided a framework for national integration; on the other, its very existence depended upon the deliberate maintenance of a bifurcation of the polity and the society.[10]

It is, nevertheless, true that there is a rich variety of form and degree in colonialism. The extent to which colonialism actually shapes the future contours and determines the substance of a given nation has rarely been carefully analyzed. Algeria, for example, owes much more to the colonial period than to any other period of its history. In each instance, the outcome depends on a number of variables: the initial political traditions of a given country; the economic standing of the colonial power itself at the time of conquest (France under the Second Empire was still a predominantly peasant society); the length of colonial domination; the extent of demographic and economic implantation; the type of colonial policy regarding, especially, the established political structure and the methods with which it is controlled and the larger strata of the population.

Algeria experienced the longest period of colonial domination (1830-1962), a third of that time being spent at war. Its fabric underwent the most systematic disruption, because the colonial system was predicated on the deliberate disorganization of the social order. Tribal organization was dismantled for two purposes: first, to inflict a blow against rural resistance; second, to dismember the collectively owned land, transferring it to individual settlers through expropriation, confiscation, and other expedient measures of the Napoleonic Code. The breakdown of tribal organization was reinforced by the administrative drive for total and permanent control. Traditionally, the district and sub-district paralleled tribal divisions and subdivisions, but these distinctions were entirely obliterated by the new administration. Dividing what was previously united in the Arab speaking population, and uniting what was previously divided in the Kabyle speaking population, the new arrangements represented a complete break with past modes of social organization. Even the people of compact areas, such as

Kabylia and the Aures, where minimal forms of self-administration had persisted, were forcefully relocated during the military efforts of the 1950's to thwart the struggle for national liberation. The French administrative legacy in Algeria and the consecutive wars made the peasant civilization "a tabula rasa," in the words of one anthropologist, "of which one could only speak as something of the past."[11]

Algeria was not only deprived of its economic base, but also of its culture. The Turkish state, as well as that of Abd-el-Kader, was destroyed. The urban literati and rural notables were deprived of their positions when they did not join in the massive exodus. With the downgrading of these "protecting strata," the society lost its essential support and "the motor for any genuine collective evolution."[12] The systematic erasure of all existing signs of Algerian nationality gravely threatened the societal identity and led a great segment of the nationalist generation to doubt even the existence of something called the Algerian nation. One prominent figure, Ferhat Abbas, who later became the head of the provisional government, wrote in 1936: "I have interrogated history; I have interrogated the living and the dead; I have visited cemeteries, and no one spoke to me of the Algerian nation."[13]

In this situation, the elite's political choices were either a plea for assimilation or simple revolt. The Algerian mass, reduced to a dust of individuals, built a whole network of resistance in order to preserve a few threads of national identity. This despair allowed the ulema—the only institution permitted under colonialism—to play a significant cultural role. But on the whole, there was no room for the development of an institutional leadership or for a mature national movement.

The French occupation of Morocco occurred a century later, and, discounting the period of the war of occupation (1912-1934), effective colonial government lasted only twenty-two years. The changes in the international context, in French policies, and the tragic condition of the Algerian experiment favored a different approach in Morocco. The system was predicated on the protection of traditional institutions and the maintenance of existing social structures: tribal patrimony was preserved, collective land was declared inalienable, and the submission of dissident communities was effected in the name of the Sultan. The monarchy was given minimal power and was used to legitimize French political control of Morocco. It was precisely on this contradictory use of the monarchy and on the disassociation between the symbols of legitimacy and the locus of power that the fate of Morocco came to rest.

The French formula required the monarchy to oppose the periphery; but once its power was secure, the colonial government revived the old contrast between the land of government and the land of dissidence in ways that challenged the cultural and political unity of the Moroccan empire. The French removed the Berber tribal territory from monarchical control and, by underwriting the customary law, offered it the option of existing separately from the national legal system. France supported the intermediary leadership and even permitted it to build small empires. Special military academies were founded to train Berber officers in the unspoken hope that they might someday assist in governing the country. This preservation of certain traditional political institutions was accompanied by a "primordialization" of politics which had debilitating effects on the national movement's capacity for constructing a civic order. The policy of partition weakened the few national elites, and in a society which remained practically unchanged, political energy was spent in maintaining the unity of the society.

Broadly sketched, these are the institutional settings in which the balance between forces tending toward the reestablishment of the old political order and toward the structural reorganization of the system can be analyzed. It is easy to understand why in Morocco the monarchy, rather than a modern national elite, played the central role as a symbol of national unity. In the national liberation movement, the poorly organized elite established some momentum by enlisting the support of the urban masses—in particular, the working classes of Casablanca. But they could never quite reach the rural society, which remained the exclusive domain of the colonial administration. France actually employed the traditional elements of society, the ruling chieftains and the religious brotherhoods against the national movement; ultimately, it even arrested and exiled the Sultan himself (1953-1955). This event triggered a widespread opposition to the French throughout the country; it removed the latent opposition of the intelligentsia to the monarchy and secured the Sultanate's future position as the axis of the entire political system.

The transformation of Algerian society, in an environment that precluded political expression, meant several things: that the challenge to France could be settled only through armed confrontation; that the revolutionary leaders who sponsored the national liberation movement would seek support from the peasantry rather than from the urban middle class, as they did in Morocco and Tunisia; and, finally, that the process of the whole political system would be redefined in a revolutionary direction. It is easier to learn about this revolutionary direction from the many crises surrounding the Algerian leadership than from the predispositions of the different classes involved.[14]

The major predicament of the Algerian Revolution, from start to finish, was the absence of institutional authority—the kind of leadership which defines the key commitments and maximizes cooperation between different groups for the fulfillment of common goals. Because of the political vacuum imposed by the French, the Algerians could neither save an embattled monarchy, nor be mobilized by a national political party. Some thought that authority could be wrested from the revolution itself. As expected, the revolution was overwhelmingly supported by the Algerian society and by the peasantry, in particular. The initial nucleus of revolutionary leaders was, in time, reinforced by the whole range of political elites—legalists, ulema, and a younger generation of intellectuals, students, and military officers.

As the revolution assumed national and international dimensions, greater attention was devoted to its ideological repercussions than to the objective conditions of the war. The war, which divided French society to the point of toppling the Fourth Republic, proved even more damaging for the Algerian elite. The intensification of the military operation led to a growing strain, first between the FLN (National Liberation Front)—an unstable coalition of political groups forced into exile—and the military components of the revolution. Then, following the construction of barbed wire barriers at the western and eastern frontiers of the country, a small part of the army broke up into *wilayas* (provincial forces), while the main bulk of the army moved across the Tunisian and Moroccan borders. The increasing fragmentation of the revolutionary front, and the fact that groups had to fight in relative isolation from one another, created a confusion within the incipient political class as to leadership and as to the rank and strength of the different sectors. For, beyond a unanimous commitment to the symbols of the revolution, there was never a consensus on the norms governing the distribution of power between the various political sectors. Because the ranking of different organizations remained unsettled even after independence, the contest between the Algerian leaders over which institution embodied the revolution was ultimately decided by the only organization that had the monopoly of force, the loyalty of its members, and a claim to national representation: the national army.

The Tunisian case falls between the two extremes of Algeria and Morocco. Unlike Algeria, which France conceived as its own creation, and Morocco, which France believed it had unified for the first time, Tunisia was a relatively coherent nation-state requiring only administrative and economic organization. Colonial administration (1881-1956) did not confront, at first, any significant rural resistance; consequently, the military component of government was underemphasized. The social and economic foundations of Tunisia were rudely shaken, but land expropriation was checked. The protecting strata were permitted to retain power under foreign rule. When the Tunisian monarchy began losing ground, modern national elites, though often persecuted, were tolerated as the *porte-parole* of the nation. As a result, political elites experienced profound generational and ideological transformation. They gradually broadened their circle of supporters, especially from among the petty-bourgeoisie and the intelligentsia, and built in 1920 a solid political organization—the Destour Party—which has remained to this day the undisputed national political authority.

The newly-established states of the Maghrib diverged, unquestionably;

in fact, national identification, after independence, was secure from pan-national appeal, as well as from internal partition. International opinion and scholarship have often missed or misinterpreted this; that the symbolic framework had been profoundly altered and that a community of political destinies linked all groups to the national frame of reference may be documented by a plethora of evidence.

Following independence, the states in the Maghrib experienced a series of inter-elite conflicts and rural unrest which were over-hastily interpreted as a reenactment of the age-old pattern of primordial dissidence.[15] Under close examination, however, most of these conflicts, far from being movements opposed to the political order, prove to be instances of active commitment to it. As a rule, regional discontent is intimately bound up with the issues debated at the center: it reflects concern for the primacy and influence of different elites within the state machinery and the flow of benefits to the various regions.

In Morocco, where most of these conflicts occurred, the political struggle became a contest between the monarchy and the political elite for control of the state apparatus. In this confrontation, rural followers needed leaders near the central government; the leaders, in turn, required a rural base to secure their bid for power. In the largest uprising, "the Rif tribesmen submitted a list of complaints to the central government. The list contained the complaints that the region was underadministered and neglected. When confronted with the alternatives of tradition, or of the benefits of modernity and industrialism, Moroccan tribesmen prefer modernity."[16]

Similarly, in Algeria, rural discontent was related to inter-elite conflict; there was opposition to the military officers and also struggle between the various factions of the FLN. These disputes had to do with which segment of the national elite would prevail and which sectors of the society would enjoy first preference in the state. To the extent that the Kabyle peasantry succeeded in its demand for more government services, it was not only because it engaged in rebellion, but because the insurrection was organized by a large segment of the urban political elite. The government completely ignored the outbreaks in the Aures Mountains, since these represented distant pressures that could quickly be resolved by the mere co-optation of local leaders in the state's agencies. Moreover, as soon as frontier hostilities began between Algeria and Morocco, dissident leaders immediately rallied to the defense of the homeland.

Why do the regions act as minorities? Why do some elite members assume the classic style of defiance in appealing to local networks of patronage? The easy temptation is to respond: the society has remained traditional. But this simply will not do. Communities in the Maghrib have deeply internalized the values of modern society, and their demands are, in essence, for the benefits of "modernization." The basic problem is that the internalization of modern values occurred when there were no institutional channels to achieve them. Thus, using "traditional" means, such as an appeal to ascriptive ties, to attain "modern" ends is no more than the practical application of available means. The classic pattern of resistance to central authority is increasingly being replaced by competition for the center's attention, so that underprivileged areas will not be relegated to second-class citizenship in the new order. This, after all, is part of "civic" politics.

At the same time, states in the Maghrib are almost immune to the ideological influence of pan-national movements. If there ever was a fertile ground for pan-nationalism, it would have originated among the nationalitarian-scripturalist groups that appeared in the early phases of the national movements. Interpreting the colonial challenge in terms of religious and cultural aggression, they were prone to take the unitarian and ideological posture of defending the entire Arab-Islamic community. While they contributed to the preservation of native identity through a defense of religion, language, and country, they really represented an early form of national consciousness: their activities were a prologue to the consolidation of national elites, who were mainly Jacobin and secular.

The alliance between the scripturalists and the secular elites during the national liberation movements proved useful in later developments. In contrast to the situation in Turkey, this alliance prevented the alienation of the masses from the reforms enacted by the center. As has been reiterated in this paper, social life in North Africa is very much characterized by a disjunction between the spiritual and the political spheres. Having pledged to defend the cultural identities of their countries, political elites manipulate religious symbolism; however, the state is organized along modern, secular lines. The important point is that the manipulation of values enables the country itself to resolve from within the problems of national identity. It is on this premise that a more complete plan for administrative and political unification was undertaken after colonialism—this time, with the tacit consent of the majority of the population.

This can be contrasted with other societies, such as Syria, and to an extent Libya, where questions of national identity are defined in terms of a whole cultural area, and where Arabism alone is the burning issue. "Syria," writes Leonard Binder:

embraces nearly five million people called Syrians—some of them Muslims, some of them Christians, some of them townsmen, some of them tribesmen . . . but the fundamental fact about Syria is not that these people call themselves, or are called, Syrians, but rather that most of them are dissatisfied with being called Syrians or with the idea of Syria. In a manner of speaking, the national ideological vocation is to do away with the idea of Syria and to lead the Arabs to the discovery of their contemporary national identity and national mission.[17]

Having shown that, in the Maghrib, the nations' claims have decisively taken priority over those of former communities, the question of the developmental content of the national polity must still be raised.

Everything in the history of colonial and pre-colonial Morocco helped the monarchy and the princely families become the major beneficiaries of independence. National unification had to overcome ethnic, cultural, and political fragmentation; thus, the unifying center cultivated the vocation of negotiation, arbitration, and compromise instead of blunt initiative and reform. The new political forces were scarcely aided by the limited innovations, such as greater social differentiation and new elite formation, that had been introduced by European domination. With the national liberation movement's failure to mobilize the rural area, and with the inheritance of a highly centralized bureaucracy, the Sultan recovered, for the first time, his full sovereignty.

The only pressures for significant change—certain demands for constitutional monarchy and for economic decolonization—emanated from the urban political parties that held aspirations for exercising power. Instead of forming an alliance with these "modern" political forces, the monarchy found it more expedient to continue its traditional reliance on support from the rural area. Several strategies were adopted to render marginal the modern political parties: sustaining rival groups to the Istiqlal and the UNFP (Union Nationale des Forces Populaires), reactivating rural protest to check party zeal, outlawing one-party systems, and relying on the army to man the administration and supervise local programs of development.[18] This amounted to the wholesale restitution of previous colonial policies. The entire strategy was designed to segment political forces, thereby safeguarding the monarchy as arbiter and preventing Morocco from pursuing a mobilizational course. Today the political arena is still composed of rival factions mutually opposed in their struggle for marginal benefits.

This strategy has a cost, however. The weakening of political parties reduces the regime's capacity for politically incorporating different groups into the society and undermines the possibility of attaining consensus on policy. To avoid those changes whose effects cannot be controlled, the countryside is condemned to stagnation; development programs are entrusted to the Ministry of Interior, whose concern for security overrides economic considerations; short-term stability is purchased through a deadlock among many veto groups; and the political system as a whole, instead of liberating the society, becomes its own prisoner. As a result, the system has been racked by permanent crisis. After a decade of attempting to establish a working relationship with the monarchy, through both progressive and conservative actions, the weakened and disorganized elite withdrew from the political system. As the monarchy has come to depend exclusively on the army, so will the future of the regime.

The strongest determination to change political structures came from

Algeria. Since there was no established authority, the two consecutive regimes realized immediately, in their quests for recognition, that responsiveness to popular demands was the best means to obtain legitimacy. When the peasants seized the lands of former settlers, the government merely endorsed the action; it broadened the nationalization of agriculture and legalized self-management in economic enterprises. That legitimacy lay primarily in revolutionary symbols must be seen in conjunction with the colonial legacy of inter-elite conflict on the one hand, and of generalized disorganization on the other. With independence, the latter was compounded as much by the mass exodus of Europeans as by the impatient, mass expectations to achieve the fruits of revolution. The problem became one of reconciling the implementation of the revolution's goals with regime stability and effective management.

The first coalition, headed by Ben Bella and supported by leftist intellectuals and partially by the army, could not deal with the dilemma. Mainly preoccupied with preempting opponents' claims to power, it adopted divisive tactics and an ultra-revolutionary posture which actually limited the government's capacity to redress the situation. Hysterical decrees—impossible to enact—were announced, and the socialist sector systematically opposed any government interference. On the basis of these inconsistencies, Ben Bella was removed. With him ended not only symbolic leadership, but also the dreams of a peasant-based, libertarian socialism, as advocated by Fanon, Harbi, Raptis, Suleyman, and others.

Since 1965, priority has been given to building the state and to economic development. Colonel Abu Midyane said, in this regard:

It is now three years since we achieved national independence and during this period, we have had to endure the advisers who have urged us on to the "withering away of the state" before that very state has even been constructed. . . . We need to build an efficient state apparatus capable of assuring discipline and revolutionary order and to remove the state's civil service from all forms of pressure and solicitations.[19]

The institutionalization of the revolution led the military leadership to totally eliminate the wartime political elite and to eradicate, through professionalization, the classic cleavages within the army itself.[20] Younger individuals, whose background and professional experience were more suitable for the regime's orientation, were brought to power and entrusted with authority over the expanding public sectors of the economy and the administrative apparatus. Despite a considerable regression on the agricultural level, Algeria is today awakening to its oil and gas potentialities, building an impressive industrial complex, and boosting the material conditions of the country. Even though the technocratic component of government is increasingly stressed over the deprived masses' demands for more consumer goods, the Algerian government is undertaking a significant investment program, mostly at the expense of foreign capital. It has even managed, in the process of confronting foreign investors, to enlist the support of sectors normally critical of the regime.

At the same time that the military leadership is providing Algeria with the first unified and effective leadership in its history, political institutions remain virtually nonexistent. Except at the local level, where communal elections are sometimes held and where candidates must be drafted, Algerians have no interest in political parties. If, with a very low capacity for political incorporation, the regime has secured acceptance for its economic achievements, it remains to be seen whether the government will use this instrumental arrangement as a springboard for the creation of a political infrastructure.

Tunisia, by contrast, commands significant political resources but lacks Algeria's economic resource base. The same Party leadership played the primary role in first obtaining independence, and then in confronting the problems of nation building and economic development. The Party acted as an institution-building-institution, sponsoring the organization of trade unions, business associations, and farmers', women's, and student organizations. These groups communicate the center's initiative to the various sectors of society and act as pressure groups on their behalf to influence governmental policy. In this way, the political system enjoys a high level of support.

Aside from the increasing secularization of Tunisian political and cultural life, the political elite favored a policy which ideally, in the words of President Bourguiba, was to be "an agreement daily negotiated with a changing reality . . . a policy that makes one step forward when the society is capable of absorbing what is being proposed."[21] At first, the changes were pragmatic and gradual enough to accommodate foreign investors and local entrepreneurs. But the growing awareness of the country's meager resources and pressures from the peasantry and the left impelled the leadership to embark upon a radical transformation of the economic and social structure. Unlike Algeria, the ten years of intensive planning and heavy investment could only be sustained from within, and this was bound to create internal polarization and a greater dependency on external sources of investment. Eventually, the leadership was forced to abandon this costly experiment and return to a reconciliatory approach.

These changes in strategy must be seen as an indication of the regime's sensitivity to the entire society. Although Bourguibism did succeed in transforming the society, it has not yet adapted itself to its own transformations. The groups recently mobilized into the political process are exerting significant pressure for a restructuring of the political system along more democratic lines. Thus, the high level of support which the regime commands has been purchased at the price of an augmented sensitivity, which ultimately constricts its own powers of social and economic transformation.

The dilemmas confronted by the Maghrib are the same ones confronted by all national societies; different theorists call them: *challenges, requirements,* or *crises.* It is precisely because, in the new states, these problems appear simultaneously, sometimes staggering the capacities of the ablest regimes, that so much passion has surfaced over results that can only be long-term at best.

This paper should have thrown into doubt the theoretical utility of employing simplistic contrasts between "tradition" and "modernity" in the study of societies such as those of the Maghrib. Variations in the "problem-structures" of these societies, the range of their potential response to these problems, the choices which are actually made, and their consequences can only be explained by referring to other variations: those in pre-colonial social, cultural, and political orders, in colonial policies and their impacts, in patterns of interelite conflicts, and in leadership commitments and resources. By focusing upon variables such as these, the comparative study of regional and cross-national, societal transformations can enrich sociological theories by putting them to the test of the plurality of histories—that is to say, the plurality of traditions, if not of modernities.

REFERENCES

1. For contrary interpretations of Algeria, see Franz Fanon, *The Wretched of the Earth* (New York: Grove Press, 1965); Gerard Chaliand, *l'Algérie est-elle socialiste?* (Paris: Maspero, 1964); David and Marina Ottoway, *Algeria: The Politics of a Socialist Revolution* (Berkeley: University of California Press, 1970); William B. Quandt, *Revolution and Political Leadership: Algeria 1954-1968* (Cambridge, Mass.: M.I.T. Press, 1969). Some of the difficulties of getting the Maghrib into focus are raised by Clifford Geertz, "In Search of North Africa," *The New York Review of Books,* April 22, 1971.

2. See Evans-Pritchard, *The Sanusi of Cyrenaica* (London: Oxford University Press, 1954); Robert Montagne, *Les Berbères et le Makhzen dans le Sud du Maroc* (Paris: Alcan, 1930); Jacques Berque, *Structures Sociales du Haut-Atlas* (Paris: Presses Universitaires de France, 1955); Ernest Gellner, *Saints of the Atlas* (Chicago: University of Chicago Press, 1969).

3. Ibn Khaldun, *The Muqaddimah,* 3 vols., trans. Franz Rosenthal (New York: Bollingen Foundation, 1958). This theory did not consider the geo-political context which should be included in any full evaluation of medieval political life. See F. Braudel, *La Méditerranée et le monde méditerranéen à l'époque de Philippe II* (Paris: Arman Colin, 1949 and 1966); F. Braudel, "Les Espagnols en Algérie 1492-1792," *Histoire et Historiens de l'Algérie* (Paris, 1931), pp. 231-266; and Abd Al-Hamid Zaghlul, *Tarikh al-Maghrib al'Arabi* (Cairo, 1965).

For an extensive analysis of the themes discussed here, see my forthcoming book, *Leadership and National Development. A Comparative Study of North Africa* (Berkeley and Los Angeles: University of California Press, Autumn 1972).

4. Clifford Geertz, *Islam Observed* (New Haven and London: Yale University Press, 1968), pp. 30-31.

5. Abdallah Laroui, *L'histoire du Maghreb, Un essai de Synthèse* (Paris: Maspero, 1970), pp. 229-267.

6. Alexis de Tocqueville, *Ecrits et Discours Politiques, Oeuvres Complètes*, Vol. 3 (Paris: Gallimard, 1962), pp. 222-224.

7. Recent North African history has not known the equivalent of the Wahabi in Arabia, the Sanusi in Libya, and the Mahdiyya in the Sudan.

8. Pellissier de Renaud, *Exploration Scientifique de l'Algérie* (Paris: 1853), p. 45.

9. Tocqueville, *Ecrits et Discours Politiques*, p. 207. A general rule might be inferred from this sort of observation: that imported bourgeoisies, or the imported middle class, do not play the liberating and unifying roles that characterized their ascendance in Europe. At home, they adopt the ideology of the Enlightenment against feudal restrictions. In the colonies, they can only succeed with a logic of domination of the native which is fertile ground for a racist ideology.

10. See Geertz, *op. cit.*, pp. 64-65.

11. Pierre Bourdieu, *Sociologie de l'Algérie* (Paris: Presses Universitaires de France, 1963), p. 125; English translation, *The Algerians* (Boston: Beacon Press, 1962).

12. Mostefa Lacheraf, *Algérie: Nation et Société* (Paris: Maspero, 1965).

13. *L'Entente* (Algiers, February 23, 1936).

14. See Franz Fanon, *The Wretched of the Earth*, and *L'An Cinq de la Révolution Algérienne* (Paris: Maspero, 1959).

15. See John Waterbury, *The Commander of the Faithful* (London: Weidenfeld & Nicolson, 1970); David and Marina Ottoway, *Algeria: The Politics of a Socialist Revolution;* and C. Geertz, "The Integrative Revolution," Geertz, ed., *Old Societies and New States* (New York: Free Press, 1963), pp. 103-157.

16. Ernest Gellner, "Patterns of Rural Rebellion in Morocco: Tribes as Minorities," *Archives Européennes de Sociologie*, 3 (1962), pp. 297-311, 299.

17. Leonard Binder, "The Tragedy of Syria," *World Politics*, 19, No. 3 (April 1967), pp. 535-537.

18. Leo Hamon, ed., *Le Rôle extra-militaire de l'armée dans le tiers-monde* (Paris: Presses Universitaires de France, 1966), especially "Le Maroc," pp. 31-67.

19. In the Algerian press, July 5, 1965 and October 20, 1965.

20. William Zartman, "The Algerian Army in Politics," in Claude E. Welsh Jr., ed., *Soldier and State in Africa* (Evanston, Ill.: Northwestern University Press, 1970), pp. 224-249.

21. *L'Action* (Tunis, July 13, 1968). See also Lars Rudebeck, *Party and People: A Study of Political Change in Tunisia* (Stockholm, 1967); and Charles A. Micaud, "Leadership and Development: The Case of Tunisia," *Comparative Politics*, 1, No. 4 (July 1969), pp. 468-484.

ABDELKADER ZGHAL

The Reactivation of Tradition in a Post-Traditional Society

THE SOCIOLOGIST who wishes to investigate what is now happening in a country like Tunisia must constantly keep in mind that we have not yet developed a systematic theory to explain the dynamics of the transition toward modernity that such a country is making. Nor do we have sufficient knowledge of pre-colonial social patterns in the Maghrib as well as of their impact on the modern Maghrib. The study of today's history need not be abandoned on these grounds, however; for—to use Balandier's expression—it is "today's history" which reveals social reality.[1] But if "today's history" often shatters the illusion of lasting stability, it remains no less true that this "illusion" expresses a dimension of social reality that exerts a certain influence, even if not a decisive one, on social dynamics. Moreover, analysis becomes more complicated when the ostensibly most innovative parts of a society behave, at a given moment, so that they create an illusion of lasting stability; such is the case of the modernist elites in Tunisia since the failure of the cooperative system in 1969. Thus, investigation of the reactivation of tradition by these modernist elites may serve to clarify certain aspects of the dialectic of continuity and change in a post-colonial or, let us say, post-traditional society. The reactivation of traditional values is not unique to Tunisia, since it appears, almost simultaneously, in other Arab-Moslem countries. In Algeria or Libya the legitimacy of power is largely assured by a policy firmly based on reactivation of traditional values, while religious demonstrations assumed greater importance in a country like Egypt after the military defeat in 1967.[2]

The Victory of the Modernist Element in the Tunisian National Movement

The Tunisian nationalist movement, in the exact sense of the term, is the product of colonialization. Before the colonial conquest in 1881, Tunisia had all the characteristics of a nation as defined by the Marxists (a common language, territory, economy, psychology, anl culture), but no nationalist ideology, in the exact sense of the term.[3] Its intellectuals had not been trained by an educational system that weaned them from traditional values, and local communities and traditional institutions still controlled or protected a large majority of the Tunisian population. Under these conditions it is not surprising that the ideology of pre-colonial Tunisia's protest movement should be similar to the ideology that arose among the merchant middle-class in European towns at the beginning of capitalism—that is to say, before the birth of nationalism in Western Europe. These two movements did not share the classical viewpoint of the nationalists who saw the language and ethnic background of the rulers as a vital issue. Both movements readily accepted heads of state of foreign extraction—as, for example, the case of the beylical family in Tunisia which is of Turkish extraction and does not even speak the native language, or that of the *podesta* in Italian towns who was traditionally recruited from outside the town where he was to perform his official duties.[4] But both movements demanded written guarantees protecting the property and honor of the people from the abuse of the centralized power as well as representative bodies to debate questions of public interest. In any case, when Tunisia was on the verge of colonialization, the notion of national citizenship was completely absent from the political thinking of even such lucid reformers as Khereddine and Ben Diaf.[5]

The nationalist movement, as such, is the product of colonialization. The colonial system produced the first generation of modernist intellectuals and the first elements of the Tunisian proletariat which at the beginning of the twentieth century gave birth to the Tunisian Youth Movement.[6] The leaders of this movement, the first Tunisian intellectuals trained in French universities, naturally came from old families of Turkish extraction which had been the cornerstone of beylical power before the colonial conquest. Viewing political action from an elitist vantage point, they were for the most part predisposed by their training and social origin to easy absorption by the colonial system, and asked the French government to function as a civilizing force. The influence of these modernists was limited, since they had their right foot in the system and their left foot in the opposition, while the majority of the population completely rejected the system.

The inverse was true of the *bourgeois* intellectuals trained in the religious university (the Zitouna). More plebeian in origin and traditionally educated, their opposition to the colonial system was total, unlike the modernists. Since their political attitude more truly reflected the feelings of the people, their influence was greater than that of the modernist intellectuals, especially after the failure of the latter group's policy of collaboration.

In 1907 the two groups (modernist and traditional) united in order to present to the French government a common program, the principal demand of which was the spread of education.[7] But in 1920, the leadership of the nationalist movement fell into the hands of the traditional intellectuals who, for the first time, called for the total independence of Tunisia and constituted a genuine political party: The Constitutional Liberal Party (Le Destour). The immediate consequences of this change in leadership were limited because no effort was made to mobilize all the social classes. Thus, along with the leaders of the Tunisian section of the French socialist Party, these *bourgeois* intellectuals did not hesitate, in 1924, to sign a petition condemning the first attempt by the Tunisian working class to organize a central national union that would be independent of the French unions.[8]

The position of this *bourgeois* elite at the heart of the Tunisian nationalist movement was undermined by the growth, after World War I, of the proletariat and the middle class. By developing industries and by mechanizing the colonists' farms, the colonial system created a proletariat separated from its traditional framework and thus receptive to nationalist sentiments. And forbidding the formation of a national union, the colonialists unwittingly encouraged the development, in the French unions, of a core of militant unionists who would later become the leaders of the most organized central union in the Arab world.[9] The emergence of a middle class was one consequence of the growth of the third sector of the economy in urban centers and of reconsolidation of small landed properties in village communities in the Sahel and in the oases of the South.

The massive participation in the Tunisian nationalist movement of this urban and rural middle class completely transformed the social basis and the ideological content of the movement. This change is not an exceptional phenomenon in the Third World. Most nationalist movements in the Arab world are at present politically and ideologically dependent upon the middle class. But in the other Arabic countries this shift took place after World War II, not in the 1930's as it did in Tunisia.

The Tunisian middle class was able to wrest the leadership of the nationalist movement from the traditional *bourgeoisie*, in part, because of the structural weakness of the Tunisian *bourgeoisie*. In undermining the economic bases of the traditional Tunisian *bourgeoisie*, the colonial system considerably weakened the social position of this group. Moreover, there existed in Tunisia in the 1930's a modernist intellegentsia of middle-class extraction which was more sensitive than that of the *bourgeoisie* to the suffering of the working class and of the people in general. Also, the cultural and linguistic homogeneity of the Tunisian population facilitated communication, in every sense of the word, among all regions and social categories.

The extraordinary 1934 congress of the Constitutional Liberal Party[10] censured the traditional and *bourgeois* leadership of the nationalist party and was held in one of the important villages of the coastal region (Le Sahel), not in the capital, which is the traditional domain of the *bourgeoisie*. Before the colonial conquest, the Sahelian peasants had been constantly threatened either by the nomadic tribes when the central power was weak or by the soldiers of the bey when the central power was stable. The change in the political system after the colonial conquest guaranteed the security of the Sahelian peasants and reinforced the status of the small property owners. As did the Kabyles in Algeria,[11] the Sahelian middle class gave unlimited encouragement to their children to attend the new schools. The colonial system reaped the harvest of its actions—the formation in the 1930's of an intellegentsia bent on destroying the colonial system. Naturally, the Sahel is not the only region that produces genuine militants, nor is the middle class the only class that trained modernist intellectuals radically opposed to the colonial system. But Tunisia's recent history cannot be understood without emphasizing the roles played by the Sahel and its village peasantry and by the middle class and its intellectuals.

At the moment of independence the Neo-Destourian Party controlled the country not by armed force, as in Algeria, nor by the former caïds, as in Morocco, but by a broad coalition forged from the urban and peasant middle class, the working class, and the youth.

Bourguiba was the spokesman and the main engineer of this coalition. Indeed, all his political skill and prestige were necessary to isolate the *bourgeois* portion of the party, which was headed by Ben Youssef and attempted to take power in the name of Islam and Arabism as soon as autonomy was proclaimed. The failure of this ideologically traditional movement led by the *bourgeoisie* reinforced the position of the modernist intellectuals and paved the way for the application of a policy of accelerated modernization during the first fifteen years of independence.

Modernization After the Failure of the Bourgeois Faction

Before independence, the modernist intellectuals were conscious that the elements of their coalition (the middle class, the working class, and the young students) in no way constituted a collective majority in the country. The traditional middle class was hostile to or at least supicious of them, while the peasantry, despite its hostility to the colonial system, was incapable of envisioning social structures apart from the traditional ones. In order to lessen the suspicion of the traditional middle class, the modernist intellectuals appointed modernist intellectuals of middle class origin to responsible positions within the party. They also adapted party structures to the traditional structures of the peasants and even, to a certain extent, to those of the city-dweller. Thus, for example, the new code of personal rights, which radically altered both the judicial situation and the status of women in Tunisia, is the work of a modernist intellectual from the traditional middle class. Moreover, the new code of personal rights was not promulgated in the name of an anti-religious set of values or even in the name of a secular one as in Turkey, but rather as a new reading, a modern reading, of religious texts. The modernist intellectuals stand for a renewal of Arab-Moslem values and not for a radical break with the past. Even before they gained control, they behaved primarily as politicians acting in reference to the balance of power and not as moralists seeking to defend principles without caring much about contingency. By 1929, before the consolidation of the nationalist movement, Bourguiba's attitude toward traditional values, including the veiling of women, was clear. For him, the most modernist statesman of the Arab world, it was a question of deciding not simply whether a particular tradition was good or bad, but whether at that moment it would have been expedient to accelerate its disappearance. The protectorate had attempted to wipe out the Tunisian personality and, after having separated it from all its foundations, to integrate it with the French personality. Thus, Bourguiba reasoned that the Tunisian personality must be made secure before its collective traditions, which constitute identity, could be moderated. Tunisian independence marked the starting point of a series of measures which not only threatened important aspects of tradition, but also were aimed at the functioning of those institutions, such as the family and the school, whose role it is to assure the transmission of values and the socialization of new generations.

The Code of Personal Rights

The first reforms dealing with the status of women were not the judicial recognition of a fairly widespread social practice (like divorce in Italy), but a voluntary decision by a modernist elite who had in mind a precise political aim. This aim went beyond the limited case of woman's status and sought to destroy all barriers to the spread of modernist innovations. Thus, the early promulgation of the code of personal rights, while borrowing certain principles from the Muslim religion, secularized the principal laws governing Tunisian matrimonial relations.

Before the promulgation of the code of personal rights in 1957, a woman's marriage, especially her first, had been traditionally outside her control, at least to a certain extent. According to the Malekite rite, the Muslim custom most widespread in the Maghrib, the father could give his daughter in marriage without asking her consent. Only after the father's death was the woman's consent formally required. After the promulgation of the code of personal rights, the consent of both partners was required regardless of whether or not the girl's father still lived.

Moreover, the code set a minimum age for the establishment of a marriage contract at seventeen years for the woman and twenty years for the man, whereas traditionally there had been no minimum age. A father could marry off his daughter no matter what her age, even though puberty had always been the traditional age for consummation of the marriage.

Before Tunisian independence the marriage contract in rural areas, particularly among populations of nomadic origin, was often a verbal agreement between two families. Since the promulgation of the code of personal rights, the marriage contract must be filed with the registry office—a preliminary condition for the control of the application of the code's new regulations. Also, a husband had previously been able to repudiate his wife at any time without the intervention of any judicial authority. A woman could request a divorce from the *cadhi* (religious judge) on grounds of her husband's sexual impotence, his prolonged absence, or his incapacity to provide for her sustenance. After the promulgation of the code of personal rights, divorce would only be pronounced by the judge upon mutual consent or upon the request of one of the partners. In the case of the latter, the judge ruled on the compensation due the wife in reparation for any injury done her or on the indemnity she owed her husband.

Before independence, polygamy was allowed, but practiced only by a small minority. The code of personal rights outlawed polygamy, and anyone who entered a new marriage before the dissolution of a previous one was liable to judicial sanctions (one year's imprisonment and a fine of 240 dinars, the equivalent of $500). The penal code also effected a certain change in the status of women since the husband's adultery became as much of an offense as the wife's. This regulation, however, was introduced much later than the promulgation of personal rights.

The promulgation of the personal rights code considerably improved the traditional status of Tunisian women, and it is not surprising that, as a corollary, independent Tunisia's official policy favored the dissemination of birth control methods. Thus, on March 16, 1960, a law was passed which for the first time in Tunisia authorized the importation and sale of birth control devices. On July 1, 1965, a new law authorized the artificial termination of a pregnancy during the first three months, provided the couple had at least five living children. In the same law, abortion was also authorized for a pregnancy which endangered the health of the mother. These legislative measures aimed to improve the status of Tunisian women by making it possible for them to plan or to limit their pregnancies. They also served to limit the birthrate of the Tunisian population at a time when the problem of unemployment was becoming more and more serious. Another effort along these lines was the December 14, 1960, law limiting the payment of government benefits to the first four children in a family.

The Reform of the Educational System

To realize the revolutionary implications of the new code of personal rights, radical reform of the educational system was necessary. The first plan of independent Tunisia dealing with educational policy aimed to have all school-age children in school within ten years (1958-1969) and to unify the educational system.[12] The traditional religious schools, called Zitounan, were eliminated and the native language was to be substituted by French in progressive stages so that the new generation would not be cut off from technology and modern values.

The results of this educational reform are impressive. Between 1956-1957 and 1970-1971, the average annual increase in the number of children in school was 27 per cent. No other economic or social sector has had a comparable growth rate. The quantitative expectations of the ten-year plan (1958-1969) have been greatly exceeded. Of course, inequality still exists according to region, social or professional class, and sex. But in 1970 the proportion of girls in primary school was 39 per cent; in secondary school (*lyceés* and modern high schools), 32 per cent; and in higher education, 20 per cent. When we add that until recently the principle of co-education was applied at every educational level, we realize the extent of the changes resulting from this reform of the educational system—particularly in a country where only fifteen years before the majority of women had been sequestered and completely under the domination of their fathers or husbands. In 1970-1971, almost one Tunisian in four was a student (1,122,000 pupils out of 5,100,000 inhabitants), attesting to the amplitude of the new educational system. Moreover, the majority of these students were of humble origin and thus receptive to the catchwords of progress and social justice.

Modernization and the Weakening of the Coalition

The liberation of women and the spread of schooling are only two aspects of a voluntary policy of modernization promoted by a modernist elite. The short-range objective of this policy was to change the Tunisian mentality so that it was primarily concerned no longer with controversies over cultural identity or relations with foreign powers, but with the needs and problems related to economic and social development. Urbanization was to alter the semi-nomadic peasants' way of life so that they would come to renounce their regional differences and to develop a modern mentality. The modernist elite mobilized every means of mass communication to reinforce the program of urbanization and to accelerate the renunciation of regional differences and the absorption of modern values.[13]

These efforts to change the Tunisian mentality owed their perceived validity to the extent that they were thought to safeguard Islam's genuine values and to consolidate Tunisia's cultural and national identity. Economic development was considered a prerequisite for the defense of the Moslem religion and the perpetuation of Arab civilization. In one of his most famous speeches, for example, Bourguiba asked the Tunisian people to cease observing the Fast of Ramadan because production fell off considerably during that period, and the nation could not allow its economic activities to slacken at that stage of the holy war against under-development.[14] To supplement his speech, the administrative schedule was changed during the month of Ramadan to allow those who did not fast to eat at noon, and strict orders were given to boarding-school directors for their students to eat normally during the month of Ramadan. Such measures were, of course, not enthusiastically accepted by everyone, but they did not meet a tide of resistance. Indeed, social change in the sense of modernization was accompanied in Tunisia by a political stability unusual for Third World countries.[15] Even the reactivation of traditional values after the policy of accelerated modernization took place almost without violence and without a radical change in the political leadership. Tunisia experienced neither the military *coup d'état* of Sudan nor the radical purge of political leadership of Egypt. Despite the remarkable continuity of the new Tunisian ruling class, however, the weakening of the modernist intellectuals' coalition played an important role in launching the movement to reactivate traditional values. The entire process was stimulated, moreover, by Bourguiba's sudden illness in 1967 and resulted in the reappearance in Tunisian politics of ideologies and social forces that had been stifled, but not eliminated, during the last fifteen years.

The Weakening of the Coalition of the Modernist Intellectuals

The different groups making up the coalition of the modernist intellectuals were affected to differing degrees by the economic and social reforms advocated by the plan of 1961, particularly by the measures taken in 1964 to strengthen the cooperative sector at the expense of the private sector. The students were the main beneficiaries of these projects since, through the growth of governmental and semi-governmental agencies, they were provided with steady and well-paying jobs. The middle class, on the other hand, felt the broadening of the cooperative system threatened its trade and small landed properties. The workers saw their salaries frozen, while the cost of living rose due to difficulties encountered in applying the economic reforms. After 1967, the decision was made to extend the cooperative system rapidly not only to all categories of arboriculturists in the agricultural zone, including the Sahel, but to merchants and artisans as well. This naturally created uneasiness among the landowners, the merchants, and the artisans, accounting in part for their opposition to the activist elements among the intellectuals in power, an administrative elite more or less alienated from their social origins. Bourguiba's personal intervention stopped the collectivization movement that threatened the traditional coalition of the modernist intellectuals. But at that moment his health did not allow him to stand up to the dissatisfaction not only of the *bourgeoisie*, but also of the middle class which, just before independence, had been the "backbone of the Neo-Destourian Party."[16]

The defeat of the activists in 1969, following Bourguiba's refusal to sign an order extending the cooperative movement to all farms, delighted large and small landowners, merchants, and artisans. The defeat revealed both the limitations of authoritarian planning and the need, in all sectors of the population, for a widening of democracy. In the new political matrix the people's vote appeared to be the main source of legitimacy, and thus the search for a clientele became a necessity for all those who hoped to play a political role within the system.

The Reappearance of Tradition

The slackening of control by the machinery of state and the spread of democracy at the level of political and parapolitical institutions provided opportunities for a large sector of the population to express, publicly and without fear, feelings more or less repressed during the period of authoritarian planning. After the failure of the cooperative system, the former militants spoke up again, vigorously denouncing what they termed the debasement of manners and morals. They attributed this phenomenon to the code of personal rights and to the educational system which granted a clearly privileged position to the French language without according enough importance to religious teaching. Women, young people, and professors were the favorite targets of former militants who, during the last ten years, had been replaced in positions of power by young technicians trained in the universities.

With the sole aim of gaining the votes of the old militants and the peasants, certain candidates who occupied positions of authority at the party level and had participated actively in the politics of modernization did not hesitate, during the last party congress, to demonstrate an exuberant attachment to tradition. Half the members of the congress were over forty years old, and nearly one member in three was a peasant. By their own espousal of traditional beliefs the modernist elite hoped to control effectively the spontaneous movement toward reactivating tradition and consequently to forestall the formation of an autonomous movement in defense of Arab-Moslem values. Their actions cannot be considered, however, simply an attempt to manipulate popular mass sentiment. In its scramble for positions of authority, at a time when the succession of Bourguiba was the pressing issue, the modernist elite adopted a strategy and a style of competition that recalled certain classic aspects of political life in Arab-Moslem society before the colonial conquest. The government in pre-colonial Arab-Moslem society was the center of temporal power and transcended the level of the tribe, yet the society itself retained the stamp of its tribal origin. At the structural level, the permanence of tribal structures was a constant threat to the stability and continuity of the state. At the cultural level, Islam's official recognition of the principle of electing a head of government according to the Bedouin tradition[17] created insurmountable difficulties with the expansion of the Moslem state. Thus, the stability and continuity of the Arab-Moslem states before the colonial conquest were constantly threatened during periods of succession. Moreover, the difficulty of establishing a principle of succession that would be effective and legitimate not only made all institutionalized forms of succession risky and unstable, but also fostered traditions of coalition and competition quite similar to those at the base of tribal social organization.

The difficulty of establishing a principle of succession for the position of head of government has become, since the illness of Bourguiba and the fall of Ben Salah, the chief obstacle to the stability and continuity of the state. The formation of factions within the ruling class since the last change of regime was not precipitated primarily by debate over development strategy for the coming decade or foreign policy. At its core was the problem of succession to the office of President of the Republic should that office become vacant. The vacillations and abrupt changes of attitude concerning a succession strategy since Bourguiba's illness suggest that the Tunisian ruling class no longer controls or manipulates the manifestations of tradition and that they are themselves, in some way, the object of manipulation by the traditional heritage. Regionalism has reappeared, for example, as a basis for the regrouping of coalitions within the ruling elite.

In truth, the members of the ruling class are sometimes not even aware of the relationship between their behavior and the aspects of tradition which they are continually criticizing. This relationship appears clearly when one compares the rules of the game which regulate political life in the Bedouin communities and the "spontaneous" strategy adopted by the members of the ruling class since Bourguiba's illness. In Bedouin societies, no single authority indisputably dominates all the groups. In this kind of social organization, coalitions between different factions are contingent, unstable, and shift constantly depending upon the issues in question; as a result, manipulation plays a large part in the strategy of all the groups. Factions tend to maintain a minimum of contact with hostile groups because they might quickly become allies, and never to place absolute confidence in allies because they are likely to change camps rapidly. Thus when Ben Salah, the man chiefly responsible for the planning policy and supposedly the dauphin of Bourguiba, wanted to monopolize all power without recognizing the existence of other factions, the members of the ruling class forgot their antagonisms with ease and united against him. The coalition that was quickly mobilized to hasten the downfall of Ben Salah naturally broke down after his defeat, splintering into two antagonistic factions. The apparent victory of one faction, which wanted to maximize the results of the Destourian Party congress for its own advantage, quickly transformed itself into a defeat, through the formation of a new coalition. The discontent of the losing faction was demonstrated, according to the tradition of the segmental community, by an ostentatious withdrawal from the coalition, but without the implication that this withdrawal necessarily constituted a definitive break.

The Future of the Traditional Movement in Tunisia

Tunisia has been, until recently, the Arab country most receptive to the values and ideas of the modern world. From the beginning of independence the personality and political acuity of Bourguiba effectively stifled nostalgia for pre-colonial traditions. But his illness struck at a time when the policy of modernization required radical investigation and reorganization of the structures of Tunisian society. The ruling class, at that moment, was confronted with two choices: it could either accept the project of radicalization connected with the planning policy, thereby strengthening Ben Salah's chances of succeeding Bourguiba as President of the Republic, or it could stop the process of collectivization and leave the office of President open to competition. The choice of the second alternative left the field open to the traditional social groups that had been directly threatened by the proposed radicalization of the planning policy. After the downfall of Ben Salah, they became the arbiter of conflicts among different factions of the ruling class. Thus, the modernist intellectuals ended by assuming the very aspects of pre-colonial tradition which they themselves had most criticized.

The traditional current will most probably grow stronger in Tunisia because the Tunisian ruling class has never, unlike that of Turkey, drawn its legitimacy from the struggle against pre-colonial traditions insofar as they were Arab-Moslem traditions. There is a clearcut distinction between the modernization policy of Bourguiba and that of Ataturk, who undertook a veritable secularization policy, calling for a sharp separation between state and church. In the Tunisian constitution Islam remains the state religion. The President of the Republic thus holds both temporal and spiritual power, since they are inseparable in the Moslem religion, and as a result the state is responsible for the "morality" of its citizens. Bourguiba undertook the enactment of modernist measures within this framework. That strategy necessarily involved constraints that limited the field of action open to the modernization policy. To be applicable, modernist measures had not only to answer the needs of the most cultured elements of the ruling class, but also to meet the aspirations of the various social groups within the coalition supporting the power elites. These modernist measures could not transgress the tolerance level—variable though it is—of traditional social groups, most especially the peasantry. Thus, after the failure of the planning policy, the government decided to reestablish the former work schedule during Ramadan and authorized cafes and restaurants to close during the day. This return to tradition during the month of Ramadan is obviously the consequence of the state's diminished power since Bourguiba's illness. But the modernist intellectuals consider this return to tradition a necessary sacrifice in order to maintain their directive role in the government.

In the future one ought to expect a strengthening of the spontaneous movement expressing the Tunisian population's attachment to Arab-Moslem civilization. The response of the government to this movement will probably be much less dogmatic than in the past; it is likely, for example, that it will encourage the construction of new mosques. Much more than in the past, the members of the ruling class will participate in religious ceremonies as a way of showing their attachment to Islam. But it is highly improbable that in the near future the return to tradition will be used as the basis of legitimacy for the ruling class, as it is in Pakistan, Saudi Arabia, and even Libya. The feeling of belonging to a nation is stronger among Tunisians than in those societies which need religion as a rallying point for rather heterogeneous groups.

The goal of this phenomenon of reactivation is not necessarily the protection of tradition *per se*, but rather the control of structural changes that affect the whole of Tunisian society and call into question the habits and situations acquired before and after independence.

Changes as important as the improvement of woman's traditional status, the extension of primary education to children of the nonpropertied classes, the increase in the number of laborers and employees in the modern sector, the sensitization of a large part of the population to the problems of economic development, and the increasing politicization of the population necessarily involve a certain dislocation. In times of crisis, one can predict a quickening of the reactivation of tradition by those elements most endangered by the process of modernization (peasants, artisans, small businessmen, former militants), and also by certain elements of the elite educated in French universities who, to conserve and even strengthen their position, play the card of tradition with the goal of gaining an audience.

REFERENCES

1. Georges Balandier, *Sens et Puissance* (Paris: Presses universitaires de France, 1971).

2. Morroe Berger, *Islam in Egypt Today. Social and Political Aspects of Popular Religion* (London: Cambridge University Press, 1970).

3. Ernest Gellner, *Thought and Change* (London: Weidenfeld and Nicolson, 1964).

4. Max Weber, *The City* (New York: The Free Press, 1958).

5. B. Tilli, "Note sur la notion d'état et la pensée de Ben Diaf," *Revue de l'Occident musulman et de la Méditerranée*, 8 (1970); "Eléments pour une approche de la pensée socio-économique de Khéreddine," *Revue de l'Occident musulman et de la*

Méditerranée, 9 (1971); "Autour du réformisme tunisien du XIX siècle. L'idée de liberté chez Khéreddine," to appear in *Cahiers de Tunisie*, 1972.

6. Ch. Kairallah, *Le Mouvement jeune tunisien* (Tunis: Etablissement Bonini, n.d.).

7. It is interesting to compare, on the question of schooling, the declarations of the Young Tunisian movement in 1907 and those of Bourguiba in 1958. See Noureddine Sraïeb, "Note sur les dirigeants politiques et Syndicalistes tunisiens de 1920 à 1934," *Revue de l'Occident musulman et de la Méditerranée*, 9 (1971). See also Bourguiba's address on June 30, 1958.

8. Abdelkader Zghal, "Construction nationale et nouvelles classes sociales en Tunisie," *Revue de l'Institut de sociologie* (Université de Bruxelles, 1967).

9. J. Berque, "Classe et histoire contemporaine des Arabes," *Cahiers Internationaux de Sociologie*, 18 (1965).

10. *Le Congrès de 1934*, Publication of the Destourien Socialist Party (in Arabic).

11. Jean Morizot, ed., J. Peyrounet, *l'Algerie Kabylisée* (Paris, 1962).

12. A. Chouikha, "Conception et résultats de la réforme tunisienne de l'enseignement de 1958," *Revue Tunisienne de Sciences Sociales*, 19 (December 1969).

13. Abdelkader Zghal, "La protection sociale et l'urbanisation des ruraux en Tunisie," to appear in *Revue tunisienne des sciences sociales* in 1972.

14. Speech on February 18, 1960.

15. Lars Rudebec, *Party and People: A Study of Political Change in Tunisia* (London: C. Hurst and Company, 1967).

16. Bourguiba, ed., Julliard, *La Tunisie et la France* (Paris, 1954), p. 10.

17. Nomination of a candidate by a representative council of all groups in each other's presence, and then approval of the chosen candidate by the whole community.

JACQUES BERQUE

Tradition and Innovation in the Maghrib

"A PRINCIPLE of unity, continuity, richness, and tradition, which exists at the beginning, anticipates the future, and remains at the end, precedes any re-constructive synthesis and outlasts any reasoned analysis." This sentence by Maurice Blondel will counterbalance the generally pejorative definitions of tradition. To accept his idea, we must view the emancipation of a people above all as a return to its tradition, to the extent that the history which be-gins at the moment of emancipation is based on principles which existed long before they were formulated. If, in the Maghrib, a general movement toward historical judgment, and increasingly deliberate efforts by the people, or the political parties, or the state to undertake collective action are now replacing what Ferhat Abbas calls "the colonial night," it does not change the fact that all social development is affected by a superabundance of what is *inherited, implicit,* and *hoped-for.* The three conditions of this superabund-ance, however, may take the regressive forms, respectively, of *atavism, ir-rationality,* and *Utopianism;* these are precisely the terms by which the best minds characterized the identity of the Maghrib during the period of colonization.

Contributions of Recent History

At the height of French power, around 1930, any analysis of tradition in the society of the Maghrib would have interpreted it as expressing the North African substratum, and would have contrasted it with the French contribution that included certain positive and negative changes. It was fashionable, in that period, to study the conflicts between cultures, but reason and history were viewed as the exclusive property of one side—that of the colonizer. A noted sociologist of the time, René Maunier, contrasted native and colonial cultures in an imaginative book, *Loi française et coutume indigène en Algérie.* Of course, Algeria was a country declared French by law, while in the Moroccan and Tunisian protectorates a certain sover-eignty and even a local personality distinct from those belonging to France were recognized. Still, the equation stated above remained operative, both in theory and in practice.

So extreme was the situation that even in the domain of law, where a reciprocal evaluation of fact and norm is required, contemporary practices relegated the society of the Maghrib to the same inferior status. Even though the *figh*, the Muslim law which both antedated and remained separate from the French system, continued to maintain its power in the background, it was considered in Algeria as merely a supplementary legal source, which the French judge, moreover, was free to interpret as he pleased. In Tunisia and Morocco, the biases of those in authority led to the same results. Certain areas of the traditional legal system were exempt from colonial incursions, such as the statute pertaining to families, or that pertaining to landholdings called "non-françisées," or "unregistered," which continued to be under the jurisdiction of the *cadi*, the traditional Muslim judge. However, these rather broad cultural safeguards, more or less residual in nature, were based on a tradition which history had gradually abandoned.

What held true in the law was also practiced against other institutions. In landholding, education, finance, administration, and in the wider sphere of manners and customs, "françisation"—a term used in Algerian legislation —presented itself as the only route to modernity, to normality, and even to morality. Colonial rule struck deeply at all of the values that sustained native life: at the rights of the indigenous population; at the language, divided into "written Arabic," "spoken Arabic," and dialects; at Muslim law, often relegated to the status of "custom"; at religion, reduced to observances or even to superstition and magic practices; and at literature, reduced to folklore. In sum, the identity of the Maghrib became little more than a collection of anachronistic relics. These kinds of colonial influences belong to the study of ethnography; history considers the way in which the events, ideas, and people of the Maghrib evolved away from their traditional life toward an accommodation, even if under protest, with the world of the colonizer, which was not only the world of industrial civilization, but also that of civilization itself, even the world of reason. However, this cultural fragmentation, which we may well consider extreme, was not solely the product of colonialism. It also corresponded in certain ways to views held by the great thinkers of the era, such as Vilfredo Pareto or Max Weber, and to the standard interpretations of Marxist thought. It was, in short, a truth of the times, nonetheless so because it may seem shocking to us today.

However, even during the colonialist era, a more careful analysis would have presented a different picture. Despite the devaluing of certain aspects of traditional life, there still remained places of refuge into which the French did not penetrate and which were even endowed by the colonial presence with new symbols and new weapons. "L'indigenat" and all that it represented—almost totally synonomous with the "traditional"—resisted by its sheer mass and by its vitality. Rapid growth of population, a vast geographical expanse that remained untouched in many districts, and whole areas of social and moral life which were sheltered from colonial incursions, all protected the native culture. Traditional values, such as religious faith and honor, if not the use of the classical language, survived and actually drew new strength from their defensive role. However, they did have to compete against innovative French policies, whose relative novelty made these traditional values more susceptible to foreign influence. The economy, for example, laid primary stress on production and consumption. The craving for knowledge and the demand for democratic rights, which became pronounced in the 1930's, were movements that directly opposed traditional forms of behavior, which were consequently labeled as *taqlîd* conformism and *jumûd* inertia. Certain traits of the personality of the Maghrib on the other hand, grew more pronounced, as though to indicate the lines of demarcation; perhaps we may attribute the continuing confinement of the harem, the marabout, confraternal worship, and even the observance of the annual fast to this reaction. Fearing their authority might be ignored or disqualified if too stringent policies were imposed on the local population, the colonizers advocated the continuance of certain traditions; but to the extent that these were viewed as conservative or reactionary by the people themselves, the colonized conspired with the colonizers to further reinforce the disastrous antithesis of rational and traditional. When independence was finally achieved, this antithesis would provoke moral and social distortions.

Reformers in the Maghrib who belonged to the *salafiya* school and advocated a return to ancestral values understood how to ward off this dangerous division which, in its most extreme form, would set atheistic modernism against old-fashioned traditionalism. At the beginning of the twentieth century, the Egyptian chaykh Abdouh imported ideas into Algeria and Tunisia which at first gave rise to bitter arguments. During the years between World War I and World War II, however, the influence of chaykh Abdel Hamid ben Badis caused these ideas to begin spreading among the active Algerian elites, while in Tunisia a liberal and enlightened attitude slowly gathered in strength. Another prominent figure, chaykh Ben Larbi al 'Alâwî, affected the very core of Morocco's ancient society—the Mosque University of Qarawiyinà Fès. In the 1930's, when the young people were seized by nationalistic fervor and forced that venerable institution to adopt a reform plan called *Nidhâm*, they were essentially struggling against all past-oriented attitudes, whether they were expressed by the colonial administration, the *caïds*, the marabouts, or the doctors of law.

From this time on, a reformist Islam, which supports nationalism and appeals to Arab solidarity, has been the major voice of political resistance. French power might have learned a lesson from the particular form taken by this resistance, which did not level its most bitter denunciations at the colonialists' efforts—real or imagined—to undermine Islam, but at the French collusion with traditionalism. In fact, the peasantry, the rural districts, and the conservative segments of the bourgeoisie largely supported the colonial regime. By their struggle against misguided *câdât* customs, against super-erogatory rites, and against obscurantism in general, reformers like Ben Badis or 'Allâl al-Fâsî were attempting to undermine the foundations of a power which they clearly saw was not directed, or no longer directed, toward progress.

Although it is based on technological innovations and on the social and intellectual forms which accompany these changes, imperialism is not able to resolve the problems that it creates because of an inherent, fundamental contradiction. Imperialism is unable to direct the modernization process honestly, and is even less able to complete this process on which it prides itself and with which, moreover, it usually collaborates, often against its own will or interests.

If this analysis, or if this feeling, is accurate and would still be applicable in the final stage—that moment when the liberation cause becomes identified with progress and the imperialist cause with regression, and the whole process follows a virtually irresistible international movement—then distinctions between the situations that have been outlined and the choices that have been proposed need to be recognized.

No movement in the Maghrib has been, or is, able to be contemptuous of the support of traditionalist forces, whether it accepts this support or struggles against it. It is class origin and educational background which determine whether the leaders view this necessity as purely tactical or as innately valuable to their country's heritage. On this point the progressives can be separated from the traditionalists. Both sides are forced to recognize the strength of the old Maghrib, which is closely tied to inherited modes of belief and worship, but they differ in the attitude which they adopt toward it; unquestionably, the difference can take violent forms.

A rupture may easily appear between the defenders of a regime rein-forced by religion, such as the Moroccan Istiqlal, and the defenders of a democratic, secular government, such as the Tunisian Neo-Destour. In Algeria the Westernism of Ferhat Abbas, though modified by a loyalty to Islam, caused him to oppose the religious reformism of the *Ulema* as strongly as he opposed the explosive associations inspired by a revolutionary social-ism that appealed simultaneously to the proletariat and to a peasantry steeped in tradition. One is reminded of the famous "warriors of Djebels," who fought as much for ancestral honor as for any ideology, even that of nationalism. Independence, once it has recovered its balance, will have the task of clarifying these complex issues.

As a corollary, no movement in the Maghrib has been, or is, able to disregard either international alliances or the changes introduced by the French regime in the style, institutions, behavior, and very identity of the country. In the critical sectors of society, the intelligentsia or the trade-unionists, for example, there is undeniably a complex blend of realities. In many cases, urbanization or economic change has caused a direct tele-scoping of modern and traditional behavior patterns. The swelling numbers of the proletariat in the cities, around the factories, and on the wharves of the ports has led to communication of ideas, a spreading of attitudes, and motivations which resist being redirected into any religious ideology, even a reformist one, and yet which are possessed of a vigorous popular strength. What will be the outcome of these relatively new conflicts?

In Tunisia, the problem gave rise to an innovative analysis, proposed by Tahar Haddad in the 1920's, which also revealed another very interesting aspect of the crisis. During the period of violent strikes, the demands of the dockworkers' union created a schism between the organization dominated by the metropolitan C.G.T. (Confédération Général du Travail) and the national leaders, who commanded popular loyalty. The bureaucracy of the C.G.T., which shared the assimilationist perspective of the national leaders despite its anti-colonialist posture, tried in vain to condemn the secession by pointing to its disturbing ties with certain reactionary forces, such as religious faith and nationalism. What prevailed, for the first time, was the declaration of a specificity that did not respond to any practical solution. Much later, the same issues provoked the split between a proletarian movement, the P.P.A., and the French Communist party, and caused the withdrawal of Algerian leaders like Amar Ouzegane from the party itself.

The problem of specificity, as it occurs during political or union struggles, will dominate the situation in the future. To the extent that it represents more than the problem of traditionalism, in its concern for revolutionizing or at least reforming behavior patterns and in its being directly engaged with the new conditions of life in the Maghrib, the issue of specificity helps pose the question of traditionalism in a better way and leads us to tighten the definition in order to better understand current changes.

Today: The "Double Sector"

In the Maghrib today, a distinction is commonly made between a "modern sector" and a "traditional sector" in the economy: the former includes the concrete results of the state's effort to promote modernity—factories, self-managing farms, cooperatives, offices, schools, and the values and customs which naturally express these changes—while the latter encompasses everything which has not yet undergone the effects of modernization. Nevertheless, it is inaccurate to speak of a wide split between one sector and the other. Although the traditional sector experiences effects "induced" by the newly-activated zones, which fuel themselves with its materials, its manpower, and even its ideas, the fact that it stands in contrast to the modern sector leads to contradictory kinds of treatment. Sometimes it is viewed as an anachronism, a mere residue, and sometimes it is seen as a preserve; yet it is always considered the base or the common foundation of society. Its inertia, whose potential for violent eruptions is, nonetheless, never underestimated, weighs heavily on all current efforts for change. On the other hand, the traditional sector possesses real virtues: its ties with the national past; its authenticity, even if in a state of decline; its vitality, even if somewhat diminished in force; its capacity to endure indefinitely without capitulating; its instinctive desire for greater well-being and for freedom.

The seriousness of this problem, which creates such a dualism for the peoples of the Maghrib, may readily be calculated, since the split appears not only in the economic sphere, but also in all categories of social existence. This dualism is viewed geographically in the opposition of a vast "Interior," the *bled*, or "le pays par excellence," to rural hamlets and those townspeople directly involved in the process of change. Demography, social stratification, and customs likewise feel the impact of this duality. Even the national psyche is affected to a point where it is wracked by contradictions.

If this analysis is accurate, no plan for progress will succeed in these countries unless it is rooted in what is fundamental and already accepted by a majority of the people. The only other alternative is to cling to the patchwork techniques and the sporadic, distorting changes which history rightly attributes to colonialism. To restate the problem: *either modernism will be based upon the traditional, or it will remain colonial in form, which means it will not exist at all.*

The economic sphere, like other areas of life, offers evidence that supports this theory. Industrialization and modernization of agriculture imply access to newly developed techniques and to the social and intellectual structures which correspond to them; until recently, however, these advances have not merged with the environment. Occasionally, sullen or violent reactions obstruct the movement toward modernization, and the disgrace, or even the debasement inflicted on the traditional economy by these reactions is like a heavy ransom. How can the situation be remedied? The governments of the Maghrib are trying to deal with this issue, but despite the energies they expend, the two sectors have still failed to unite.

For at least a generation, Islam in the Maghrib has leaned toward making reasonable adjustments, an attitude which represented a break from many former institutions, practices, and feelings. As was the case with Christianity, but in a still more violent manner because of the colonial situation and its consequences, these variations required corresponding sociological and political changes. Islam "maraboutique" or "confrerique," for example, is commonly branded as reactionary and is rejected by most enlightened people; the rites practiced in the countryside incur severe criticism. In Morocco, a movement related to the Moslem Brotherhood in the East tries to draw not only constitutional principles from the Koran, but also a social ethic and even a system of socialism. In Algeria, another movement acts as the self-appointed guardian of *givam* religious values, so that it may disagree, openly or covertly, with the revolutionary state. In a more general way, the attitudes of *çabr* (patience) and *rid̄a* (harmony with the transcendental) which used to predominate, and in which many Westerners could see nothing but fatalism and resignation, are currently repudiated.

However, it is clear that if customs remain dominated by religious belief, the reasoning behind various motivations is equally affected by sentiment. The suggestive force of any social imperative always depends on its popular resonance; conversely, new laws can always excite resistance. It is uncertain whether, in Tunisia, the explosive reactions to government propaganda against ritual fasting were motivated by devotion to religious principles or by political opposition. Does the rigorous moral stance officially taken by the Algerians, including prohibition of alcoholic beverages and segregation of women, spring from a past-oriented morality, or from a justified fear that the dispersal of national energies might lead to the loss of national identity? A clear separation of the issues would be difficult.

Once again, we turn to the law for more precise distinctions. A legislator in the Maghrib views as "traditional" everything that does not reflect the established and decreed norms, whether these are preserved from the time of French rule or established since independence. Manners, customs, and statute law thus relate to actual law much as they do in Europe. A slight difference exists, however, because the body of unwritten norms survives to the same extent that a "traditional sector" survives in the spheres of social and moral reality. It is clear that this traditional sector exerts a conservative force. Recent studies have shown that the liberal legislation dealing with marriage or birth control, which has been adopted in some of these countries, Tunisia, for example, is hampered by prevailing customs. Nearly everywhere, as the distance from administrative centers increases, rural society is rebuilding itself on what might be called its true foundations.

This situation is not unique to the Maghrib, for any unwritten law may prevail over official codifications because of an ethnological truth whose thrust is not necessarily reactionary. This is the case with the form of democracy based on *jemâ 'a-s* (rural communities or collectives), which still functions implicitly in many regions, both Arab and Berber, exerting a more genuinely modern influence than many of the innovative measures promoted by the centralized government. In any case, these situations are ambiguous and deserve to be studied intensively, taking each sociological category separately.

For example, what can be called "traditional" in the realm of language?

Certainly the Arab or Berber speakers, who are completely unschooled but who meet daily needs and even produce artistic creations of great interest, fall into the traditional category. Works of poetry, music, and sculpture that are based on local traditions and enjoy wide popular support, especially in the countryside, stand in contrast to the works of art that draw their major inspiration from Western tradition. With language, as with other aesthetic spheres, certain standards and certain genres are suited for the dialogue with modernity, whether the appropriate techniques are found in French culture or in classical Arab culture. In this area, modernism risks cutting itself off from the mass of the people, a problem of which writers and artists are acutely conscious. They hope to resolve it by becoming more directly aware of the essential realities of the country, an approach which presupposes the use of the most scholarly techniques. Consequently, experimentation with the most advanced foreign methods would contribute to restoring authentic elements of the tradition. Thus, artists are showing the way to other people actively involved in the affairs of the Maghrib, but the synthesis they envision is a difficult one, vulnerable both to undeserved failure and to unfair repudiation.

An additional difficulty, moreover, is created by the fact that the "traditional" in the Maghrib, as it applies to either institutions or customs, is not always synonomous with the "national." French colonialism was so long-lived that it created certain systems for implementing policies and certain modes of expression and thought which still exert an influence on the current generation, sometimes being adopted, while at other times being resented as undesirable after-effects. Modernism in the Maghrib stands in opposition to not merely one, but to two kinds of tradition—colonial and pre-colonial. Both may appear to exert negative influences, but in a characteristically ambiguous way, both are defensible because they have a positive side: the former, its connection with world culture, and the latter, its ties to ancestral values. This kind of ambiguity permeates the culture of the Maghrib.

A Critique of Continuity

The term "culture" has so many accepted meanings that we should already have justified our usage of it. In this article, culture has meant, and will continue to mean, the collective identity that is based on a relationship with a territorial substratum, in which reciprocally dependent systems of behavior and expression interact to eventually reflect the society's fundamental ethos. On the subjective level, this identity creates the feeling of a "we," which is itself contained within a still broader identity. Thus a peasant from Chaouïa in Morocco superimposes on the "we" of his community the "we" of the province, of Morocco, of the Maghrib, and of Arab Islam, since the latter, if only by its rites and ceremonies, invests even the events of his daily life with the ideas and reference points of the civilization it expresses.

If this is true, the failure of modernization during the colonial era may be seen as the result of its intention, if not to completely assimilate the identity (the "we") of the Maghrib, at least to win it over gradually. The change did take place, producing a more or less radical modification of values and behavior. Facts, ideas, a language based on French culture and more generally on industrial civilization were introduced *en masse*, yet instead of being won over to the Other, the identity of the Maghrib gained a strength which initially sustained the battle for independence and today supports the struggle to achieve modernity.

The Maghrib is gradually taking its place in the world industrial market, a declared goal of its national governments which will supposedly bolster the collective identity and furnish it with new weapons. But the evidence in this matter is inconclusive. The personality of these peoples draws much of its character from a continuity based partly on ancestral heritage, and partly on distinctive qualities. Theoretically, these different patterns could —and should—be reconciled; this is the intention of political leaders in the Maghrib, when they use the concept of specificity. Consequently, while they will speak of "particular forms of socialism," they will also stress the role of the "human element" in development, the inappropriateness of imported methodologies, and the necessity of original approaches, and they believe that these methods will bring success. In fact, what appear to be contradictions break out between modernization on the one hand, and certain features of continuity or particularity, springing largely from tradition, on the other.

Continuity, a guarantee of survival for the collective identity, is often thought to exercise too much power, not only because it preserves the underdeveloped status of the Maghrib, but also because its welter of institutions, forms of behavior, and ideas seems quite incompatible with the future. The partisans of continuity themselves will have to distinguish between the achievements and incentives for effective action contained in their heritage, and those elements which inhibit or impede progress.

One of the most difficult questions centers on the role of religion, not as a metaphysical system, but as an organizer of society. Its right to this role is contested, not only by comparing it to European models, but also by referring to its own process of internal evolution. For some time the reformist policies of the Ulemas have genuinely aimed at making religious faith and rites more reasonable; yet, on the one hand, the problem of customs and habits goes far beyond that of mere doctrine, and on the other, the violent turn taken by many struggles in the Maghrib, if it has not directly damaged religious faith, has at least suggested other values for social organization: social and economic democracy, or even revolution. Many of these ideals, it is true, may be inferred from Islam in its original, pure form, and thus the potential for an Islamic socialism does exist, as proponents of a certain school of belief claim. However, the real dispute—if not the stated one—

centers on the odds and risks of a socialism belonging to the industrial era, whose problems, systems, and processes are incongruous with local ways of life. It is even possible that future secularization will be influenced by the tradition in the Maghrib of carefully separating the spiritual and the temporal spheres.

The value placed on the Arab cultural legacy found in the Maghrib is another expression of continuity. Its power emanates from the fact that it is founded on a widely-recognized classical tradition and that it establishes an affinity with similar movements active in other Islam-Mediterranean nations; its weakness lies in its neglect of those areas of past or present reality which do not form part of that legacy. Ethnological planning in the Maghrib, for example, does not meet the favorable response one expects from regimes which need population growth, especially in rural areas. There is nothing in the Maghrib which corresponds to the *indegenista* movement in Mexico, or to widescale efforts of the same sort in India, Black Africa, and elsewhere. Fortunately, however, positions on this issue are beginning to shift.

Moreover, science, or even applied knowledge (the fields of psychology and education, for example) do not carry the sole responsibility for making these difficult choices; if politics wants to be based on real forces, it must also assume some of this burden. The old form of solidarity in the Maghrib, the *jemâ'a*, has clearly been reassumed in the Algerian commune, while Morocco and Tunisia seem more hesitant in this respect. Until very recently, Tunisia has carried on policies which did not shrink from attacking the traditional practices of urban commerce, but this opposition to the existing liberalism, justly accused of actually being mercantilism, clashes with forms of behavior that are firmly established and are even prestigious. The Muslim *medina* or town has always been mercantile in character. Planning today does not deal only with economic variations; to a certain extent it affects the sphere of social values and has thus recently caused certain repercussions.

Because the attention of officials is generally focused on policies which are likely to have an immediate impact, they are prone to neglect, and indeed to attack, any facts or behavior which they consider unfavorable to the desired outcome. Nomadism and stock-raising, and all other manifestations of a decentralized approach toward the economy and toward local customs are nearly everywhere sacrificed to a more thorough centralization. As a result, there is a crisis in what may be called Bedouin values, whose profound importance in the structure of North Africa should not be underestimated. Undoubtedly, choices and sacrifices analogous to those which Europe effected in the nineteenth century are, to some extent, inevitable. But the problem is more difficult for nations which are "re-emerging," and which must re-establish their own identity in the face of, and among, better equipped national identities quarreling over a world reshaped by technology.

Neutralize or rid oneself of unproductive kinds of behavior—an admirable goal! Yet, to what extent will irreparable damage be inflicted on certain distinctive qualities and, gradually, on the inherent value of the national personality?

The conflict exists and is experienced with either bitterness or sadness. It takes the simple form of a polarization between Islam and a secular socialism, and there seem to be no better solutions unless reality can be divided and treated in new ways. Will new answers be found? In the Maghrib as elsewhere, these questions remain unresolved.

Theoretical Perspectives

The real problem for the peoples of the Maghrib, as for other peoples, is the need to reach a compromise between their own particular character and general, worldwide currents of change. To save this special character does not require merely conserving their heritage, but somehow combining a legacy which remains intact in large areas of geographical, social, and psychic reality with a dynamic of development. It would be false to reduce the particular to the traditional, for any vital continuity implies choices, ruptures, and innovations, but it would be no less false to deny the role of tradition in both the dynamic and the continuity.

On the other hand, there is the fallacy of that antithesis, too often flaunted, between a modernity which may only be achieved through foreign influence and a tradition which can only turn in upon itself. Positive and negative, and indigenous and borrowed elements mingle on every plane in these situations, although preservation and development of the collective identity are, finally, the condition and the criterion by which success may be measured.

Collective identity resides more in a system than in any of its particular features; the content may change without harming the system itself. Yet, how may the system appropriate to an individual society be determined? Certainly it cannot be derived only from what presents itself as traditional, which often merely represents a distorted and decadent stage in the evolution of social continuity. The system results from multi-disciplinary investigations that seek to weld together coherent elements of a positive influence from different epochs and experiences. These immutable elements are unquestionably relative, both to the variables imposed by historical situations, and to the contents which fill them. But finally their inherent variations assume a long-term form, which outlasts several generations. Despite all imaginable changes of framework, of the economy, of attitudes, and even of manners and customs, there is little chance that the inhabitant of the Maghrib tomorrow will differ from the inhabitant of today in any more fundamental way than the latter differs from his father, or even from his ancestors who lived before the colonial period.

However, what has changed and will change still more are the conditions under which an inhabitant of the Maghrib discusses his own problem. The possibilities offered by modern analytical methods, and the demands of a deepening consciousness may create new anxieties, but they already offer better formulations of the problems. Far from making it impractical, the fact that this research must be conducted under the pressure of necessity, in the midst of internal and external confusion, not only gives it a dynamic quality, but also endows it with a range of worldwide experiences and reforms. By allowing action and analysis to interact, the inhabitant of the Maghrib in the last third of the twentieth century will use an approach that may not be sufficient, but is certainly necessary if he is to solve in his own way a problem which concerns us all.

Notes on Contributors

HEINZ BECHERT, born in 1932 in Munich, is Professor of Indology and Director of the Seminar for Indian and Buddhist Studies, at the University of Göttingen. He is the author of *Bruchstücke buddhistischer Verssammlungen* (Berlin, 1961), *Buddhismus, Staat und Gesellschaft*, vols. 1 and 2 (Frankfurt, Wiesbaden, 1966-1967), of which volume 3 is forthcoming, *Singhalesische Handschriften* (Wiesbaden, 1969), and *Über die Marburger Fragmente des Saddharmapundarika* (Göttingen, 1972).

JACQUES BERQUE, born in 1910 in Algeria, is Professor at the Collège de France, and holds the Chair of Social History of Contemporary Islam. His publications include *The Arabs: Their History and Future* (New York, 1964), *French North Africa: The Maghrib between Two World Wars* (New York, 1967), and *Egypt: Imperialism and Revolution* (London, 1972).

S. N. EISENSTADT, born in 1923 in Warsaw, is Professor of Sociology at Hebrew University, Jerusalem. He is the author of *From Generation to Generation* (Glencoe, Ill., 1956), *The Political Systems of Empires* (New York, 1963), *Modernization, Protest and Change* (Englewood Cliffs, N.J., 1966), *Israeli Society* (London, 1968), *The Protestant Ethic and Modernization* (New York, 1968), *Political Sociology* (New York, 1971), and *Social Differentiation and Stratification* (Glenview, Ill., 1971).

ERNEST GELLNER, born in 1925 in Paris, is Professor at the London School of Economics. Mr. Gellner is the author of *Words and Things* (Boston, 1959), *Thought and Change* (Chicago, 1965), *Saints of the Atlas* (Chicago, 1969), and of the forthcoming *Legitimation of Belief*, to be published in London in 1973.

J. C. HEESTERMAN, born in 1925 in Amsterdam, is Professor of Indology at Leiden University. Mr. Heesterman is the author of *The Ancient Indian Royal Consecration* (The Hague, 1957) and co-editor of *Pratidanam: Indian, Iranian and Indo-European Studies* (The Hague, 1968). He has written articles on Indian religion and sociology for the *Indo-Iranian Journal*.

ELBAKI HERMASSI, born in 1937 in Tunisia, is Assistant Professor of Sociology at the University of California, Berkeley. He is the author of *Leadership and National Development in North Africa. A Comparative Study* (Berkeley, 1972). Mr. Hermassi has done research on social movements at the École Pratique des Hautes Études, Paris, and has taught at Tunis University.

EDMUND LEACH, born in 1910 in Sidmouth, England, is Professor of Social Anthropology and Provost of King's College, The University of Cambridge. He is the author of *Rethinking Anthropology* (London, 1961), *A Runaway World?* (London, 1968),

Claude Lévi-Strauss (New York, 1970) and *Genesis as Myth* (London, 1970). Mr. Leach is President of the Royal Anthropological Institute for 1971-73.

ŞERIF MARDIN, born in 1927 in Istanbul, holds the Chair of Turkish Political Life at Ankara University, and is Visiting Professor at Columbia University. Mr. Mardin is the author of *The Genesis of Young Ottoman Thought* (Princeton, 1962), and a number of articles on ideology as a facet of modernization. He is working on a forthcoming study of the modernization of communications.

ASHIS NANDY, born in 1937 in India, is a Fellow of the Centre for the Study of Developing Societies in Delhi. Mr. Nandy is co-author of a forthcoming volume on entrepreneurship, *Opportunity and Response,* and has published articles in the fields of political psychology and the culture of science. He is presently working on a biography of the Indian mathematician Srinivasa Ramanujan, and on a study of images of the future among Indian decision makers.

S. J. TAMBIAH, born in 1929 in Ceylon, is Lecturer in Social Anthropology at the University of Cambridge and a Fellow of King's College. Mr. Tambiah is the author of *Buddhism and the Spirit Cults in North-east Thailand* (Cambridge, 1970) and of several articles on religion and social organization in Southeast Asia.

NUR YALMAN, born in 1931 in Istanbul, is Professor of Social Anthropology at Harvard University. He is the author of *Under the Bo Tree* (Berkeley, 1967) and "On Land Disputes in Eastern Turkey," in Tikku, ed., *Islam and its Cultural Divergence* (Urbana, 1971). Mr. Yalman has served on the faculties of the University of Cambridge and the University of Chicago, and has done field work in Turkey and Ceylon.

ABDELKADER ZGHAL, born in 1931 in Tunisia, is Director of the Sociology Section of the Centre d'Études et de Recherches Économiques et Sociales at Tunis University. Mr. Zghal is the author of *Modernisation de l'agriculture et populations semi-nomades* (The Hague, 1967). His recent works deal with modes of peasant political participation in the pre-colonial Maghrib and the impact of this heritage on the post-colonial Maghrib.

INDEX

253